STUDIES AND TEXTS

43

# THE EARLY COUNCILS
OF POPE PASCHAL II
1100-1110

BY

UTA-RENATE BLUMENTHAL

PONTIFICAL INSTITUTE OF MEDIAEVAL STUDIES
TORONTO 1978

ACKNOWLEDGMENT

This book has been published with a
grant in aid of publication from
the De Rancé Foundation.

CANADIAN CATALOGUING IN PUBLICATION DATA

Blumenthal, Uta-Renate, 1935-
   The early councils of Pope Paschal II, 1100-1110

(Studies and texts — Pontifical Institute of Mediaeval Studies ; 43 ISSN 0082-5328)

Bibliography: p.
Includes index.
ISBN 0-88844-043-X

1. Councils and synods — History.    2. Paschalis II, Pope, d. 1118.
I. Title.    II. Series: Pontifical Institute of Mediaeval Studies.
Studies and texts — Pontifical Institute of Mediaeval Studies ; 43.

BX825.B58                262'.5'2                C77-001675-8

*Copyright 1978 by*
PONTIFICAL INSTITUTE OF MEDIAEVAL STUDIES
59 Queen's Park Crescent East
Toronto, Ontario, Canada M5S 2C4

PRINTED BY UNIVERSA PRESS, WETTEREN, BELGIUM

*For my family*

# Contents

| | |
|---|---|
| Preface | IX |
| Table of Abbreviations | X |
| Sigla | XII |
| Note on the Latin Texts | XIII |
| Introduction | 1 |

**1 The Councils from 1100 to 1105**

| | |
|---|---|
| The Council of Melfi, October 1100 | 7 |
|     The Sources and Previous Scholarship | 7 |
|     The Participants | 8 |
|     The Canons | 10 |
|     Other Notable Decisions of the Council | 10 |
| The Lateran Council, Lent 1102 | 11 |
|     The Sources and Previous Scholarship | 11 |
|     The Participants | 16 |
|     The Canons | 17 |
|     Other Notable Decisions of the Council | 20 |
| The Lateran Council, Lent 1105 | 23 |
|     The Sources and Previous Scholarship | 23 |
|     The Participants | 28 |
|     The Canons | 29 |
|     Other Notable Decisions of the Council | 30 |

**2 The Council of Guastalla, 22 October 1106** — 32

| | |
|---|---|
| The Sources and Previous Scholarship | 36 |
| The Participants | 38 |
| The Canons | 43 |
|     Previous Editions and their Manuscripts | 43 |
|         The *Liber Pontificalis* | 43 |
|         The Correctores Romani | 47 |
|         Baronius and the Conciliar Editors | 48 |
|         The Edition of Ludwig Weiland | 50 |
|         The Boso Tradition | 51 |
|         The Paraphrase of C.2 | 54 |
|         C.4 Redaction 1 | 54 |
|         C.4 Redaction 2 | 56 |
|         C.6 as Part of the *Breviarium Gestorum* of 1112 | 57 |

|   |   |
|---|---|
| New Guastalla Texts .............................. | 57 |
|     Manuscripts .............................. 65 | |
|     The Edition .............................. 68 | |
| Other Notable Decisions of the Council ............... | 71 |

## 3 The Council of Troyes, 23 May 1107

|   |   |
|---|---|
| 3 The Council of Troyes, 23 May 1107 ............... | 74 |
| The Sources and Previous Scholarship ................ | 76 |
| The Participants .............................. | 78 |
| The Canons .................................. | 82 |
|   Previously Known Texts ........................ | 82 |
|   The Arsenal Tradition ......................... | 84 |
|     Manuscripts .............................. 88 | |
|     Text .............................. 90 | |
| Other Notable Decisions of the Council ............... | 97 |

## 4 The Councils of 1108 and 1110

|   |   |
|---|---|
| The Council of Benevento, October 1108 ............. | 102 |
|   The Sources and Previous Scholarship ................ | 102 |
|   The Participants .............................. | 102 |
|   The Canons .................................. | 103 |
|   Other Notable Decisions of the Council ............. | 106 |
| The Lateran Council, 7 March 1110 .................. | 106 |
|   The Sources and Previous Scholarship ................ | 106 |
|   The Participants .............................. | 107 |
|   The Canons .................................. | 109 |
|     Edition .................................. | 109 |
|       The Manuscripts of Class A .............. 112 | |
|       The Manuscripts of Subgroup A ............ 114 | |
|       The Manuscripts of Class B .............. 116 | |
|       The Manuscripts of Subgroup B ............ 117 | |
|       The Text .............................. 118 | |
|   Fragments of the 1110 Decrees in Canonical Collections | 121 |
|   Other Notable Decisions of the Council .............. | 122 |
| Conclusion .................................. | 123 |
| Appendix 1. A Council of Dubious Authenticity: Benevento, Autumn 1102 ................ | 130 |
| Appendix 2. The Guastalla Canons and Gratian's *Decretum* .. | 132 |
| Appendix 3. Fragments .......................... | 135 |
| Bibliography .................................. | 139 |
| Index of Incipits of Paschalian Canons .............. | 159 |
| Manuscript Index .............................. | 160 |
| General Index .................................. | 162 |

# Preface

This book is the first monograph to deal with the synods of Paschal II, the least known and most misunderstood pope of the period of the Gregorian reform. The absence of earlier studies meant that I had to sift through numerous early printed works, in particular those of the great conciliar editors. For many years now, I have also followed up hints in manuscript catalogues and examined hundreds of manuscripts in European libraries.

I am grateful for some financial support from Columbia University and the Vanderbilt University Research Council. My special thanks go to the librarians of various ecclesiastical, municipal and national institutions for their gracious welcome and assistance, sometimes under the most difficult circumstances. I should like to mention in particular the great kindness of the late Dr. Luigi Pancrazi at Cortona. I am also grateful to Barbara Ajami, Professor Johanne Autenrieth, Martin Bertram, Phoebe Drews, Father Gérard Fransen, Father Antonio García y García, Professor John Gilchrist, Carla-Maria Gläser, Dr. Wolfgang Hagemann, Cynthia M. Pyle, Msgr. Ruyschaert, Father Alfons Stickler, and especially to Professor Stephan Kuttner and Professor Horst Fuhrmann who kindly read a draft of the manuscript and aided generously with comments and advice.

Most of all, however, I want to thank here my teachers at Columbia University: Malcolm Bean, Paul O. Kristeller, John H. Mundy and Robert Somerville. Without Professor Somerville's patient encouragement, aid and inspiration in particular the book would never have been written.

Nashville
December 1975

# Table of Abbreviations
(See Bibliography for full details)

| | |
|---|---|
| *Abhandlungen Berlin* | *Abhandlungen der Preussischen Akademie der Wissenschaften, philosophisch-historische Klasse.* |
| Abhandlungen Göttingen | Abhandlungen der Gesellschaft der Wissenschaften zu Göttingen, philologisch-historische Klasse. |
| AUF | *Archiv für Urkundenforschung.* |
| Ans. | Anselm II, bishop of Lucca. *Collectio canonum.* |
| BEC | *Bibliothèque de l'Ecole des Chartes.* |
| Brackmann GP | Brackmann, Albert, ed. *Germania Pontificia.* |
| DA | *Deutsches Archiv für Erforschung des Mittelalters.* |
| Deusd. | Deusdedit. *Collectio Canonum.* |
| DHGE | *Dictionnaire d'Histoire et de Géographie Ecclésiastiques.* |
| Dion. | Dionysius Exiguus. |
| F | Fuhrmann, Horst. *Einfluss und Verbreitung der Pseudoisidorischen Fälschungen.* |
| Grat. | Gratian. *Decretum.* |
| H | Hinschius, Paul, ed. *Decretales Pseudo-Isidorianae.* |
| Holtzmann, PUE | Holtzmann, Walter, ed. *Papsturkunden in England.* |
| JK and JL | Jaffé, Philip. *Regesta pontificum Romanorum*, 2nd ed. by G. Wattenbach and S. Loewenfeld, F. Kaltenbrunner, and P. Ewald. The abbreviation JK is used for letters through the year 589 (2nd ed. Kaltenbrunner) and the abbreviation JL for letters through the years 883-1198 (2nd ed. Loewenfeld). |
| Kehr IP | Kehr, Paul, ed. *Italia Pontificia.* |
| LP | *Liber Pontificalis*, ed. Louis D. Duchesne. |
| LThK | *Lexikon für Theologie und Kirche.* |
| MGH SS | Monumenta Germaniae Historica, Scriptores. |
| MGH Const. 1 | *Constitutiones et acta publica*, ed. Ludwig Weiland. |
| Nachrichten Göttingen | *Nachrichten der Gesellschaft der Wissenschaften zu Göttingen, philologisch-historische Klasse.* |
| QFIAB | *Quellen und Forschungen aus italienischen Archiven und Bibliotheken.* |

| | |
|---|---|
| Rep. Font. | *Repertorium Fontium Medii Aevi.* |
| Realenzyklopädie | *Realenzyklopädie für Protestantische Theologie und Kirche.* |
| RHCOc | *Recueil des historiens des croisades - occidentaux.* |
| 74 T | Gilchrist, John T., ed. *Diversorum patrum sententie.* |
| Sitzungsberichte Göttingen | *Sitzungsberichte der Gesellschaft der Wissenschaften zu Göttingen, philologisch-historische Klasse.* |
| Sitzungsberichte Vienna | *Sitzungsberichte der Akademie der Wissenschaften Vienna, philosophisch-historische Klasse.* |
| 13L | Collection in Thirteen Books of ms Vat. lat. 1367. |
| ZRG Germ. Abt. | *Zeitschrift der Savigny Stiftung für Rechtsgeschichte Germanistische Abteilung.* |
| ZRG Kan. Abt. | *Zeitschrift der Savigny Stiftung für Rechtsgeschichte Kanonistische Abteilung.* |

# Sigla

| | |
|---|---|
| An | *Annalista Saxo* |
| B | Brussels, BR 11 196 - 11 197 |
| Bl | Bamberg Lit. 140 |
| Bp | Bamberg Patr. 30 |
| C | *Chronicon Colonense* |
| Co | Cortona 43 |
| Cr | *Chronica monasterii Casinensis* |
| E | *Ekkehard* |
| Fa | Florence, Bibl. Mediceo-Laurenziana Ashburnham 53 |
| Fb | Frankfurt Barth. 50 |
| Fc | Florence, Bibl. Naz. Centrale Conv. Sop. A.4.269 |
| Fm | Florence, Bibl. Mediceo-Laurenziana San Marco 499 |
| G | Göttweig 53 |
| Go | Göttweig 85 |
| Gu | Graz UB 351 |
| H | *Annales Hildesheimenses* |
| M | Munich Clm. 3739 |
| Ma | Madrid Bibl. Nac. 4207 |
| Mb | Metz 221 |
| N | Naples XII A.37-39 |
| Nb | Naples XII A.27 |
| O | Orléans 315 |
| P | Parma 976 |
| Pa | Paris, Bibl. de l'Arsenal 717 |
| Pi | Pistoia 135 |
| Pn | Paris BN 11851 |
| Ra | Rome, Biblioteca Vallicelliana C.16 |
| Rf | Rome, Biblioteca Vallicelliana F.54 |
| Rv | Rome, Biblioteca Vallicelliana C.24 |
| S | Segni fragment |
| Sm | Schaffhausen 46 |
| U | *Codex Udalricus* |
| V | Vienna 1705 |
| Va | Biblioteca Vaticana Vat. lat. 1346 |
| Vb | Biblioteca Vaticana Vat. lat. 4977 |
| Vba | Biblioteca Vaticana Barb. lat. 897 |
| Vc | Biblioteca Vaticana Vat. lat. 3831 |

| | |
|---|---|
| Ve | Biblioteca Vaticana Vat. lat. 1361 |
| Vl | Biblioteca Vaticana Barb. lat. 538 |
| Vp | Biblioteca Vaticana Palat. 587 |
| Vy | Vienna 2186 |
| Wa | Wolfenbüttel Guelf. 9.4 Aug. 4° |
| Wg | Wolfenbüttel Gud. 212 |
| Wh | Wolfenbüttel Guelf. Helmst. 308 |

## Note on the Latin Texts

Editions of texts presented here are prepared according to the rules established by the Institute of Medieval Canon Law.* Insignificant spelling variants are omitted from the apparatus. 'ę' is transcribed as 'ae'. All previously printed texts follow the style of the original.

* S. Kuttner, "Notes on the Presentation of Text and Apparatus in Editing Works of the Decretists and Decretalists," *Traditio* 15 (1959) 452-464, and idem, "Some Methodological Considerations," *Traditio* 11 (1955) 435-439.

# Introduction

Even more than that of his predecessor, Urban II, the pontificate of Pope Paschal II (1099-1118) is a period of new developments in church politics and ecclesiastical thought.[1] It is marked at once by the high point of the investiture controversy, at the time the dominant aspect of the Gregorian struggle for the *libertas ecclesiae*,[2] as well as by the solution of this conflict between 'regnum' and 'sacerdotium' in England, France, and Hungary.[3] The agreements of February 1111[4] failed to bring about a reconciliation between the papacy and the Holy Roman Empire, but they lay at the heart of the eventual truce of 1122, the so-called Concordat of Worms.[5] Nevertheless, the pontiff primarily responsible for these developments, Paschal II, is a shadowy figure. With the exception of a few brief doctoral dissertations from the nineteenth or early twentieth century, no monograph about this pope exists.[6] At the same time, historical writings on the period,

---

[1] For Urban II see Alfons Becker, *Papst Urban II. (1088-1099)*, MGH Schriften 19/1 (Stuttgart 1964) 16.

[2] This is generally recognized: e.g. Augustin Fliche and V. Martin, eds., *Histoire de l'église depuis les origines jusqu'à nos jours*, vol. 8, Augustin Fliche, *La réforme grégorienne et la reconquête chrétienne (1057-1123)*, (Paris 1950) 340; Hubert Jedin and John Dolan, eds., *Handbook of Church History*, vol. 3, Friedrich Kempf et al., *The Church in the Age of Feudalism*, trans. A. Biggs (New York 1969) 393.

[3] See Kempf, *The Church in the Age of Feudalism*, pp. 393-394, and for Hungary J. D. Mansi, *Sacrorum conciliorum nova et amplissima collectio...* 20 (Venice 1775) 1211-1212.

[4] MGH Const. 1 nos. 83-101, pp. 134-152.

[5] Edited by Adolf Hofmeister, "Das Wormser Konkordat," *Festschrift Dietrich Schäfer* (Jena 1915) 64-148, repr. separately with a preface by R. Schmidt (Darmstadt 1962). The bibliography is large. Particularly noteworthy are Ernst Bernheim, *Das Wormser Konkordat und seine Vorurkunden* (Breslau 1906), and Robert L. Benson, *The Bishop-Elect* (Princeton 1968) esp. 228-250. Cf. now also P. Classen, "Das Wormser Konkordat in der deutschen Verfassungsgeschichte," in *Investiturstreit und Reichsverfassung*, ed. J. Fleckenstein, Konstanzer Arbeitskreis für mittelalterliche Geschichte, Vorträge und Forschungen 17 (Sigmaringen 1973) 411-460.

[6] The most detailed bibliography for older literature is found in *Realenzyklopädie für protestantische Theologie und Kirche* 14: 717-724 (C. Mirbt). See also Carl-Joseph von Hefele and H. Leclercq, *Histoire des Conciles* 5/1 (Paris 1912) 465 n. 3. Recent bibliographies are given by Theodor Schieffer, LThK 8 (1963) 128-129 and Kempf, *The Church in the Age of Feudalism*, pp. 392-398 and esp. p. 542. Most useful as points of departure for Paschal's pontificate are Hermann Guleke, *Deutschlands innere Kirchenpolitik von 1105 bis 1111* (Dorpat 1882); Gerson Peiser, *Der deutsche Investiturstreit unter König Heinrich*

of course, cannot help but refer to Paschal and the result is a peculiar diversity of opinion. His defenders like Augustin Fliche apologize for his assumed deficiencies by pointing to his sanctity, although sanctity aside, Fliche's judgment[7] differs little from that of, for instance, Haller, one of Paschal's critics.[8] For N. H. Cantor Paschal was "a dour old monk" and "a fanatical high Gregorian," "second in importance only to Hildebrand himself."[9] P. Zerbi argued that Paschal proposed a rigid separation of church and world, going further than even Pope Gregory vii in his desire to assure the purity of the church.[10] The great historian Hauck, finally, admitted Paschal's intellectual brilliance, but stressed his weakness.[11]

The reason for these differences of opinion among historians is not far to seek.[12] Even the most rapid survey of the appropriate pages of Jaffé's *Regesta*[13] shows that Paschal's long reign was also a very active one. Although Paschal's official *Registrum* is lost[14] Jaffé and his continuator, S.

---

*v. bis zum päpstlichen Privileg vom 3. April 1111* (Berlin 1883); Wilhelm Schum, "Kaiser Heinrich v. und Papst Paschalis ii. im Jahre 1112," *Jahrbücher der Akademie zu Erfurt*, n.s. 8 (1877) 191-318. Mr. Carlo Servatius, University of Saarbrücken, has just completed a dissertation that should fill the gap with respect to a biography. Not seen.

[7] *La réforme grégorienne*, p. 339: "... est un saint qui fera preuve d'un absolu désintéressement et d'une totale abnégation de soi-même."

[8] Johannes Haller, *Das Papsttum*, vol. 2, 2nd ed. (Esslingen 1962) 472.

[9] *Church, Kingship, and Lay Investiture in England: 1089-1135* (Princeton 1958) esp. 122-124.

[10] "Pasquale ii e l'ideale della povertà della chiesa," *Annuario dell'Università cattolica del Sacro Cuore* (Milan 1964-65) 207-229.

[11] *Kirchengeschichte Deutschlands*, vol. 3 (Leipzig 1896) 893 n. 2.

[12] Cf. Franz-Josef Schmale, *Studien zum Schisma des Jahres 1130* (Cologne and Graz 1961) 17-22. Schmale is extremely reticent and careful whenever he refers to Paschal in the course of his discussion of the background of the antipope Anaclete ii. E.g. "Verschwiegen werden darf natürlich nicht, dass zumal bei Johannes von Gaeta und vielleicht ebenso bei Abt Pontius von Cluny andere Gründe als die des Petrus, also etwa tatsächlich die Paschals, für ihre Haltung bestimmend gewesen sein können" (ibid. p. 19 n. 13). Schmale nowhere indicates what Paschal's ecclesiastical and political theories might have been; this is noticeable even though the question lies outside the framework of Schmale's inquiry.

[13] 1: 702-772.

[14] Paschal's was not the only one to perish. Until 1198, knowledge of papal correspondence depends almost entirely on whatever was preserved by recipients. Only a few of the papal registers survived by odd chance, mostly as fragments, those of Gregory i, John viii, Stephen v, Gregory vii, Anaclete ii, and Alexander iii. Some traces of Paschal's register can be found in the *Liber Censuum* (ms Vat. lat. 8486), ed. Paul Fabre and Louis D. Duchesne (vol. 1-2 Paris 1889-1910, vol. 3 [ed. G. Mollat] Paris 1952), and in two other Vatican codices: ms Ottob. lat. 3057 and ms Vat. lat. 1984. The Ottobonianus contains the *Digesta pauperis scholaris Albini* (cf. Paul Fabre, *Etude sur le Liber Censuum de l'église romaine* [Paris 1892] esp. 10-20); ms Vat. lat. 1984 contains the register excerpts among several additions known in part as the so-called Annales Romani (cf. Louis D. Duchesne, *Liber Pontificalis* 2: xxii-xxiii and 329-350).

Loewenfeld, were able to list about 800 letters and privileges. The Göttinger Papsturkunden project,[15] initiated in 1896 by Paul Kehr, has contributed significant additional material for Paschal. Manuscript research continues to add to the number of known letters and other documents.[16] They are invaluable,[17] but the majority are concerned with purely administrative matters, such as grants and reconfirmation of privileges for monasteries and bishoprics. They will, therefore, with respect to Paschal's politics, yield little more than the statement that he continued and accelerated in this area the policies of his predecessor, Pope Urban II.[18]

Other major sources of great historical value for the pontificates of this period are chronicles, hagiographic writings as well as conciliar acta and canons. There is no need to emphasize the difficulties connected with the use of this material.[19] Many of the chronicles are edited in the *Scriptores* series of the *Monumenta Germaniae Historica*. These pioneer works constitute a most helpful starting point, but in many cases cannot meet the exacting requirements of modern textual criticism. As examples may be mentioned the chronicle of Ekkehard of Aura and the Chronicon of Montecassino. It is fortunate that both have recently been analyzed and in one case at least partially reedited.[20] The situation with regard to conciliar

---

[15] Cf. Leo Santifaller, *Neuere Editionen mittelalterlicher Königs- und Papsturkunden* (Vienna 1958) 66-69; Theodor Schieffer, "Der Stand des Göttinger Papsturkunden-Werkes," *Jahrbuch der Akademie der Wissenschaften Göttingen* (1971) 68-79 and idem, DA 30 (1974) 643-644.

[16] Recent publications of letters are those by Denis Bethell, "Two letters of Pope Paschal II to Scotland," *Scottish Historical Review* 49 (1970) 33-45; Stephan Kuttner, "Some Roman Manuscripts of Canonical Collections," *Bulletin of Medieval Canon Law*, n.s. 1 (1971) 7-29; Robert Somerville, "An Unknown Letter of Pope Paschal II," *Speculum* 47 (1972) 737-741; Horst Fuhrmann, "Zwei Papstbriefe aus der Überlieferung der Rechtssammlung 'Polycarpus'," *Aus Reichsgeschichte und Nordischer Geschichte* (Stuttgart 1972) 131-140.

[17] See, for example, Georg Schreiber, *Kurie und Kloster im 12. Jahrhundert*, 2 vols. (Stuttgart 1910; repr. Amsterdam 1965). In a future study I plan to examine Paschal's citations from canon law in his letters.

[18] For Urban see Alfons Becker, "Urban II. und die deutsche Kirche," in *Investiturstreit und Reichsverfassung*, ed. J. Fleckenstein, Konstanzer Arbeitskreis für mittelalterliche Geschichte, Vorträge und Forschungen 17 (Sigmaringen 1973) 241-275.

[19] E.g. Herbert Grundmann, *Geschichtsschreibung im Mittelalter: Gattungen-Epochen-Eigenart* (Göttingen 1965); Jörg Kastner, *Historiae fundationum monasteriorum: Frühformen monastischer Institutionsgeschichtsschreibung im Mittelalter*, Münchener Beiträge zur Mediävistik und Renaissance-Forschung (Munich 1974); for the use of hagiographical writings see Georg Jenal, *Erzbischof Anno II. von Köln (1056-75) und sein politisches Wirken*, Monographien zur Geschichte des Mittelalters 8/1 (Stuttgart 1974) esp. 56-60 and 97-99 with bibliography.

[20] For Ekkehard see below chapter 1, n. 36; Hartmut Hoffmann, Göttingen, is preparing a new edition of the chronicle of Montecassino. His "Studien zur Chronik von Montecassino," DA 29 (1973) 59-162 can already be consulted.

material is even bleaker. Beginning with the *Annales Ecclesiastici* of Cardinal Baronius,[21] material has been gathered to document Paschal's councils; conciliar editors from Severinus Binius (1573-1641)[22] to the archbishop of Lucca, Giovanni Domenico Mansi (1692-1769), have continued the work of Baronius.[23] As R. Somerville has pointed out in his work on Urban's council of Clermont in 1095, "the amount and diversity of the collected sources is staggering."[24] Quantity does not always make for quality, and this is certainly true for the material assembled for Paschal's councils. Sixteen synods are listed for his pontificate, but for the vast majority of them Mansi and his predecessors relied on brief chronicle accounts of dubious authenticity. There are few signs of critical analysis of the sources, which were thrown together haphazardly. This situation improved little in the nineteenth century when interest in papal councils was renewed.

---

[21] See A. Pincherle, *Dizionario biografico degli Italiani* 6 (1964) 470-478; A. Molieu, DHGE 6 (1932) 872-877.

[22] Binius, a priest from Cologne, published two editions of his work: *Concilia generalia et provincialia, graeca et latina quaecunque reperiri potuerunt.* They appeared in Cologne in 1606 and 1618 respectively. The second edition incorporated material from Baronius' *Annales*. For Binius see H. Quentin, *Jean-Dominique Mansi et les grandes collections conciliaires* (Paris 1900) 21-24.

[23] Mansi's *Sacrorum conciliorum nova et amplissima collectio* encompasses 31 volumes, of which, however, only the first 14 were published before his death in 1769. The letters and councils from the period of Paschal II are found in 20: 977-1238 and 21: 1-162. Mansi's personal contributions to Paschal scholarship in these volumes are reprinted from his six volume supplement to the Venetian revision of Labbe-Cossart's *Sacrorum conciliorum collectio*. Mansi's supplement, *Sanctorum conciliorum et decretorum collectio nova* (Lucca 1748-52) is also known as *Ad concilia Veneto-Labbeana supplementum*. In between the works of Binius and Mansi there appeared in 1636 a 'de luxe' reprint of Binius' 1618 text: *Concilia generalia et provincialia graeca et latina, quae reperiri potuerunt omnia*, 9 vols. (Paris); in 1644 the *Conciliorum omnium generalium et provincialium collectio regia*; between 1671 and 1672 the work of the Jesuit scholars P. Labbe and G. Cossart: *Sacrosancta concilia ad regiam editionem exacta...* 18 vols.; Jean Hardouin's *Acta conciliorum*, 12 vols. (Paris 1714-1715) and *Sacrosancta concilia ad regiam editionem exacta* by Niccolò Coleti, 23 vols. (Venice 1728-33). The various collections are discussed by Quentin, *Mansi*; Alphonsus M. Stickler, *Historia iuris canonici latini*, 1: *Historia Fontium* (Turin 1950; repr. 1974) 294-298; A. van Hove, *Prolegomena ad codicem iuris canonici*, 2nd ed. (Mechlin and Rome 1945) 391-393. The connection between these works in general as well as with the council of Clermont has been elucidated by Robert Somerville, *The Councils of Urban II*, 1: *Decreta Claromontensia* (Amsterdam 1972) ch. 1, pp. 6-19.

[24] Somerville, *Decreta Claromontensia*, p. 6; see ibid. pp. 6-19 for critical considerations concerning the quality of the collections; cf. also Somerville, "The Council of Pisa, 1135," *Speculum* 45 (1970) 98-114, esp. 98-100 and R. L. Kay, "Mansi and Rouen: a Critique of the Conciliar Collections," *Catholic Historical Review* 52 (1966) 155-185.

J. von Pflugk-Harttung[25] and L. Weiland[26] edited conciliar texts based at least in part on manuscript research done by themselves or their collaborators. Weiland, indeed, edited canons for four of Paschal's councils: the council of Guastalla in 1106, the council of Troyes in 1107, and the Lateran councils of 1110 and 1112.[27] But although his work is useful and far more readable than Mansi's, it is lamentably incomplete. This is not intended as a derogatory remark; the difficulties and obstacles in the path of conciliar endeavors can scarcely be exaggerated.[28] Unless an official version for at least some of the decisions of a papal council is preserved, as for example in the registers of Gregory VII,[29] or, by chance, in letters sent out by the papal chancery, information for the eleventh and twelfth centuries frequently depends on more or less reliable entries scattered through chronicles and across the fly leaves of manuscripts that often defy attempts at identification.[30]

Yet, beginning with the assemblies of Pope Leo IX, the great papal synods laid the theoretical framework for papal policy. For this reason it appeared well worthwhile to examine the texts for the councils held by Paschal II between the pontiff's accession in August 1099 and his capture by King Henry V of Germany in February 1111. It is inevitable that this dramatic event[31] has excited the interest of historians but it is an insufficient basis on which to evaluate Paschal's pontificate. The key to Paschal's policies has to be sought primarily in the first ten years of his pontificate, rather than in the later period which is dominated by the events of the spring of 1111.[32] The following examination of the councils which

---

[25] J. von Pflugk-Harttung, *Acta pontificum romanorum inedita: Urkunden der Päpste vom Jahre 748-1198*, 3 vols. (1 Tübingen 1881, 2 and 3 Stuttgart 1884-86).

[26] MGH Const. 1.

[27] Ibid. nos. 395-400, pp. 564-574.

[28] See the contributions by Somerville, *Decreta Claromontensia*, and in connection with provincial legislation C. R. Cheney, "Textual Problems of the English Provincial Canons," *La Critica del Testo, Atti del 2° Congresso internazionale della Società Italiana di Storia del Diritto* (Florence 1971) 1: 165-188 (repr. in *Medieval Texts and Studies* [Oxford 1973] 111-137). Both authors include bibliographies. See now also F.-J. Schmale, "Systematisches zu den Konzilien des Reformpapsttums im 12. Jahrhundert," *Annuarium Historiae Conciliorum* 6 (1974) 21-39.

[29] *Das Register Gregors VII.*, ed. Erich Caspar, MGH Epistolae selectae 2, 2 fasc. 1920-23.

[30] Cf. my "Ein neuer Text für das Reimser Konzil Papst Leos IX. (1049)?" DA 32 (1976) 23-48.

[31] Kempf, *The Church in the Age of Feudalism*, pp. 397-398; MGH Const. 1: 134-152.

[32] It is well known that they constitute a subject of investigation in their own right. Cf. Gerold Meyer von Knonau, *Jahrbücher des Deutschen Reiches unter Heinrich IV. und Heinrich V.*, Jahrbücher der Deutschen Geschichte 17, 7 vols. (Leipzig 1890-1909) 6: 138-

Paschal held during these years is a first step toward such an evaluation. Given the chaotic condition of the available conciliar material, a critical analysis of known texts in conjunction with a search for new texts still in manuscript[33] was necessary. Nevertheless, many questions concerning Paschal's councils remain unanswered for the time being; it is also likely that future research will unearth additional sources for Paschal's pontificate. Still, the disproportion between the large number of conflicting interpretations and the lack of critical analysis even of available conciliar texts has made my investigation seem well worthwhile.

This study is not a biography of Paschal II and even the form of continuous narrative is dispensed with for the sake of textual clarity.[34] Discussions of the episcopate are included solely when demanded by the analysis of conciliar texts.[35] Somerville's hypothetical reconstruction of an eleventh- or early twelfth-century church council brings out the great variety of information that has to be taken into account when discussing papal synods.[36] For Paschal's councils this information is divided into four sections:[37] sources and previous scholarship, participants,[38] canons, and any other notable decisions of the council. The last topic requires some comment, for it covers a selection of *acta*, chosen only from the point of view of their significance for the interpretation of Paschal's policies during the early years of his pontificate.

---

205 with bibliography; Hauck, *Kirchengeschichte*, 3: 890-899; Fliche, *La réforme grégorienne*, pp. 356-371; Kempf, *The Church in the Age of Feudalism*, pp. 395-398.

[33] My research concentrated particularly on manuscripts in Italian and French libraries. Some Spanish, German, English, and Austrian libraries were also visited but extensive research in these latter countries was unfortunately not possible. Other countries, for example those in eastern Europe, have not been visited.

[34] Such a narrative is also readily accessible in the pertinent volumes of Knonau's *Jahrbücher* which are indispensable and not yet superseded. The most recent English biography of Paschal is that by H. K. Mann, *The Lives of the Popes*, vol. 8, 2nd ed. (London 1925) 1-108.

[35] A very important study of the cardinalate under Paschal II is part of a dissertation by Rudolf Hüls, "Das Kardinalskollegium in seiner Entstehungszeit und die Regioneneinteilung Roms," Göttingen 1975.

[36] *Decreta Claromontensia* chapter 2 and idem, "The Council of Clermont (1095), and Latin Christian Society," *Archivum Historiae Pontificiae* 12 (1974) 55-90.

[37] A brief historical introduction is given where necessary.

[38] Papal privileges for ecclesiastical institutions and synodal judgments are important sources for the names of participants. They are taken from the editions that are available at present. These are indicated in Jaffé's *Regesta pontificum romanorum* and in the volumes comprising the Göttinger Papsturkunden project. Cf. in general Georgine Tangl, *Die Teilnehmer an den allgemeinen Konzilien des Mittelalters* (Weimar 1932; repr. Darmstadt 1969) esp. 183-192.

# 1

# The Councils from 1100 to 1105

## THE COUNCIL OF MELFI, OCTOBER 1100

### The Sources and Previous Scholarship

The first synod held by Paschal II during his pontificate took place at Melfi in southern Italy[1] in October 1100.[2] Few records are left, and nothing was known about the council before Mansi called attention to it in the mid-eighteenth century. In the second volume of his *Ad concilia Veneto-Labbeana supplementum*[3] he published what have remained to this day the primary sources for Paschal's first council: the entry under the year 1100 in

---

[1] Melfi was one of the most important centers of the Norman dukes of Apulia. Duke Roger had been invested by Paschal on 14 August 1100, and the assembly at Melfi is a further expression of the cooperation between Paschal and the Normans at the beginning of his pontificate. The pontiff was dependent on Norman military support in order to subjugate Benevento. For the relationship between the papacy and the Norman principalities to the south of Rome see in general Paul Kehr, "Die Belehnungen der süditalienischen Normannenfürsten durch die Päpste (1059-1192)," *Abhandlungen Berlin* 1934-35, pp. 1-52, esp. 9 and 33-35; Otto Vehse, "Benevent als Territorium des Kirchenstaates bis zum Beginn der avignonesischen Epoche. I. Teil," QFIAB 22 (1930-31) 87-160; H.-W. Klewitz, "Studien über die Wiederherstellung der römischen Kirche in Süditalien durch das Reformpapsttum," QFIAB 25 (1933-34) 105-157; Josef Deer, *Papsttum und Normannen: Untersuchungen zu ihren lehnsrechtlichen und kirchenpolitischen Beziehungen*, Studien und Quellen zur Welt Kaiser Friedrichs II. 1 (Cologne 1972).

[2] Mansi 20: 1131-1134.

[3] Cf. ibid.; Mansi's work is also known as *Sanctorum conciliorum et decretorum collectio nova*. See vol. 2 (Lucca 1748) 179-184.

the *Annales Beneventani monasterii Sanctae Sophiae*[4] and two letters from the papal chancery, JL 5841,[5] and JL 5864.[6]

According to Jaffé's *Regesta*,[7] letters JL 5839 and JL 5840, addressed to Diego Gelmirez, bishop-elect of Santiago de Compostela and to King Alfons VI respectively, were also sent from Melfi at this time, but the text of the letters does not prove any direct connection with the council. Nothing is known about the arrival of a Spanish delegation which might have participated in the assembly and carried the letters home.[8]

## The Participants

JL 5841, a privilege for Bishop Stephen of Mazzara (d. ca. 1125), dated

---

[4] The critical edition of the *Annales Beneventani* is that published by O. Bertolini, "Gli Annales Beneventani," *Bullettino dell'Istituto Storico Italiano per il Medio Evo e Archivio Muratoriano* 42 (1923) 1-163. (The text of the *Annales* together with an edition of the *Catalogus Beneventanus Sanctae Sophiae* is found in an appendix, pp. 100-163.) The *Annales* are preserved in three early twelfth-century manuscripts: Vatican City, Vat. lat. 4928 (Bertolini's MS C.1; it is described on pages 17-21), Vat. lat. 4939 (Bertolini's MS C.2; it is described on pages 21-24), Naples, Bibl. Naz. VI E 43 (Bertolini's MS C.3; it is described on pages 27-30). All three of the manuscripts were written almost simultaneously at the monastery of St. Sophia in Benevento (24 and 29): C.1 in 1113 or immediately afterwards (31), C.2 in 1119 (31), and C.3 between 1099 and January 1118, the date of the death of Pope Paschal II (29). Each of the three manuscripts represents a distinct redaction. (Bertolini uses the designation A.1-A.3, corresponding to MSS C.1-C.3 [11]. A fourth redaction, originally accepted as genuine by G. H. Pertz [*Annales Beneventani*, ed. G. H. Pertz, MGH SS 3 (1839) 173-185, 173 MS 2] was found to be an eighteenth-century forgery [11-12 n.1 and the references given there].) The redactions share a common source. Bertolini concluded: "Certo non siamo in grado di determinare con precisione il valore dei rapporti intercedenti tra la fonte comune e i testi che se ne valsero, in quanto solo per gli attuali Annales Beneventani e per il Cat. IV [Catalogus Beneventanus] è grande la probabilità che i monachi li abbiano compilati direttamente sulle tabelle chronologiche esistenti nel loro monastero, da cui essi trascrivevano le note storiche marginali per ordinarle secondo gli anni cui loro pareva fossero apposte, o per ridurle a forma catalogistica" (85). The marginal annotation in the chronological tables at St. Sophia began in the late eighth or early ninth century (87) and was continued until 1128 (88). The value of the *Annales Beneventani* lies in the fact "che essi rappresentano un testo contemporaneo o quasi agli avvenimenti registrati" (11).

[5] JL 5841 was edited by R. Pirrus, *Sicilia sacra disquisitionibus et notitiis illustrata* (Leiden s.d.). The letter is found ibid. part 3: 954. A marginal note in this section of *Sicilia Sacra* (Mazarensis Ecclesiae episcopalis Notitia Sexta; its preface is dated 1641) identifies the editor's source: "autogr. in eccl. Maz. exscrip. lib. monar. fol. 52." See now Kehr IP 10: 252 no. 2.

[6] Kehr IP 8: 157 no. 153.

[7] 1: 706.

[8] The *Historia Compostellana* (PL 170, 889-1236) recorded the protracted struggle of Diego to obtain the metropolitan dignity for Compostela. Diego, the candidate of King Alfons VI of Castille and León, was made subdeacon by Paschal in March 1100 (JL 5822). Cf. Karl Jordan, "Zur päpstlichen Finanzgeschichte im 11. und 12. Jahrhundert," QFIAB 25 (1933-34) 61-104, pp. 83-87.

Melfi, 15 October 1100,[9] was given by the hand of the chancellor John of Gaeta and signed by a group of eminent ecclesiastics. Although the privilege itself does not specifically refer to the synod of Melfi, its date permits the conclusion that the signatories of JL 5841 were among the participants of the council. They were Alberic, cardinal priest of S. Pietro in Vincoli,[10] Oddo, cardinal bishop of Ostia,[11] John, cardinal bishop of Tusculum,[12] Archbishop Albert of Siponto (d. 1116), Robert, cardinal priest of S. Eusebio,[13] Bishop Robert of Messina (d. 1109), Bishop Roger of Syracuse (d. 1104), and Milo, cardinal bishop of Palestrina.[14]

In JL 5864, from 31 March 1101, Paschal confirmed a judicial decision by the council of Melfi in favor of the monastery of Montecassino.[15] As this *actum*[16] shows, the abbess of the monastery of S. Maria at Capua, who had lost her rights in the daughter-house of S. Maria de Cingla to the monks of Montecassino through a decision of Pope Urban II,[17] had appeared as plaintiff at Melfi.[18] Montecassino was represented by John of Gaeta.[19] After the council had requested the advice of two secular judges, 'Romani iudices' Petrus and Raimbald,[20] a committee represented by Bruno of Segni[21]

---

[9] It is probable that the bishop of Mazzara attended the synod.

[10] H.-W. Klewitz, "Die Entstehung des Kardinalkollegiums," ZRG Kan. Abt. 25 (1936) 115-221, 217, no. 36.

[11] Ibid., 210, no. 1.

[12] Ibid., 211, no. 12.

[13] Ibid., 216, no. 27 with references to further literature.

[14] Ibid., 211, no. 9.

[15] Kehr IP 8: 157, nos. 152-153 = Mansi, 20: 1132-1134.

[16] Specific judgments at a council were part of the *acta* of a council and are distinct from general canons. See Somerville, *Decreta Claromontensia* p. 25.

[17] Kehr IP 8: 156 no. 151.

[18] "In Melphitana siquidem synodo, quam, largiente Domino, nostrae ordinationis anno secundo solemniter celebravimus, Abbatissa ... reclamavit" (JL 5864 = Mansi 20: 1133).

[19] Ibid.

[20] Petrus and Raimbald (other forms of the latter name are Rembald, Rambald, and Renbald) had already been employed by Pope Urban II; see Theodor Hirschfeld, "Das Gerichtswesen der Stadt Rom vom 8. bis 12. Jahrhundert wesentlich nach stadtrömischen Urkunden," AUF 4 (1912) 419-562, esp. 537. Cf. also Kehr, "Papsturkunden in Campanien," *Nachrichten Göttingen* (1900) 311-312, no. 5.

[21] H. Hoffmann, *Dizionario Biografico degli Italiani* 14 (1972) 644-647; to the bibliography should now be added Gérard Fransen, "Réflections sur l'étude des collections canoniques à l'occasion de l'édition d'une lettre de Bruno de Segni," *Studi Gregoriani* 9 (1972) 515-533, and Klewitz, "Kardinalskollegium," pp. 139-145. Fundamental are Bernhard Gigalski, *Bruno, Bischof von Segni, Abt von Montecassino: Sein Leben und seine Schriften*, Kirchengeschichtliche Studien 3/4 (Münster 1898) and Réginald Grégoire, *Bruno de Segni, exégète médiéval et théologien monastique*, Centro italiano di Studi sull'alto medioevo 3 (Spoleto 1965).

declared that Urban's decision was just and should remain in force.[22] In short, with the help of JL 5864 it is known that in addition to the chancellor and to the signatories of the Mazzara privilege[23] the abbess of S. Maria of Capua, Bishop Bruno of Segni, Petrus, and Raimbald attended the council of Melfi.

## The Canons

No trace of conciliar legislation at Melfi is preserved.

### Other Notable Decisions of the Council

The most important decision of the synod of Melfi was the excommunication of the city of Benevento recorded in the first redaction of the *Annales Beneventani*, written in 1113 or soon afterwards:[24]

> Paschalis papa descendit in Apuliam et fecit synodum in Melfim mense octobri, et excommunicavit Beneventanam civitatem, et permansit in excommunicationem menses .xi. dies .xxi.[25]

The excommunication was an open declaration of war[26] against the city. Benevento, since 1051 part of the papal states,[27] was at the time governed by Anso, son and successor of Dacumarius. While Dacumarius had been careful to maintain at least the semblance of papal overlordship,[28] Anso began to rule independently in the manner and style of Lombard princes.[29] With the help of Duke Roger of Apulia, Paschal successfully attacked

---

[22] The abbess had not been content with the decision of the Roman law judges (Mansi 20: 1134; Hirschfeld could show that the *Institutes*, the *Codex* and the *Digestum vetus* were well known and used at the papal curia in the late eleventh and early twelfth century, "Gerichtswesen," p. 508): "Caeterum Abbatissa illa vehementius insistente fratribus nostris, episcoporum quibusdam praecepimus, ut in partem euntes ex consilio responderent, utrum causa haec retractanda ulterius videretur. Regresso Brunone Signino episcopo proloquente dixerunt rationabile, ac justum sibi domini Papae judicium videri, ratumque id habendum tamquam canonico ordine pertractatum" (Mansi 20: 1134; Kehr IP 8: 157 no. 152).

[23] JL 5841.

[24] See above n. 4.

[25] P. 151 (redaction A.1); Holtzmann IP 9: 25 no. 29. Redactions A.2 and A.3 omit the excommunication of Benevento.

[26] Vehse, "Benevent," p. 115. Cf. in general Peter Partner, *The Lands of St. Peter* (Berkeley 1972), esp. 138-154.

[27] Vehse, "Benevent," p. 94.

[28] Ibid., p. 111. Vehse pointed out that the titles *praesides* or *praeses* as well as *rector*, which were used by Dacumarius, were titles of an official and not of an independent ruler.

[29] Ibid., p. 115.

Benevento in December 1101, expelled Anso,[30] and re-integrated Benevento into the papal states, bringing one of the aims of the reform papacy to a successful conclusion.[31]

## THE LATERAN COUNCIL, LENT 1102[32]

### THE SOURCES AND PREVIOUS SCHOLARSHIP

Paschal's first synod of international significance was the Lateran council of 1102, held during Lent in the tradition of Pope Gregory vii. It was better known than the preceding council of Melfi, and C. Baronius had already collected and edited sources for this synod in the twelfth volume of the monumental *Annales Ecclesiastici* (1607).[33] He made use of a passage from the 'Abbas Urspergensis,'[34] and included chapter 28 of book 4 of the

---

[30] Holtzmann IP 9: 25 no. 30. For Paschal's 1101 campaign, see now also Hartmut Hoffmann, "Petrus Diaconus, die Herren von Tusculum und der Sturz Oderisius' ii. von Montecassino," DA 27 (1971) 1-109, 21-23.

[31] The significance of Paschal's pontificate for Benevento has been analysed by Vehse, "Benevent," esp. 116-124. This scholar concluded: "Als Paschal am 21. Januar 1118 starb, hinterliess er das Papsttum im festen Besitz des kleinen Territoriums im Süden. Die Zielsicherheit und Energie, die er durch seine Reform der Beneventer Verhältnisse und sein wiederholtes Eingreifen in die Geschicke der Stadt bewiesen hat, steht in merkwürdigem Widerspruch zu der Schwäche, die er in der grossen Politik oft zeigte" (ibid., 124).

[32] The chronicle of Ekkehard of Aura provides an approximate date: "Transacta post haec media quadragesima ... synodus magna Romae est habita" (*Frutolfs und Ekkehards Chroniken und die Anonyme Kaiserchronik*, ed. Franz-Josef Schmale und Irene Schmale-Ott, Ausgewählte Quellen zur deutschen Geschichte des Mittelalters 15 [Darmstadt 1972] 180 [hereafter cited as Ekkehard]). In 1102, Easter fell on 6 April. Lent, therefore, began on 23 February, Quadragesima Sunday (C. R. Cheney, *Handbook of Dates*, London 1945). The middle of the 40-day fast was 14 March, a Friday. When Paschal excommunicated Henry iv on Maundy Thursday, 3 April, he referred to the synod in the past tense: "nos quoque in proxima synodo nostra iudicio totius aecclesiae perpetuo eum anathemati tradidimus" (Ekkehard, p. 180). The synod, therefore, seems to have taken place sometime between 9-15 March and 3 April.

[33] Baronius, *Annales* 12: 21-24.

[34] Ibid., pp. 21-22. The chronicle to which Baronius and the succeeding conciliar editors referred as 'Abbas Urspergensis' is the chronicle edited as *Chronicon Universale* of Ekkehard of Aura by Georg Waitz (Ekkehardi Uraugiensis Chronica, MGH SS 6 [1844] 1-267) and now as *Frutolfs und Ekkehards Chroniken* by Schmale and Schmale-Ott (see above n. 32). The following articles in particular provide some insight into the complicated structure and textual transmission of the chronicle: Franz-Josef Schmale, "Überlieferungskritik und Editionsprinzipien der Chronik Ekkehards von Aura," DA 27 (1971) 110-134; Irene Schmale-Ott, "Untersuchungen zu Ekkehard von Aura und zur Kaiserchronik," *Zeitschrift für bayerische Landesgeschichte* 34 (1971) 403-461 (includes an analysis of the known data for Ekkehard's life); see also Rep. Font. 4: 334-335 (forthcoming) and Irene Schmale-Ott, "Die Rezension C der Weltchronik Ekkehards," DA 12 (1956) 363-387.

*Chronica monasterii Casinensis.*[35] The *Chronica*, however, most likely reported one of the judicial decisions of the Lateran council of 1105. The pertinent section describes the violent disagreement between the citizens of Capua, led by their Archbishop Sennes (d. 1118), and the monks of Montecassino for whom Bruno, bishop of Segni from 1079-1123, had consecrated the church of Sant'Angelo in Formis. The account shows that Bruno did so while a monk at Montecassino,[36] in other words between 1102/1103 and 1107, when he was elected abbot of the monastery. The Roman council that according to the chronicle settled the quarrel in favor of Montecassino must therefore have been the council of 1105.

Employing the *Decretales* of Pope Gregory IX, Baronius' *Annales Ecclesiastici* also included among the sources for the council of 1102 a decretal of Paschal II to the archbishop of Palermo[37] (incipit: Significasti reges) as well as the full text of the letter (JL 6570). This text the cardinal transcribed from a Vatican manuscript "qui inscribitur liber Censuum"[38] where the letter is addressed to the archbishop N. of Poland (incipit: Significasti frater).[39] It is probable that the admonition was sent neither to Palermo nor to Poland, but instead to Spalato (Split).[40] The later arch-

---

[35] Baronius, *Annales* 12: 22, where the reference given reads: "Petr. Diac. Chron. Cass. lib. 4 c.30." The chronicle is here used in the edition by Wilhelm Wattenbach, MGH SS 7 (1846) 551-844. For a discussion of it see now Hoffmann, "Chronik von Montecassino" with bibliography.

[36] "[Abbas] ... cappellam ... fecit a Brunone Signensi episcopo et huius coenobii monacho dedicari..." (MGH SS 7: 774). For the council of 1105 see ch. 1, pp. 23-29. Cf. E. Sthamer, "Das Chartular von Sant'Angelo in Formis," QFIAB 22 (1930-31) 1-30.

[37] [JL 6570] = Comp. 1, 1.4.21, and 10, 1.6.4: Paschalis Panormitano Archiepiscopo, *Significasti — uisitant.*

[38] Baronius, *Annales*, 12: 23. Baronius used the *Liber Censuum* redaction of Nicolas of Aragon also known as Nicholas Roselli.

[39] The manuscript tradition of the decretal letter includes numerous variants with regard to the addressee. See X.1.6.4 with Friedberg's apparatus. Paul Hinschius, *System des Katholischen Kirchenrechts* 3 (Berlin 1883) 203 n.6, argued for a Hungarian addressee. See also the following note.

[40] This was first proposed by G. Fejer (*Codex diplomaticus Hungariae ecclesiasticus ac civilis* 2 [Buda 1829] 32) as indicated by Friedberg (*Quinque Compilationes Antiquae*, ed. E. Friedberg [Leipzig 1882] 3 = Comp. 1, 1.4.21) and accepted by Jaffé (*Regesta* 1: 767-768 under JL 6570) and Duchesne (*Liber Pontificalis* 2: 374 n.). Walther Holtzmann, as his unpublished papers show, was inclined to accept this suggestion although he pointed out that the references to the Saxons and Danes found in some manuscripts do not fit this context. The archbishop of Spalato from 1100 to 1110 (Holtzmann: 1102-1110) was a Roman, Crescentius by name, who had been nominated by Paschal. (On the see of Spalato cf. *Liber Censuum* 1: 138b, n.1.) Crescentius participated in the council of 1102 (see below p. 17). I would like to thank Professor Kuttner of the Institute of Medieval Canon Law, Professors R. Somerville and S. Chodorow for copies of Holtzmann's notes on the decretals of Paschal II in twelfth-century collections.

bishop of Split, Crescentius, participated in the council of 1102. According to JL 6570, however, he cannot have received the pallium at the synod since it was taken to him by papal legates. As closer examination shows, a connection between JL 6570 and the council of 1102 is unlikely. Baronius linked the undated decretal letter to a profession of obedience that, as reported by Ekkehard of Aura,[41] was instituted by the 1102 synod,[42] writing:

> Quam autem audisti superius recitatam fidei professionem exhibere eam tenebantur etiam cum iuramento Episcopi, Archiepiscopi et omnes, a quibus Romanus Pontifex exigere vellet. Accidit autem ea occasione, ut cum accepturus pallium Panormitanus Archiepiscopus, ad idem iuramentum praestandum exigeretur ab Apostolicae Sedis Apocrisarijs, et id facere detrectaret; eum Paschalis Papa corripuerit, ut apparet ex Decretali epistola ipsius ad eumdem Archiepiscopum data.[43]

Later scholars were apparently less convinced that the decretal referred to the 1102 council and omitted it. This general skepticism was justified, as the complete text of JL 6570 shows.[44] Baronius seemingly confused the oath that a newly elected metropolitan rendered to the pope in exchange for the pallium[45] with the general profession of obedience and the connected abjuration of heresy promulgated by the synod of 1102.[46]

---

[41] Ekkehard, p. 180.

[42] See below pp. 20-23.

[43] Baronius, *Annales*, 12: 22. Baronius' opinion is also clearly expressed in his introduction to JL 6570: "Eodem quoque argumento [X, 1.6.4] eadem praecedente occasione [council of 1102] idem Paschalis Papa tunc scripsisse ad Archiepiscopum Poloniae reperitur his verbis in codice Vaticano, qui inscribitur liber Censuum, ex collectione Cencii Cameralis" (ibid., p. 23).

[44] It is most accessible in PL 163, col. 428.

[45] On the metropolitan/episcopal oath and its development see in general Hinschius, *Kirchenrecht* 2 (Berlin 1878) 30 and n.3 as well as vol. 3 (Berlin 1883) 201ff; Theodor Gottlob, *Der kirchliche Amtseid der Bischöfe*, Kanonistische Studien und Texte 9 (Bonn 1936) esp. pp. 42ff. and pp. 160ff.; E. H. Kantorowicz, "Inalienability," *Speculum* 29 (1954) 488-502, esp. pp. 491-494; idem, *The King's Two Bodies* (Princeton 1957) pp. 348-350; Benson, *Bishop-Elect*, p. 169; Deér, *Papsttum und Normannen*, esp. pp. 65-70; Girgensohn, "Miscellanea Italiae pontificiae," *Nachrichten Göttingen* (1974), esp. pp. 172-187 and 194-196 with further bibliography. JL 6570 replies to the objections raised by the archbishop of Spalato against such metropolitan oaths, apparently on the grounds that the Scriptures prohibited the swearing of an oath. (See *Realenzyklopädie* 5: 239-244 s.v. Eid for the theological aspects of the oath.) Bishop Otto of Bamberg (1103-1139) also seems to have referred to this oath when he wrote to his canons in 1106 announcing his consecration by Paschal: "Et quod nulli, a Romano pontifice consecrato, nostris temporibus contigit, sine obligatione alicuius iuramenti consecratus sum" (ed. Ph. Jaffé, *Monumenta Bambergensia*, Bibliotheca rerum germanicarum 5 [1869] 248 no. 131). For St. Otto, apostle of Pomerania and former chancellor of Henry IV, see H. Burkard, DHGE 6 (1932) 463, no. 8 and below ch. 2, n. 43.

[46] Below, pp. 20-23.

But the decretal apart, Baronius' edition of the council of 1102 remained standard[47] until Mansi revised Labbe-Cossart.[48] His *Supplementum* added two items to the inherited material for this Lateran council. Both are letters; one was sent by Paschal to Anselm of Canterbury (JL 5908)[49] and the other by Archbishop William II of Auch (1126-1166/70) to the members of his diocese.[50] Unfortunately, Mansi is also responsible for some of the confusion surrounding the synod, for the letter of the archbishop of Auch does not belong to the year 1102, and JL 5908 to Anselm was attributed by Mansi erroneously to the year 1101.

To begin with the letter from the archbishop of Auch, Mansi's source was Pierre de Marca's *Histoire de Béarn*. De Marca had discovered the letter in the chartulary of the abbey of Lescar.[51] Misled by some of de Marca's comments,[52] Mansi failed to notice that the letter from Auch 'Ex eodem Chartario'[53] had nothing to do with the preceding item, 'E Chartario Lascurrensi,'[54] apart from the fact that both mention a Peace and Truce of God, and that they were published from the same chartulary. The Peace 'E Chartario Lascurrensi' is dated 1104[55] whereas the *decretum pacis* "ex

---

[47] Binius 3/2: 436-437; Labbe-Cossart 10: 727-728; *Collectio Regia* 26: 746-747; Hardouin 6/2: 1861-1864; Coleti 12: 1095-1098.

[48] Mansi 20: 1135-1136 and 1147-1150.

[49] It is edited by F. S. Schmitt, *S. Anselmi Cantuariensis archiepiscopi opera omnia* (Edinburgh 1945, 6 vols.) ep. 222 (4: 124).

[50] Pierre de Marca, *Histoire de Béarn* (Paris 1640) 397-398; 2nd ed. by V. Dubarat (Pau 1912) 2 vols., 2: 80 (hereafter only the second edition will be cited).

[51] The chartulary of the Abbey of Lescar was destroyed in 1787. Several extracts made from the original exist in manuscript. Extracts by P. de Marca in Paris, BN MS lat. 12751, p. 744; extracts by A. Oïhenart (the exact dates of this historian, poet, and avocat of the Parlement de Navarre are unknown; he wrote during the first half of the seventeenth century. [*Nouvelle Biographie Générale* 37-38 (1863) 566-567]) are also preserved at the Bibliothèque Nationale in Paris, Collection Duchesne, vol. CXIV, fols. 21-26; other excerpts are at the library of Tarbes (MS Glanage VI, pp. 98-114). See Henri Stein, *Bibliographie générale des cartulaires français*, Manuels de bibliographie historique 4 (Paris 1907), 282.

[52] *Histoire*, Book 5, chapter 14 (77-8) contains the following comment of de Marca: "C'est un acte assés curieux, qui s'est conservé dans le Chartulaire de Lascar, qui fait voir que le Concile General, assemblé à Rome, avoit ordonné à tous les Metropolitains de publier en leurs Provinces la Paix et la Trefue de Dieu ... Le nom du Pape, ni l'année n'y sont pas consignés, mais le nom de l'Archévesque Guillaume Legat du Pape, monstre assés que c'estoit Guillaume II siegeant du temps du Pape Paschal II et que le Concile General, dont il entend parler, est celui qui fut tenu à Rome l'an M.CII. contre l'Empereur Henri IIII...." The commentary is supposed to accompany only annotation no. 12: "E Chartario Lascurrensi" (1104) but includes items from paragraph 13: "Ex eodem Chartario."

[53] Ibid., p. 81, paragraph 13.

[54] Ibid., pp. 80-81, paragraph 12.

[55] See Hartmut Hoffmann, *Gottesfriede und Treuga Dei*, MGH Schriften 20 (Stuttgart 1964) 102 where further references can be found.

eodem Chartario" was issued by William II of Auch, archbishop from 1126 to 1166/70. As the text of the *decretum* shows, the archbishop announced to his diocese the Peace statute promulgated at the Lateran Council of 1139 held by Pope Innocent II.[56] Given the dates of the pontificate of William II of Auch, he could not possibly have repromulgated for his archdiocese a decision of the Lateran council of 1102, since he refers to a Roman general synod which had just taken place.[57]

It is generally accepted that Paschal's letter to Anselm of Canterbury (JL 5908) to which Mansi referred in the supplement, was sent in April 1102.[58] Mansi alone was persuaded that the letter belonged to the year 1101.[59] Since JL 5908 with the incomplete dating formula "data Lateranis xvii kalendas maii" reported the decisions of a council held by Paschal in the Lateran,[60] Mansi concluded that Paschal had assembled a synod in 1101 as well as in 1102.[61] The scholar based his decision on considerations derived from book 3 of the *Historia novorum in Anglia* by Eadmer, monk of Christ Church, Canterbury, companion and secretary of Archbishop Anselm:[62]

---

[56] Ibid., pp. 121-122; for the peace decrees of the Second Lateran Council of 1139 see *Conciliorum oecumenicorum decreta*, ed. J. Alberigo et al. (Basel 1962) 175-176.

[57] "Nunc praesertim urgente Apostolici mandati auctoritate ... oportet nos super bono Pacis et Treugvae Dei, subditis nostris propensiorem curam impendere. Inde est quod iuxta statuta Generalis Concilij Romae nuper celebrati, Pacem et Treugam Dei in Provincia nostra ex parte Dei, et Domini Papae, et nostra ab omnibus inconcusse et inviolabiliter praecipimus observari. Forma Pacis et Treugvae Dei talis est..." (Marca, *Histoire de Béarn*, 2: 80).

[58] E.g., Schmitt, *Opera* ep. 222 (4: 124); Hefele-Leclercq, *Histoire des Conciles* 5/1: 475-476; Jaffé, *Regesta* under JL 5908; see also Holtzmann, PUE 1: 222, introduction to no. 5.

[59] Mansi 20: 1135-36.

[60] "Qua de re in synodo nuper apud Lateranense consistorium celebrata ... decreta renovavimus."

[61] Mansi 20: 1135-36. Mansi was uncertain whether the text from the chronicle of "Conrad Abbas Urspergensis" did not perhaps belong to the same council as JL 5908 ("An Concilium istud Romanum idem reputandum sit ac Romanum illud, quod Labbeus ex Urspergensi in sequentem annum 1102 refert, definire non ausim"), but ultimately left the usual Ekkehard-Montecassino material as a block under the year 1102 (Mansi 20: 1147-1150), since, as he argued, annual Lenten councils were customary and two might have been held in succession. (Ibid., 1136: "Constat utique Romanos eorum temporum pontifices quotannis circa Martium vel Aprilim concilia habere consuevisse; quare duo per duos succedentes annos concilia iisdem circiter mensibus constitui commode possunt.")

[62] *Eadmeri historia novorum in Anglia*, ed. M. Rule, Rerum Britannicarum Medii Aevi Scriptores (Rolls Series) 81 (London 1884). The earlier edition of Eadmer by John Selden was based on a manuscript of very poor quality (London, BM Cotton. Titus A.ix): *Eadmeri monachi Cantuariensis historiae novorum sive sui saeculi libri vi* (London 1623). The first four books of Eadmer's work have recently been translated. (*Eadmer's History of Recent Events in England*, trans. G. Bosanquet; London 1964.) All subsequent references to the

[JL 5908] ad S. Anselmum anno 1101 datam fuisse. Id vero ex Eadmero lib. III. Novorum non difficili opera eruitur. Nam epistolam illam dedit Paschalis quo tempore a rege Henrico episcopi Romam missi sunt ad pontificem; illi vero reduces in Angliam, alias ab his quarum meminimus, posteriores literas retulerunt signatas Beneventi II. idus Decembris. Reipsa vero constat pontificem anno 1101 elabente Beneventi egisse....[63]

An analysis of book 3 of Eadmer's *Historia novorum*, however, proves clearly that the letters in question were written in 1102,[64] and that the generally accepted date for JL 5908, 15 April 1102, is indeed correct. The letter is a valuable addition to the sources for the Lateran council of 1102.

## THE PARTICIPANTS

The chronicler Ekkehard of Aura provided some general information concerning the assembled ecclesiastics. Although no names are given, he mentioned bishops from Apulia, the Campagna, Sicily and Tuscany as well as representatives from north of the Alps.[65] Ekkehard was not an eyewitness, but he arrived in Rome shortly after the synod's conclusion,[66] and

---

*Historia novorum* will be to the Rule edition. On Eadmer and the manuscripts of his writings see R. W. Southern, *Saint Anselm and His Biographer: a Study of Monastic Life and Thought 1059 - c. 1130* (Cambridge 1963) 229-240; Rule's edition is criticized ibid., pp. 298-313.

[63] Mansi 20: 1135. Mansi was obliged to assume that the "posteriores literae" (JL 5928 and JL 5929, both dated Benevento, "II. idus Decembris" [Schmitt, *Opera* ep. nos. 281 and 282 (4: 196-199)]) also belong to Paschal's correspondence from the year 1101, since they are connected with the delivery of JL 5908.

[64] In the winter of 1101/1102 King Henry I of England and Archbishop Anselm had sent a joint embassy to Paschal that was composed of the archbishop-elect of York, Gerard, Bishops Herbert of Thetfort-Norwich and Robert of Chester as well as Baldwin of Bec and Alexander of Canterbury (Eadmer, *Historia novorum*, pp. 132-133). They returned with JL 5908 and other letters in August 1102 (ibid., pp. 134-137) and quarreled publicly among themselves about whether or not Paschal had entrusted the bishops in the group with secret verbal messages for Henry (ibid., pp. 137-138). As a consequence of the quarrel, Anselm sent a new embassy to Rome (ibid., p. 140) that returned with JL 5928 and JL 5929 giving the lie to the bishops by the time of Henry's Easter court of 1103, a few days before Anselm left for his second exile, when he finally opened the letters (ibid., pp. 146-151).

[65] "Transacta post haec media quadragesima convenientibus universis Apuliae, Campaniae, Siciliae, Tuscaniae totiusque simul Italiae presulibus, ultramontanorum autem quam plurimorum patrum legatis synodus magna Romae est habita..." (Ekkehard, p. 180).

[66] For the date of the synod see above n. 32 and Ekkehard, p. 181, nn. 93-95. Ekkehard of Aura came to Rome at the beginning of Easter week, or 1 April, on his return from a pilgrimage to the Holy Land which he had undertaken in the company of illustrious crusaders from northern Italy, France and southern Germany in 1101. See Schmale-Ott, "Untersuchungen," pp. 405-406. An excellent brief summary of the ill-fated expedition can be

his report seems reliable. Two privileges, JL 5898 for Bishop John of Fiesole, and JL 5899 for Abbot Godfrey of Vendôme were apparently issued in conjunction with the synod on 11 March 1102. They indicate that in addition to the petitioners the cardinals of Palestrina, Albano, S. Clemente and the bishop of Spalato, Crescentius, were among the participants as were the papal notary Peter and the Chancellor John of Gaeta.[67] Another Italian at the council was Cardinal Bernard degli Uberti, abbot of Vallombrosa, papal legate, and after 1106 bishop of Parma.[68]

## The Canons

Ekkehard of Aura was aware that the council had promulgated legislation,[69] but it is a letter of Paschal to Anselm of Canterbury, JL 5908, that preserves the content of one of the canons: "Qua de re in synodo nuper apud Lateranense consistorium celebrata patrum nostrorum decreta renovavimus, sancientes et interdicentes, ne quisquam omnino clericus hominum faciat laico aut de manu laici ecclesias vel ecclesiastica dona suscipiat." Lay homage is of particular interest in the present context. JL 5908 is transmitted both among the correspondence of Anselm[70] and in Eadmer's *Historia novorum*.[71] Eadmer's text shows a variant, as noticed by

---

found in Hans Eberhard Mayer, *The Crusades*, trans. John Gillingham (Oxford 1972) 69-70; more detailed is Marshall Whithed Baldwin, *The First Hundred Years, A History of the Crusades*, ed. Kenneth M. Setton, 1 (Philadelphia 1958) 350-363.

[67] For Godfrey of Vendôme see in addition to JL 5899 also the remarks of Ernst Sackur, ed., *Goffridi abbatis Vindocinensis libelli*, MGH Libelli de lite 2 (1892) 676-700, p. 677. The other known participants were signatories of JL 5898.

[68] *Dizionario Biografico degli Italiani* 9 (1967) 292-300 (R. Volpini), p. 295; Klaus Ganzer, *Die Entwicklung des auswärtigen Kardinalats im hohen Mittelalter*, Bibliothek des Deutschen Historischen Instituts in Rom 26 (Tübingen 1963), pp. 51-55.

[69] "... synodus magna Romae est habita, ubi preter antiqua patrum instituta more solito reverenter confirmata etiam sepedictum nostri temporis scisma inter precipuas hereses computatur..." (Ekkehard, p. 180).

[70] All the manuscripts are early and of great authority. See F. S. Schmitt, "Zur Entstehungsgeschichte der handschriftlichen Sammlungen der Briefe des Hl. Anselm von Canterbury," *Revue Bénédictine* 48 (1936) 300-317; idem, "Zur Überlieferung der Korrespondenz Anselms von Canterbury: Neue Briefe," ibid., 43 (1931) 224-238; André Wilmart, "La tradition des lettres de S. Anselme," ibid., 43 (1931) 38-54.

[71] P. 135. It should be noted that MS London, BM, Cotton Claud. E V of the Pseudo-Isidorian Decretals in the redaction of Lanfranc of Canterbury contains on fol. 246v among its additions a copy of Eadmer's version of JL 5908 together with the Canterbury forgeries. For the frequently discussed codex see now Schafer Williams, *Codices Pseudo-Isidoriani*, Monumenta iuris canonici series C: Subsidia vol. 3 (New York 1971) no. 27, pp. 29-30 with bibliography. The best description of the contents of the manuscript is by Heinrich Boehmer, *Die Fälschungen Erzbischof Lanfranks von Canterbury* (Leipzig 1902) 62-64 n. 2; cf. Holtzmann, PUE 1: 83 and 84.

Mansi;[72] the crucial words "hominium faciat laico aut" are omitted and only the prohibition of lay investituture remains. R. W. Southern suggests that Eadmer altered Paschal's letter in order to bring it into harmony with Paschal's post-1106 policies when he permitted lay homage in England.[73] Eadmer's *Vita Sancti Anselmi*,[74] a work written much later than the *Historia*, lends support to Southern's argument. In the *Vita* Eadmer omitted in the account of the Roman council of 1099[75] the reference to the prohibition of lay homage which he had still included in the *Historia*.[76] Incontrovertible proof that Eadmer did indeed alter the text of JL 5908 is furnished by a second letter sent by Paschal to Anselm around 15 April 1102, JL 5909. Just as JL 5908 in the Anselmian transmission, JL 5909 contains an explicit condemnation of lay homage although no reference to the synod is made: "Liberam esse ecclesiam Paulus dicit. Indignum est igitur ut clericus, qui iam in dei sortem assumptus est et iam laicorum dignitatem excessit, pro terrenis lucris hominium laico faciat."[77] Lay homage had perhaps first been prohibited by Pope Urban II at the council of Clermont in 1095.[78] At the Roman council of 1099[79] which the English archbishop attended, the prohibition was apparently repeated, since Anselm, who because of his attendance felt himself bound by the canons of 1099, frequently referred to this council in his correspondence with Paschal concerning lay homage.[80] Lay homage was the main point of contention between the king and Anselm, and it was Paschal's 'dispensation' regarding this particular

---

[72] Mansi 20: 1136.
[73] Southern, *Saint Anselm*, esp. p. 299 n. 3 and p. 310.
[74] Eadmer, *The Life of St. Anselm, Archbishop of Canterbury*, ed. and trans. by R. W. Southern (Oxford 1962).
[75] Ibid., p. 115.
[76] Eadmer, *Historia novorum*, p. 114.
[77] Schmitt, *Opera* ep. 223 (4: 128).
[78] Somerville, *Decreta Claromontensia*, p. 145, no. 19. Somerville's planned edition of the remainder of the councils of Pope Urban II will show whether this pontiff perhaps repeated at Clermont a decree that was earlier promulgated elsewhere. On the significance of lay homage cf. Z. N. Brooke, "Lay Investiture and Its Relation to the Conflict of Empire and Papacy," *Proceedings, British Academy* 25 (1939) 217-247, esp. pp. 236ff.
[79] The council of 1099 has not yet been edited. The canons published in Mansi (20: 961-964) are identified there as a repetition of the canons from the council of Piacenza held by Pope Urban II in 1095. Until a critical examination of the council is available, Eadmer and the letters of the archbishop of Canterbury (see below n. 80) are the only evidence that Urban repeated the Clermont canon against lay homage at the Roman council of 1099. JL 6073 admits the prohibition, but implicitly denies the concomitant excommunication.
[80] Schmitt, *Opera* ep. 218 (4: 120), ep. 217 (4: 118-119) and also ep. 214 (4: 111-114) as well as ep. 388 (5: 331-332).

issue that made the agreement of 1107 between Henry and Anselm possible.[81]

The prohibition of lay homage at the council of 1102, although short-lived, as it turned out, aroused the interest of ecclesiastics on the continent. Excerpts from JL 5908 have been found in several canonical manuscripts. One of them is the oldest and best manuscript of the unedited *Collection in Ten Parts*, [82] Paris, BN lat. 10743, from the first decades of the twelfth century. The codex contains as 4.24.7 (p. 227) with the inscription "Paschalis II Anselmo Cantuariorum archiepiscopo" the following excerpt:

> In synodo nuper apud Lateranense consistorium celebrata patrum nostrorum decreta renouauimus sancientes et interdicentes ne quisquam omnino clericus hominium laico faciat.[83]

Perhaps related to the *Collection in Ten Parts* is a small compilation of canonical texts, primarily from the late eleventh and early twelfth centuries which form an appendix in MS 364 of the Bibliothèque municipale of St. Omer,[84] discovered by G. Fransen.[85] On fol. 162v the excerpt from JL 5908, as found in MS Paris, BN lat. 10743, is transcribed.

The St. Omer codex is a copy of the canonical collection *Panormia* by Ivo of Chartres.[86] Two further twelfth-century manuscripts of this collection,

---

[81] Paschal absolved Anselm from the observation of Urban's prohibition of investiture and homage: "Te autem, frater in Christo venerabilis et carissime, ab illa prohibitione sive, ut tu credis, excommunicatione absolvimus, quam ab antecessore nostro, sanctae memoriae Urbano papa, adversus investituras aut hominia factam intelligis" (JL 6073; Schmitt, *Opera* ep. 397 [5: 340-342]).

[82] Stickler, *Historia iuris canonici*, p. 186; van Hove, *Prolegomena*, p. 334; P. Fournier - G. Le Bras, *Histoire des collections canoniques en occident*, 2 (Paris 1932; repr. Aalen 1972) 296-302; Paul Fournier, "Les collections canoniques attribuées à Yves de Chartres," BEC 58 (1897) 433-42. The collection is a revision made by the Archdeacon Walter of Thérouanne shortly after 1123 of the *Collection in Nine Books* in MS Wolfenbüttel Gud. 212. See R. Somerville, "The Council of Beauvais, 1114," *Traditio* 24 (1968) 493-503, 498 with bibliography ibid., n. 33 and idem, *Decreta Claromontensia*, pp. 60-63.

[83] The same text is found in the remaining manuscripts of the *Collection in Ten Parts*: Berlin, DS, Phillipps 1746 (Rose 95) 4.24.2 (fol. 72va); Cambridge, Corpus Christi College 94, 4.24.7 (fol. 71r); Florence, B. Naz., C.S. D2 1476, 4.25.2 (fol. 90v); Vienna, ÖNB 2178, 4.25.2 (fol. 87v).

[84] *Catalogue Général*, Quarto series, 3: 177. The codex is the former MS 333 of the Abbey of St. Bertin and dates from the second half of the twelfth century.

[85] "Trois notes" *Traditio* 26 (1970) 444-447. See also Somerville, *Decreta Claromontensia*, pp. 68-69.

[86] See Stickler, *Historia iuris canonici*, pp. 180-184; van Hove, *Prolegomena*, pp. 331-332; Fournier-Le Bras, *Histoire des collections canoniques* 2: 85-108; P. Fournier, "Les collections canoniques attribuées à Yves de Chartres," BEC 57 (1896) 645-698; BEC 58 (1897) 26-77; 293-326; 410-444; 624-676.

Paris BN lat. 4284[87] and Vatican City, Reginensis lat. 972,[88] also contain a set of additions which include 1102 material. Among canons from councils, papal letters, sentences from the church fathers, especially Augustine, and letters of Ivo of Chartres, a long excerpt from JL 5908 is transmitted. The appendices in mss Paris, BN lat. 4284 and Vatican, Reg. lat. 972 are not connected to the *Collection in Ten Parts*, and the excerpt from JL 5908 differs, particularly in length,[89] but the purpose in every case was undoubtedly to preserve the 1102 decision which supported the position of Archbishop Anselm in the investiture conflict. It is worth noting that the codices,[90] all by the way linked to northern France, also contain an excerpt from another of the pontiff's letters to Anselm of Canterbury, JL 5928, that equally serves to strongly condemn lay investiture.[91] This interest in the prohibition of lay homage clearly reflects support for a rigorous continuation of Roman reform policies at least among some French ecclesiastics.

Other Notable Decisions of the Council

Ekkehard of Aura, who formulated the chronicle account for the year 1102 early in 1106 at the latest,[92] included two items of particular interest for his contemporaries as well as for the historian. The first was the solemn excommunication of Henry iv which Paschal pronounced publicly according

---

[87] See *Catalogus codicum manuscriptorum Bibliothecae Regiae* 3 (Paris 1744) 574.
[88] Montfaucon no. 92. See *Les manuscrits de la Reine de Suède au Vatican, Réédition du Catalogue de Montfaucon et côtes actuelles*, Studi e Testi 238 (1964), p. 10.
[89] The inscription reads in both manuscripts: "Paschalis episcopus servus servorum dei venerabili fratri et coepiscopo Anselmo Cantuariorum." The text: "Nuper in synodo apud lateranense consistorium celebrata patrum nostrorum decreta renovavimus sancientes et interdicentes ne quisquam omnino clericus hominium laico faciat aut de manu laici ecclesiastica dona suscipiat. Hec est symoniace pravitatis radix ... explicit: procuretur eternam." See Schmitt, *Opera* ep. 222 (4: 125), lines 19-29, where this text differing slightly in the beginning forms a complete paragraph. The text is found in ms Paris, BN lat. 4284 on fol. 164r and in ms Vatican, Reg. lat. 972 on fol. 103v. The appendices in these manuscripts are identical. See Stephan Kuttner and Robert Somerville, "The So-Called Canons of Nîmes (1096)," *Tijdschrift voor Rechtsgeschiedenis* 38 (1970) 175-189, p. 178 n. 18.
[90] ms St. Omer 364 is the exception, containing only the excerpt from JL 5908.
[91] For the full text of this letter see Schmitt, *Opera* ep. 281 (4: 196-198). The excerpt is found in ms Paris, BN lat. 4284 on fol. 164r and in ms Reg. lat. 972 on fol. 103v-104r. The *Collection in Ten Parts* contains a slightly briefer excerpt: Paris, BN lat. 10743, 4.29.6 (pp. 231-232); Berlin, DS, Phillipps 1746 (Rose 95) 4.28.6 (fol. 73vb); Cambridge, Corpus Christi College 94, 4.29.6 (fol. 73r); Florence, B. Naz., C.S. D2 1476, 4.29.6 (fol. 103r); Vienna, ÖNB 2178, 4.29.6 (fol. 89r-89v).
[92] See Schmale-Ott, "Untersuchungen," pp. 406-407.

to ancient custom[93] on Maundy Thursday (3 April 1102) in the Basilica of St. Peter in the presence of Ekkehard:[94]

> Quia, inquit, tunicam Christi scindere, id est aecclesiam rapinis et incendiis devastare, luxuriis, periuriis atque homicidiis commaculare non cessavit, primo a beatae memoriae Gregorio papa, deinde a sanctissimo viro Urbano predecessore meo propter suam inoboedientiam excommunicatus est atque condempnatus; nos quoque in proxima synodo nostra iudicio totius aecclesiae perpetuo eum anathemati tradidimus. Id notum volumus omnibus et maxime ultramontanis esse, quatinus ab ipsius se contineant iniquitate.[95]

The second item to attract special attention in Ekkehard's report is a formula of anathema introduced by the synod that is combined with a profession of obedience to Paschal and his successors:

> Anathematizo omnem heresim et precipue eam, quae statum presentis aecclesiae perturbat, quae docet et astruit anathema contempnendum et aecclesiae ligamenta spernenda esse. Promitto autem oboedientiam apostolicae sedis pontifici domno Paschali eiusque successoribus sub testimonio Christi et aecclesiae, affirmans quod affirmat, et dampnans quod dampnat sancta et universalis aecclesia.[96]

Theodor Gottlob, discussing the development of the oath of office or *promissio*[97] required from ecclesiastics who came into close contact with the Apostolic See, points out that the written profession of obedience that had to be signed by the participants of the Lateran council of 1102 is a document aiming to assure ecclesiastical unity and acceptance of papal measures undertaken in connection with the investiture controversy.[98] He contrasts this sworn declaration with the ordinary oath of office, presumably

---

[93] Gratian, *De cons.* D.3 c.17; R. Somerville, "Honorius II, Conrad and Lothar III," *Archivum Historiae Pontificiae* 10 (1972) 341-346, pp. 345-346 and n. 25; for the ceremony and its significance see also LThK 6 (1961) 197-199 s.v. Kirchenbann and ibid., 1 (1957) 494-495) s.v. Anathema as well as Hinschius, *System des Katholischen Kirchenrechts* 5 (1893) 1-13.

[94] "Ibi etiam quam sententiam in imperatorem ... promulgaverit, nos quoque inter innumeras diversarum gentium catervas proxima coena Domini in aecclesia Lateranensi ab ipsius ore didicimus..." (Ekkehard, p. 180).

[95] Ibid. Henry IV was excommunicated by Pope Gregory VII in 1076, 1080 and 1081. Urban II repeated the excommunication in JL 5393 of 18 April 1089, and probably again at the council of Piacenza in 1095. Cf. Alfons Becker, "Urban II. und die deutsche Kirche," p. 244.

[96] Ekkehard, p. 180.

[97] The required *promissio* had the characteristics of an oath from early times on. See Gottlob, *Amtseid*, pp. 8-10.

[98] Gottlob, ibid., pp. 49ff., refers in this connection to Paschal's letter JL 6570.

modelled on the oath of Archbishop Wibert of Ravenna,[99] which Paschal demanded when the pallium was granted.[100]

The clergy assembled in the Lateran in 1102 presumably already supported papal policies. The signed *professio*, therefore, can only have served two purposes; (1) to show that the church stood united behind Paschal in the face of the continuing schism of the German church under Henry IV; and (2) to forestall a possible desertion of the papal cause through adherence to yet a third imperial anti-pope.[101] The Lateran synod was designed to create clear fronts. This is demonstrated by all of the surviving evidence: the only canon, the definition of the current schism as heresy, the excommunication of Henry IV, and the oath of obedience, adapted very skilfully by the curia to the requirements of Paschal's pontificate and widely used to reconcile schismatics with the Roman church. The *Annales S. Disibodi*,[102] a mid-twelfth century chronicle of largely derivative character from the German Benedictine monastery at Disidenbodenberg in the archdiocese of Mainz[103] spell out this purpose: "Venerabilis autem Paschalis et apostolicae sedis antistes statuit, ut quicumque de scismate hereticorum ad unitatem et concordiam sanctae ecclesiae katholicae reverti vellent, prius omnem heresim anathematizarent; sicque promissa apostolicae sedis pontifici Paschali eiusque successoribus obedientia, sub testimonio Christi et ecclesiae, paci et unitati reconciliarentur. Ordo reconciliationis huiusmodi est: Anathematizo...."[104] A further instance of the use made of the formula is a letter sent by Paschal shortly after the council of Guastalla held in October 1106 to Archbishop Bruno of Trier, instructing him to reconcile Bishop Otbert of Liège (1092-1117) "et Leodicensem clerum sive populum" to the church according to the 1102 *promissio* (JL 6099). Continued use is also demonstrated by the Iusiurandum Wirziburgensium,

---

[99] The text of Wibert's oath is transmitted in Deusdedit's canonical collection, *Die Kanonessammlung des Kardinals Deusdedit*, ed. Victor Wolf von Glanvell (Paderborn 1905; repr. Aalen 1967) 4. 423, and passed from this collection into the "Digesta pauperis scholaris Albini," 10. 46 (published in *Liber Censuum* 2: 94), and the *Liber Censuum* (1: 417).

[100] See the bibliography given above, n. 45.

[101] The second successor of Wibert of Ravenna (d. 1100), Albert, had just been defeated. See Jaffé, *Regesta* 1: 773.

[102] See Rep. Font. 2 (1967) 328; subsequent references are to the partial edition (a. 891-1200) by G. Waitz, MGH SS 17 (1861) 4-30.

[103] See M.-A. Dimier, DHGE 14 (1960) 519-520.

[104] MGH SS 17: 17. The formula of anathema is found under the year 1099. The entry, however, comes close to being a synopsis of the whole of Paschal's pontificate. Furthermore, the text shows that the formula dates from after the death of Wibert of Ravenna (September 1100).

preserved in the Codex Udalrici[105] and dated by Jaffé "from after February 1105."[106] As in the case of Liège the oath was used at Würzburg to bring the city back into the papal fold.[107] The oath for the readmission of schismatics to communion with the Roman church was long customary[108] of course, and Paschal apparently simply set out to continue the traditions of Pope Urban II as a text first published by Pflugk-Harttung might indicate,[109] yet the widespread use of the formula during his pontificate deserves to be noted.

## THE LATERAN COUNCIL, LENT 1105[110]

### The Sources and Previous Scholarship

If any one council were to be chosen to demonstrate the very limited usefulness of the *Amplissima Collectio* of Mansi for Paschal's councils, it could well be the council held by the pontiff in the Lateran during Lent, 1105. Texts which belong to this synod are nowhere collected under a distinct rubric, but instead are attributed to pseudo-councils of 1103 and 1104.[111] For the sake of clarity the history of the available sources will therefore be presented under three headings: 1103, 1104, 1105.

---

[105] See in general Wattenbach-Holtzmann, *Deutschlands Geschichtsquellen*, rev. ed. F.-J. Schmale, 2: 439-442 and 3: 137*; R. Somerville, "Honorius II," esp. 343; Peter Classen, "Heinrichs IV. Briefe im Codex Udalrici," DA 20 (1964) 115-129. Schmale and Somerville partially rejected the thesis presented by Franz-Josef Schmale, "Fiktionen im Codex Udalrici," *Zeitschrift für bayerische Landesgeschichte* 20 (1957) 437-474.

[106] *Monumenta Bambergensia*, ed. Jaffé, p. 230, no. 119.

[107] "Anathematizo omnem heresim; praecipue illam, quae praesentis ecclesiae statum conturbat et astruit: ligamenta ecclesiae esse spernenda, sub testimonio Christi et ecclesiae. Promitto autem fidem et obedientiam Romanae sedis pontifici Pascali et R[uperto] Wirzeburgensis ecclesiae episcopo; dampnans, quod dampnat, affirmans, quod affirmat sancta universalis ecclesia" (ibid.). For the events at Würzburg in the spring of 1105 see Knonau, *Jahrbücher* 5: 232.

[108] Gottlob, *Amtseid*, pp. 9ff.

[109] Cf. A. Brackmann GP II/1 (1923) 33 no. 19 and p. 132 no. 31; J. von Pflugk-Harttung, "Briefe aus den Jahren 1047-1146," *Neues Archiv* 6 (1881) 626-636, 628-629. The Jaffé no. is JL 5825. The formula begins: "Ego N. illius loci dictus episcopus seu cuiuslibet ordinis clericus anathematizo omnes hereses et scismata cum suis auctoribus, precipue Wibertum, quondam Ravennatensem episcopum...," showing that the anti-pope was still living at the time of composition.

[110] The date can be established with the aid of Paschal's letters JL 6028 and 6029.

[111] No evidence that Paschal held a council either in 1103 or 1104 has come down to us. The possibility that a synod met at Benevento in December 1102 is discussed in Appendix 1.

## 1103

A passage in the *Historia Mediolanensis* by Landulf of S. Paulo[112] is the only source which was once thought to indicate that Paschal held a council in 1103. Introduced into the conciliar collections by Labbe and Cossart, the text was reproduced by Hardouin as well as Coleti and Mansi.[113] Mansi retained the text under the year 1103, although he correctly pointed out that the report in the *Historia Mediolanensis* really referred to a council held in 1105: "Si duo anni transierunt post experimentum ignis, quod factum est exeunte anno 1102 vel ineunte 1103,[114] ac deinde Liprandus provocatus ad synodum Romanam venit, haec igitur habita anno 1105, et eadem est ac Lateranensis de qua infra."[115] Mansi's argument is valid and therefore no evidence for a papal council in 1103 exists.

## 1104

The idea that Paschal II presided at a synod in 1104 also originated with the work of the Jesuit scholars Labbe and Cossart. In the tenth volume of the *Sacrosancta concilia* they placed Paschal's letter JL 6028 to Anselm of Canterbury[116] under the year 1104.[117] Since this letter refers to a papal council they consequently assumed that a synod had been held by the pontiff in 1104. Their error was soon emended. In the annotations to his edition of Baronius' *Annales Ecclesiastici* Pagi pointed out very clearly that JL 6028 belongs to the year 1105. His argument, based on Eadmer's *Historia novorum*, cannot but be accepted.[118]

---

[112] *Landulphi Junioris sive de Sancto Paulo Historia Mediolanensis ab anno MXCV usque ad annum MCXXXVII*, Rerum Italicarum Scriptores, 2nd ed., vol. 5/3, ed. C. Castiglioni (Bologna s.d.). For a biography of Landulf see ibid., vii-x. As the editor points out, Landulf's purpose was to write an apologia both for himself and his beloved uncle Luitprand; "Nel nipote è manifesta la preoccupazione di presentare Liprando, come un santo degno degli onori degli altari. Senza voler menomamente togliere alcunchè alle benemerenze da Liprando acquistate nella diuturna lotta per la causa santa, ci pare però doveroso rilevare che il di lui zelo era spesso indiscreto e intollerante, e che tutti i fatti prodigiosi attribuitigli dal nipote riconoscente, a cominciare dalla stessa famosa prova del fuoco, non sono suffragati da altre testimonianza storiche" (ibid., p. vii). Landulf's historical contributions have to be evaluated with these remarks in mind.

[113] Labbe-Cossart 10: 1833-1834; Hardouin 6/2: 1871-1872; Coleti 12: 1107; Mansi 20: 1159-1162.

[114] See *Historia Mediolanensis*, p. 10 n. 1 and E. Cazzani, *Vescovi e Arcivescovi di Milano* (Milan 1955) 135.

[115] Mansi 20: 1159-1160n.

[116] Schmitt, *Opera ep.* 353 (5: 293).

[117] Labbe-Cossart 10: 741; Hardouin (6/2: 1875-1876), Coleti (12: 1115-1116) and Mansi (20: 1183-1184) reproduced the dates of Labbe-Cossart.

[118] Baronius, *Annales Ecclesiastici cum critica historico-chronologica*, ed. A. Pagi, vol. 18 (Lucca 1746) 172, observatio P. Antonii Pagi ad An. Chr. 1105 n. 4. Pagi's argument applies equally to JL 6029 dealing with the same matters.

But while Pagi corrected Labbe and Cossart, he himself was in error when he published among the annotations to the work of Baronius under the year 1104 a passage from the continuation of the *Gesta Treverorum*,[119] indicating that Archbishop Bruno of Trier[120] had gone to Rome and encountered Pope Paschal II at a synod: "Anno igitur ordinationis suae tercio mense Marcio Romam profectus apostolorum gratia et percipiendae benedictionis magistri sui causa, invenit domnum Pascalem universali sinodo praesidentem, papatus sui iam annum octavum agentem."[121] Pagi corrected the pontifical year to read "annum quintum" since this corresponded to the third year of Bruno's episcopate: January 1104 to January 1105, implying a council had been held in March 1104.[122] It would, however, be equally possible to alter the year of Bruno's episcopate to bring it into harmony with the eighth year of Paschal's pontificate: August 1106 - August 1107.[123] Paschal celebrated two councils during this time, the synods of Guastalla and Troyes. The *Gesta* indicate that Bruno travelled south. The council at which he encountered the pontiff is, therefore, the council of Guastalla, held around 22 October 1106. Furthermore, the *Gesta Treverorum* make it clear that Bruno set out for Rome at the behest of Henry V. "Magister suus" in the text[124] has to refer either to Emperor Henry IV or to Henry V. There is no evidence that Henry IV sent ambassadors to Rome in 1104, the date Pagi suggested for Bruno's journey, but many sources confirm that the archbishop of Trier was entrusted twice with the office of ambassador by Henry V in 1106.[125] His first embassy in

---

[119] The chronicle was edited by G. Waitz, MGH SS 8 (1848) 111-204. The most recent bibliography is found in Wattenbach-Holtzmann, *Deutschlands Geschichtsquellen* 2: 619-623 and 3: 170*-171*. Additional publications concerning the *Gesta Treverorum* are indicated below n. 128.

[120] Bruno of Brettheim-Laufen, 13 (6?) Jan. 1102 - 25 April 1124. See G. Allemang, DHGE 10 (1938) 970-971; Horst Schlechte, *Erzbischof Bruno von Trier* (Leipzig 1934); N. Gladel, *Die trierischen Erzbischöfe in der Zeit des Investiturstreits* (Kaldenkirchen 1932) 61-104.

[121] MGH SS 8: 192.

[122] *Annales Ecclesiastici*, ed. Pagi, 18: 165.

[123] The manuscripts of the *Gesta Treverorum* all read "octavus" for the pontifical year of Paschal II. The one exception, Waitz' codex B 1, reads "nonus" instead of "octavus." "Quintus" is not found in any of them. Pagi was familiar with the text published by Luc d'Achery (1609-1685) in the *Spicilegium*.

[124] MGH SS 8: 192.

[125] Allemang's article (DHGE 10: 970-971) argues that Bruno had led the original embassy sent by Henry V to Paschal II early in 1105, and states that it was this embassy that was captured at Trent. Allemang confuses two embassies. As soon as Henry had separated from his father at Christmas 1104 he sent messengers to Paschal requesting absolution from the oath he had rendered his father at the time of his coronation in 1098 (Knonau, *Jahr-*

the early spring of 1106 came to an abrupt end in the mountains near Trent.[126] His second mission was completed successfully when he participated in the council of Guastalla in October 1106. It may be concluded that the events which are described in the chronicle occurred at this synod.[127] The *Gesta Treverorum* seem to be incorrect not for Paschal's pontifical year, as Pagi had assumed, but for the episcopal year of Bruno.[128]

## 1105

In addition to the sources for the council of 1105 which are identified in the preceding analysis among material gathered under the dates 1103 and 1104,[129] two other items contribute information concerning the Lateran council of 1105: a passage in the *Chronicon monasterii Casinensis* which was discussed earlier,[130] and a letter (JL 6175) addressed by Paschal to the clergy of the Church of the Holy Sepulchre at Jerusalem, King Baldwin (1100-1118) and the people of Jerusalem.[131] The letter, written in 1107 after the death of Patriarch Daimbert,[132] describes his suffering and his restitution to the see of Jerusalem by a council:

---

*bücher* 5: 215 n. 7; Peiser, *Investiturstreit*, pp. 8-9). The messengers are not known by name, but Bruno certainly was not among them, since he remained loyal to Henry IV until the fall of 1105. The messengers were not captured but reached the pape safely.

[126] Knonau, *Jahrbücher* 5: 294-296 and Schlechte, *Bruno von Trier*, p. 34. Schlechte's argument that it was probably Cardinal Legate Richard of Albano who served as the first link between Bruno and Pope Paschal II in October 1105 (ibid., p. 33) appears acceptable.

[127] This was suggested earlier by Hefele-Leclercq, *Histoire des conciles* 5/1: 497. W. von Giesebrecht rejected the identification of Bruno's journey, described in the *Gesta*, with his attendance at Guastalla, but without good reason as Peiser showed who accepted Hefele-Leclercq's dating of the episode (*Investiturstreit*, pp. 27-29 n. 39). See in particular Horst Schlechte, *Bruno von Trier*, pp. 35-38.

[128] In addition to the prolegomena of Waitz (MGH SS 8: 111-129) cf. on the *Gesta Treverorum* in general Heinz Thomas, "Studien zur Trierer Geschichtsschreibung des 11. Jahrhunderts, insbesondere zu den Gesta Treverorum," *Rheinisches Archiv* 68 (1968); Harry Bresslau, "Zur Kritik von Gesta Trevirorum Contin. I, cap. 3ff.," *Jahrbücher des deutschen Reichs unter Konrad II.*, Jahrbücher der deutschen Geschichte 2 (Leipzig 1884) Exkurs I, pp. 514-518; particularly helpful in the present context are the remarks by Gladel, *Trierische Erzbischöfe*, pp. 106-108, Exkurs: "Die Glaubwürdigkeit der gesta Trvirorum, additamentum et continuatio prima caput 9ss." Frequent chronological errors, according to Gladel, should not detract from the overall value of the *Gesta* for local history.

[129] They are Landulph's *Historia Mediolanensis* and JL 6028.

[130] Above, pp. 11-12.

[131] The letter is preserved in the cartulary of the church, *Cartulaire de l'Église du Saint Sépulcre de Jérusalem*, ed. E. de Rozière (Paris 1849) 8-11, no. 10.

[132] Archbishop of Pisa, 1099-1102 and Patriarch of Jerusalem. The majority of the sources for Daimbert's life (see J. G. Rowe, "Paschal II and the Relation Between the Spiritual and Temporal Powers in the Kingdom of Jerusalem," *Speculum* 32 [1957] 470-501, esp. 486 n. 84) and the majority of historians (cf. ibid.) accept 1107, the date given by William

... Si quidem in Daibertum bone memorie, fratrem nostrum et coepiscopum, acerrime conspiratum esse [noscitur], ad quod noegocium decidendum nostre sedis [legatum], presbiterum cardinalem Robertum, misimus....[133] Ceterum frater ille (Daimbert) ad sedem apostolicam veniens, non defecisse sed regio se fatebatur timore propulsum, apud nos itaque iudicium executus est. Interim apud vos Evremarum[134] novimus legati nostri favore ad regimen episcopatus electum. Nos autem, in Lateranensi ecclesia Daiberti satisfactione suscepta, suo eum officio et Ierosolimitane sedi restituimus synodali iudicio; Evremarum vero a Ierosolimitana sede removimus....[135]

Since the date of the restitution of the patriarch is not mentioned, opinions differ as to when a papal council discussed and decided the case of Daimbert of Pisa-Jerusalem. The older argument in favor of a Jerusalem council in 1107[136] contradicts the known facts. Jaffé, Hefele-Leclercq, and now Rowe[137] seem to be correct in claiming that Paschal reinstated Daimbert at the council of 1105. A few considerations will bear this out.

---

of Tyre (*Historia rerum in partibus transmarinis gestarum*, RHCOc 1: 457), as the date of death for Daimbert. J. G. Rowe thought that William's entry ought to be dated 1105, using a Pisan chronicle as evidence, but without evaluating this chronicle's authenticity as contrasted with the other sources. Rowe admits that the problem is a difficult one. It cannot be investigated here, and this author therefore accepts the conventional date, 1107. To the bibliography given by Rowe should now be added Mayer, *The Crusades*. Daimbert's position in the Holy Land is also briefly discussed by Joshua Prawer, *Histoire du Royaume Latin de Jérusalem*, trans. G. Nahon, vol. 1 (Paris 1969) 261-264. S. Runciman's account of Daimbert's activities is very subjective. Runciman follows in general Albert d'Aix, who, as Runciman admits, is prejudiced against Daimbert, and blames William of Tyre for "besmirching" the name of Daimbert's opponent, Arnulf (*A History of the Crusades* [Cambridge Engl. 1951 and 1952; reprinted New York 1964 and 1965] 1: 299n; 2: 81ff. in the reprint).

[133] Robert, cardinal presbyter of the title of S. Eusebius, was also known as Robert of Paris. Becker, *Urban II*, p. 110 n. 363 and especially Klewitz, "Kardinalskollegium," p. 216.

[134] Evremar of Chocques, diocese of Arras. See Baldwin, *The First Hundred Years*, p. 383.

[135] Rozière, *Cartulaire* no. 10 = JL 6175.

[136] This had been assumed by Baronius (12: 63-64; cf. ibid., 38 for Daimbert's arrival in Rome under the date 1104) and all conciliar editors including Mansi (20: 1215-1216). The erroneous statement found its way also into Baldwin, *The First Hundred Years*, p. 383. It is based on a passage in William of Tyre's *Historia*: "Interea dominus Daimbertus, Hierosolymorum patriarcha, post longam exspectationem qua eum detinuerat dominus Paschalis papa et ecclesia romana, volens plenius edoceri, utrum rex Hierosolymorum et qui eum expulerant, vellent aliquid contra eum allegare, unde hoc videri possent de jure fecisse; postquam nemo comparuit ... jussus est ad propria redire et sedem recipere..." (RHCOc 1: 456-7 [XI.4]). This passage, just as JL 6175, does not provide a date for the events described, but also does not contain any mention of a council at Jerusalem that reinstated Daimbert. Furthermore, since Daimbert died at Messina on 16 June 1107, while preparing to return for the first time to his see which he had left in 1104, he cannot possibly have attended a council at Jerusalem in 1107.

[137] Jaffé, *Regesta* 1: 733; Hefele-Leclercq, *Histoire des conciles* 5/1, 483-4; Rowe, "Jerusalem," pp. 485-488.

Daimbert left Antioch in the company of Bohemond of Antioch in the fall of 1104,[138] and they arrived at Bari in January 1105.[139] Bohemond remained for eight months in Apulia and subsequently accompanied the papal legate Bishop Bruno of Segni to the synod of Poitiers which was held in June 1106.[140] During this time, nothing is heard about Daimbert of Pisa. It would be easy to assume with William of Tyre that the former patriarch waited for a decision by the pontiff. Paschal's letter to Jerusalem (JL 6175) shows, however, that this cannot have been the case, for, as the pope wrote, it was a synod that reinstated Daimbert. As Rowe pointed out, Paschal's itinerary leaves the spring of 1105 as the only possible date for the synod that discussed the case of Daimbert.[141]

## The Participants

JL 6175 which was just discussed provides evidence that Daimbert of Pisa-Jerusalem attended the council in the Lateran. A document, dated 8 May 1108, of the Fondo S. Eugenio of the Archivio di Stato at Siena[142] is evidence for the probable presence of several other ecclesiastics: Bruno of Segni, Robert, cardinal priest of S. Eusebio,[143] Ugo, cardinal of SS. Cosma and Damiano,[144] Abbot Henry of S. Salvatore,[145] and Bishop Roger of Volterra (1099-1131, tr. Pisa 1121).

---

[138] William of Tyre, RHCOc 1: 1 [XI.1] 450: "Aestate vero transcursa, dominus Boamundus ... in Apuliam navigavit, et cum eo dominus Daymbertus, Hierosolymorum patriarcha."

[139] R. Röhricht, *Geschichte der Kreuzzüge im Umriss* (Innsbruck 1898) 63. Cf. Prawer, *Jerusalem*, 1: 287.

[140] Mansi 20: 1205-1208. For these events see especially J. G. Rowe, "Paschal II, Bohemund of Antioch and the Byzantine Empire," *Bulletin of the John Rylands Library* 49 (1966) 165-202; Gigalski, *Bruno von Segni*, pp. 58-68; Grégoire, *Bruno de Segni*, p. 47; Th. Schieffer, *Die päpstlichen Legaten in Frankreich vom Vertrage von Meersen (870) bis zum Schisma von 1130* (Berlin 1935) 175ff.; MGH SS 7: 777, Chronicle of Montecassino 4, 31 and the relevant remarks in Hoffmann, "Studien," pp. 145-146; R. B. Yewdale, *Bohemond I, Prince of Antioch* (Princeton 1924, repr. Amsterdam 1970) 108ff.

[141] Rowe, "Jerusalem," 486 and n. 84. This is also assumed by G. Tangl, *Die Teilnehmer*, p. 184.

[142] Published by J. Ficker, *Forschungen zur Reichs- und Rechtsgeschichte Italiens* 4 (1874) 138, no. 94 and Paul Kehr, "Le Bolle Pontificie che si conservano negli Archivi Senesi," *Bullettino Senese di Storia Patria* 6 (1899) 73. See also Kehr, IP 3 (1908) 311 no. 4.

[143] Klewitz, "Kardinalskollegium," p. 216 no. 27. The cardinal is also known as Robert of Paris and was Paschal's legate to Jerusalem in 1102 when he deposed Daimbert. (A succinct recent summary is that by Rowe, "Paschal II," 172-173.) His presence in 1105 lends further support to the argument that Daimbert's case was discussed at the council of 1105.

[144] Klewitz, "Kardinalskollegium," p. 219 n. 4.

[145] On the history of the monastery of S. Salvatore see W. Kurze, "Der Adel und das

In spite of the shortcomings of the *Historia Mediolanensis*,[146] Landulf's statements can partially be accepted as authentic. The ordeal of the priest Luitprand, Landulf's uncle, and rector of the church of San Paolo in Compito, Milan,[147] is presumably one of the prodigious feats which were invented by the nephew,[148] but not the suit between Luitprand and Archbishop Grossolan of Milan.[149] The litigation, whether involving an ordeal or not, was decided in the presence of the pontiff in Grossolan's favor during the Lateran synod of 1105.[150] In addition to the chief contenders, Grossolan and Luitprand, Landulf mentioned as having attended the council "Landulphus de Vareglate, qui post ipsam sinodum fuit Astensis episcopus."[151]

The quarrel between the monks of Montecassino and Archbishop Sennes of Capua over the consecration of the church of Sant'Angelo in Formis as reported in the chronicle of Montecassino was also resolved in 1105, and the archbishop of Capua can thus be added to the list of participants.[152]

## The Canons

No canons have been preserved.

---

Kloster S. Salvatore all'Isola im 11. und 12. Jahrhundert," QFIAB 47 (1967) 446-573. A brief regest of the document in question is found ibid., p. 542, n. 45.

[146] Above n. 112.

[147] *Historia Mediolanensis*, pp. vii-viii and n. 1.

[148] Ibid., pp. vii and xv. An analysis of the *Historia* has shown that there is no reason to depart from scholarly consensus, and Castiglioni's conclusions are here accepted.

[149] See Gams, *Series episcoporum* sub Savona and Mediolanensis. Grossolanus, the Latin form for his Greek name Chrysolaus, became bishop of Savona in 1098 and was transferred to Milan in 1102 where he had been elected archbishop. He was expelled in 1112 and died in Rome 6 August 1117. Still valuable for the history of Grossolan is G. Giulini, *Memorie spettanti alla storia, al governo, ed alla descrizione della città, e della campagna di Milano* 4 (Milan s.d.) esp. 466-527 and 5: 1-64. See also O. Masnovo, "Pier Grosolano e il suo epitafio," *Archivio Storico Lombardo*, ser. 5, 49 (1922) 1-28, so far the only attempt, if not very convincing, to evaluate the scant and biased sources for his episcopate. Cf. P. Guerrini, "Un cardinale Gregoriano a Brescia, il vescovo Arimanno," *Studi Gregoriani* 2 (1947) 361-385, 382. The most recent contribution is E. Cazzani, *Vescovi e Arcivescovi di Milano* (Milan 1955) 133-139.

[150] Cazzani, *Vescovi e Arcivescovi di Milano*, p. 135. The date was mentioned by Landulf (*Historia Mediolanensis*, p. 20); "Putavi non pretereundum scilentio, quod durante lite Grosulani, scilicet 1105, 7 idus maiis invente sunt reliquie...." For the events of the council see ibid., pp. 13-14.

[151] *Historia Mediolanensis*, pp. 13-14 and A. Bellini, "Il beato Landolfo da Vergiate," *Archivio Storico Lombardo* 49 (1922) 332-349.

[152] See above, p. 12.

## Other Notable Decisions of the Council

JL 6028, the letter of Paschal to Anselm of Canterbury erroneously dated 1104 by Labbe and Cossart,[153] reports the decision of a synod to excommunicate councillors of King Henry I of England and all those who had received investiture from his hand:

> Unde in concilio nuper habito ex communi fratrum et coepiscoporum sententia deliberatum est regis consiliarios, qui ad investiturae flagitium illum impellunt, et eos qui ab eo investiti sunt, ab ecclesiae liminibus repellendos, quia de libera facere conantur ancillam. Quam nimirum sententiam nos sancti spiritus iudicio in comitem de Mellento et eius complices promulgavimus, et eandem ipsam in eos qui sunt investiti a rege, eiusdem spiritus sancti iudicio confirmamus. Regis vero sententia ea ex causa dilata est, quia suos ad nos nuntios in praeteriti Paschae tempore debuit destinare.[154]

The date preserved is "VII. Kal. Aprilis," 26 March. In 1105, Easter fell on 9 April, and the date, therefore, seems to contradict the last phrase from the letter quoted: "Regis vero sententia ea ex causa dilata est, quia suos ad nos nuntios in praeteriti Paschae tempore debuit destinare." Unless the date is indeed wrong this sentence from Paschal's letter would mean that the assembled ecclesiastics agreed to wait for messengers from England whom the king was supposed to have sent to Rome almost a year earlier.[155] This is possible but difficult to prove.[156] In any event the clause was clearly intended to give Henry I another chance before he would himself be excommunicated.[157]

It is certain that these decisions and deliberations occurred in the year 1105 at the Lateran council. As noted by Pagi, Eadmer gives all the indications needed to identify the year: "In secundo autem anno adventus nostri a Roma Lugdunum, ipse papa, coacto Lateranis generali concilio, comitem de Mellente, cujus saepe superius habita mentio est, et complices ejus qui regem ad investiturae flagitium sicut dicebatur impellebant, necne illos qui ab eo investiti fuerant, a liminibus sanctae ecclesiae judicio Spiritus

---

[153] See above pp. 24-25.
[154] Schmitt, *Opera*, ep. 353 (5: 293) = JL 6028.
[155] See R. W. Southern, *Saint Anselm and His Biographer*, p. 175 n. 1.
[156] Pagi accepted this implication without hesitation. See above n. 118.
[157] It generally caused surprise that Anselm, after the pope had made a move in JL 6028 to support him, decided to excommunicate the English king himself. Professor Southern has shown, however, that Anselm threatened to excommunicate Henry I simply on the basis of the king's seizure of the Canterbury diocesan lands. (Southern, *Saint Anselm and His Biographer*, pp. 175-176.)

Sancti reppulit, et hoc ipsum per epistolam (JL 6028) quam ecce supponimus Anselmo sub celeritate innotuit."[158] Anselm left England for Rome shortly after Easter 1103.[159] From Bec and Chartres, where he stayed until August 1103,[160] he went to Rome,[161] but was back at Lyons for Christmas of the same year.[162] The second year of Anselm's coming to Lyons, as Eadmer expressed it, would cover almost the complete calendar year 1105. JL 6028, therefore, was received by Anselm at Lyons sometime in 1105 and reported the decisions which had been made in March 1105[163] "ex communi fratrum et coepiscoporum sententia," or in the words of JL 6029,[164] "in concilio quod praeterita Quadragesima celebravimus." Both of Paschal's letters are evidence for the council's decision to support Archbishop Anselm of Canterbury and to continue the strict prohibition of lay investiture. It should be noted that homage is not mentioned, perhaps, but not necessarily, a sign that negotiations concerning the latter were under way.

---

[158] Eadmer, *Historia novorum*, p. 163.
[159] Ibid., pp. 147-148.
[160] Ibid., p. 151.
[161] Ibid., p. 152.
[162] Ibid., p. 157.
[163] The date was never questioned except by the conciliar editors. Eadmer mentioned the swiftness with which Paschal informed Anselm of the decisions of the council. He must be correct, for even though this historian's information is not always reliable, as has been seen, it is difficult to imagine that Paschal, who at least since Anselm's Roman visit of 1103 was aware of the archbishop's plight, would have waited for a year or two before he informed him of a decision that might help him and which would not be kept a secret anyway. Cf. Fliche, *La réforme grégorienne*, p. 342 and the following note.
[164] JL 6029 (Schmitt, *Opera*, ep. 354, 5: 294) addressed to Archbishop Gerard of York, corroborates JL 6028, but does not contain dating elements except for a reference to Lent during which the council had been held. Since Anselm was in exile at Lyons, Paschal requested Gerard to proclaim the excommunications.

# 2

# The Council of Guastalla, 22 October 1106

On 12 December 1104, King Henry v (1104-1125) rebelled and departed secretly from the camp of his father, Emperor Henry iv (1154-1106).[1] This break between father and son altered the position of the papacy in Germany, where until then the papal party had been on the defensive.[2] Much of the support for the younger Henry, who immediately sent messengers to Paschal,[3] came from adherents to the papal cause, and for the moment Henry v made this cause to a large extent[4] his own.[5] Paschal fully supported the king and his revolt,[6] insisting, however, on the observance of the decrees of the council of Piacenza, held by his predecessor, Urban ii, in 1095.[7] The victories of Henry v and his sup-

---

[1] For general information see Knonau, *Jahrbücher* 5: 203; Fliche, *La réforme grégorienne*, p. 345.

[2] Becker, *Urban II.*, pp. 139-165 and idem, "Urban ii. und die deutsche Kirche," passim as well as Carl Henking, *Gebhard III., Bischof von Constanz: 1084-1110* (Stuttgart 1880) passim. Valuable are the comments and notes in Kurt Hils, *Die Grafen von Nellenburg im 11. Jahrhundert*, Forschungen zur Oberrheinischen Landesgeschichte 19 (Freiburg 1967) 103-135.

[3] Christmas 1104/New Year 1105; Knonau, *Jahrbücher* 5: 215 n. 7; Fliche, *La réforme grégorienne*, p. 346.

[4] It is often noted that Henry v, even at this stage of his career, continued to invest bishops. See especially Guleke, *Kirchenpolitik*. In an appendix ("Regesten der Wahlen geistlicher Reichsfürsten zwischen 1105 und 1111") Guleke showed that Henry v maintained his control over the German church unopposed by either nobility or ecclesiastics. Cf. Fliche, *La réforme grégorienne*, p. 346.

[5] A full narrative of the developments in Germany after Henry's rebellion against his father is found in Knonau, *Jahrbücher* 5: 203-273. Knonau gives valuable references to the sources and includes a critical discussion of previous scholarship.

[6] JL 6070. For a discussion of the letter's date see Knonau, *Jahrbücher* 5: 215-16, esp. 216 n. 8. Knonau's date, first half of 1105, is here accepted.

[7] JL 6050: "De ordinationibus clericorum qui in nostri temporis schismate ordinati sunt, non aliud scribendum duximus quam in Placentina synodo per sanctae memoriae Ur-

porters together with their reforming synods of Quedlinburg and Nordhausen early in 1105 thus became victories for the papacy also.[8]

The synod of Guastalla,[9] held by Paschal around 22 October 1106, was a reflection of the new situation in Germany and an attempt by the pontiff to bring about a permanent reconciliation between Rome and the empire. A council had been planned from the very first. Paschal's letter to King Henry v of early 1105, preserved in paraphrase in the *Chronica monasterii Casinensis*,[10] already suggested that he intended to hold a synod to deal with German affairs, if necessary even in Germany, in order to support Henry v on account of the latter's obedience to the Apostolic See:[11]

> Si enim sicut suarum apostolicae sedi litterarum allegatione promittebat, plena mentis devotione sibi suisque legitimis successoribus obedientiam exhibere curasset, quam sive reges sive imperatores catholici suis praedecessoribus exhibuerunt, ipse profecto eum ut catholicum imperatorem haberet, et honorem eius per Dei gratiam servaret, atque augere curaret. Nam si in coepta vellet probitate persistere, magna Romano imperio salus per apostolicae sedis obedientiam proveniret; quam ob causam non solum in partes illas venire, sed extremis quoque periculis personam suam exponere paratus esset.

The letter may have constituted Paschal's first contact with Henry v.[12] Its rather general proposal for a synod was made more explicit and urgent in

---

banum praedecessorem nostrum deliberatum est." Cf. below n. 14. The best available edition of the canons of Piacenza is that by L. Weiland (MGH Const. 1: 560-563). Cf. Knonau, *Jahrbücher* 5: 255-6.

[8] For the synods see ibid. pp. 272-3; A. Hauck, *Kirchengeschichte* 3: 879-882; Guleke, *Kirchenpolitik*, pp. 19-24 and 47. The synods met in the presence of the king, promulgated reform legislation and replaced imperially nominated bishops with ecclesiastics loyal to both the pope and the king. The schism in Germany had come to an end, argued Hauck.

[9] Cf. below n. 20.

[10] JL 6070; *Chronicon monasterii Casinensis* 4, c. 36 = MGH SS 7: 779.

[11] Ibid. According to Ekkehard, an embassy sent from the diet of Mainz, Christmas 1105/New Year 1106, was to invite Paschal "si fieri possit" to come across the Alps (Ekkehard, pp. 204 and 272). The invitation was perhaps encouraged by Paschal's suggestion. The German participants of the council of Guastalla again urged the pope's visit and believed that he would come to Germany. (See ibid. p. 292, where Mainz is suggested.) According to the same chronicler who was an eyewitness on both occasions, Henry v and the papal legates expected the pontiff to celebrate Christmas 1106 in this country: "Rex Heinricus natalem Domini Ratispone celebravit, presentibus scilicet legatis domni apostolici Paschalis, cuius adventum ipse iam aliquandiu apud Augustam Alemanniae metropolim caeterasque superiores partes prestolatus fuerat" (Ekkehard, p. 294). The *Annales Patherbrunnenses* (ed. Paul Scheffer-Boichorst, Innsbruck 1870; see Rep. Font. 2: 313 and Wattenbach-Holtzmann, *Deutschlands Geschichtsquellen* 2: 584-587) say that Paschal was expected at Mainz (p. 116). See also Knonau, *Jahrbücher* 6: 31-33 and n. 43 where further references are given.

[12] Cf. above n. 6.

Paschal's letter of November 1105 (JL 6050) to Archbishop Rothard of Mainz.[13] Here Paschal no longer proposed to come to Germany himself. He emphasized that it was a council either presided over by himself in Italy or by papal legates in Germany that must decide the cases of excommunicated bishops:

> Porro episcopos qui sub excommunicatione in eodem schismate manus impositionem susceperunt, ad concilii sententiam deferendos arbitramur. Tantum enim tantarum personarum malum generaliter deliberatione aut curandum est aut detruncandum (JL 6050).

The standing papal legate in Germany, Gebhard of Constance, and Archbishop Rothard of Mainz were evidently not authorized to reconcile excommunicated bishops. Accordingly, the synod of Nordhausen held in the early summer of 1105 only arranged for the reconciliation of ecclesiastics who had been consecrated by schismatics,[14] and reserved the decision concerning the schismatics themselves, the 'pseudoepiscopi', for the pope as we learn through the eyewitness account of Ekkehard of Aura.[15] Rothard, in-

---

[13] 1088-1109. In addition to Knonau see for Rothard M. Stimming, *Mainzer Urkundenbuch* (1932), for JL 6050 ibid. pp. 328-329, no. 423; Heinrich Büttner, "Das Erzstift Mainz und die Klosterreform im 11. Jahrhundert," *Archiv für Mittelrheinische Kirchengeschichte* 1 (1949) 30-64; Peter Rassow, "Über Erzbischof Ruthard von Mainz (1089-1109)," in *Die geschichtliche Einheit des Abendlandes* (Cologne and Graz 1960) 255-262, and in connection with JL 6050 also idem, "Der Kampf Kaiser Heinrichs iv. mit Heinrich v.," *Zeitschrift für Kirchengeschichte* 47 (1928) 451-465. Paschal wrote in this letter: "De concilii autem loco vel tempore, si vestris in partibus celebrandum sit, tua interest, communicato fratrum consilio, nobis citius indicare. Optamus enim et vehementer opportunum est, ut vel apud vos per legatos nostros vel in Italia per nos largiente Domino peragatur. In quo de sacerdotii ac regni scandalo propulsando, pace stabilienda, communi per Dei gratiam deliberatione tractemus."

[14] Cf. c. 10 of Urban's council of Piacenza (MGH Const. 1: 562) which could have served as basis for the action of the legate: "Qui vero ab episcopis quondam quidem catholice ordinatis sed in hoc scismate a Romana aecclesiae separatis consecrati sunt, eos nimirum, cum ad aecclesiae unitatem redierint, servatis propriis ordinibus, misericorditer suscipi iubemus, si tamen vita eos et scientia commendat." As has been seen earlier (above n. 7) Paschal referred to these decrees in his letter JL 6050. In certain manuscripts of the canons of Piacenza c. 10 contains an addition: "et si his nostris decretis cognitis mox ab errore ad catholicam ecclesiam transierint et nobis nostrisque legatis per omnia obedire promiserint." This policy, also, was continued by Paschal. On Gebhard's activity see in general also O. Schumann, *Die päpstlichen Legaten in Deutschland zur Zeit Heinrichs iv. und Heinrichs v. (1056-1125)*, (Marburg 1912) esp. pp. 67-74 and 81-83.

[15] That Ekkehard of Aura was present at Nordhausen has been concluded by Schmale-Ott, "Untersuchungen" 407. The chronicler's account (Ekkehard, p. 190) is illuminating: "In quo concilio (Nordhausen) super sententiis instantibus patrum decretis primo relectis, quaeque poterant ad presens laudabiliter corrigebantur, quaedam vero, quae et graviora videbantur, ad apostolicam audientiam differebantur. Symoniaca quippe heresis patrum con-

deed, reinstated Bishop Udo of Hildesheim,[16] but was for this and other reasons suspended from office at the council of Troyes in 1107.[17] In March 1106, finally, Paschal decided to hold the necessary synod himself during the month of October in Italy. The formal invitation sent to Archbishop Rothard of Mainz and his suffragans is preserved and illustrates the convocation procedures for a general synod.[18] Countess Mathilda of Tuscany was Paschal's hostess. According to one source, the council had originally been called to gather at Piacenza,[19] and it seems that Paschal changed the meeting place at the last minute to Guastalla, a little town nearby,[20] since

---

suetudine condempnata, Nycholaitarum quoque fornicaria commixtio ibidem est ab omnibus abdicata: ieiunium .... Romano more celebrandum a prescriptis presulibus apostolica auctoritate indicitur, et pax Dei confirmatur; his vero qui a pseudoepiscopis fuerant consecrati, per catholicam manus impositionem reconciliatio proximo ieiunio danda fore promittitur." The Pseudo-Isidorian stipulation that the deposition of bishops were *causae maiores* reserved to the pope alone was used for the first time at the Roman synod of 864. See Fuhrmann, *Einfluss und Verbreitung* 2: 257-259 and esp. n. 58.

[16] For Udo and the restitution by Rothard see Knonau, *Jahrbücher* 5: 227; A. Bertram, *Geschichte des Bisthums Hildesheim* 1 (Hildesheim 1899) 127 and particularly Wolfgang Heinemann, *Das Bistum Hildesheim im Kräftespiel der Reichs- und Territorialpolitik vornehmlich des 12. Jahrhunderts*, Quellen und Darstellungen zur Geschichte Niedersachsens 72 (Hildesheim 1968) especially pp. 49-59.

[17] JL 6145 (M. Stimming, *Mainzer Urkundenbuch*, pp. 338-339, no. 432): "... ad concilium nec venisti nec canonicas excusationes pretendisti. Hildinisheimensem publice criminosum, post synodicam prohibitionem officio restituisti ...." It cannot be determined to which synod Paschal was referring in the latter part of the citation.

[18] JL 6076 (Jaffé, *Monumenta Bambergensia*, p. 247 no. 130): "... duximus et magna consultatione deliberavimus: ut in proximis Octobribus Idibus (Oct. 8-15) synodalem vobiscum debeamus celebrare conventum. Idcirco tam te, karissime frater, quam omnes Moguntinae ecclesiae suffraganeos litteris praesentibus praemonemus: ut, convocatis dyocesium vestrarum qui digniores videntur abbatibus, convocatis etiam clericorum personis quibus concilii tractatus necessarius est, praenominato in tempore citra Alpes nobiscum convenire omni occasione seposita procuretis; quatinus, largiente Domino, ablatis de medio scismatum causis, ecclesiae ac regno pacis reformetur integritas." The synod is described in the same letter as *generalis tractatus* and *synodalis conventus*. *Generalis tractatus* is probably a synonym for the expression *concilium generale* that is used by Ekkehard of Aura (p. 244). For the meaning of "general council" under the reform papacy see H. Fuhrmann, "Das Ökumenische Konzil und seine historischen Grundlagen," *Geschichte in Wissenschaft und Unterricht* 12 (1961) 672-695.

[19] "Nos igitur videntes, quod nullo modo adquiescerent, communicato cum amicis nostris consilio Romanum pontificem, qui in Placentia urbe Italiae generale concilium indixerat, per me ipsum ipse adii. Quo cum quibusdam fratribus meis cum pervenissem et non ibi sed potius in alio loco qui Wardastallum dicitur reperissem, benignissime nos suscepit" (Seherus, *Primordia Calmosiacensia*, ed. P. Jaffé, MGH SS 12: 324-347, 336). Seher, abbot of the monastery of Chaumouzey in the diocese of Toul and author of the chronicle, died in 1128. See Potthast, *Wegweiser durch die Geschichtswerke des europäischen Mittelalters* (2 vols., 2nd ed. Berlin 1896) 2: 1006.

[20] The reason for this change is not known. Guastalla was part of Mathilda's patrimony, Piacenza a commune under her influence. No sign of hostility on the part of the commune of

the German delegation, led by Bruno of Trier as 'legatus regis,'[21] also disembarked at Piacenza.[22] It is unlikely that he had not been correctly informed about the location of the synod.

## THE SOURCES AND PREVIOUS SCHOLARSHIP

Cardinal Baronius was familiar with the council of Guastalla and included in the *Annales Ecclesiastici*[23] pertinent sections from the chronicle of Ekkehard of Aura,[24] the *Vita Mathildis* by Donizo,[25] and from Udalschalk's *De Eginone et Herimanno*.[26] The last chronicle account includes two letters Paschal had written in connection with the see of Augsburg (JL 6103 and JL 6119). A third letter (JL 5971) was published by Baronius together with a set of canons for the synod from a Vatican manuscript "qui liber Censuum inscribitur."[27]

---

Piacenza is found in the sources. On the contrary, Bishop Aldo of Piacenza accompanied the pontiff to Troyes (below ch. 3, n. 38). Furthermore, the synod of Guastalla had the approval of the German king, who sent representatives. Last but not least Piacenza stood high in Paschal's favor. It was freed from its dependence on the archdiocese of Ravenna (cf. *Liber Censuum*, ed. Fabre-Duchesne, 1: 115, col. a: "Le privilège était considérable, et l'honneur très envié").

[21] On Bruno's activity as royal ambassador at Guastalla see Schlechte, *Bruno von Trier*, pp. 35-37.

[22] *Translatio S. Modoaldi*, ed. P. Jaffé, MGH SS 12 (1856) 284-310, p. 296. The chronicle was probably written between 1105 and 1138 by an unknown author in the monastery of Helmarshausen in Paderborn, Hesse. A description and bibliography can be found in Wattenbach-Holtzmann, *Deutschlands Geschichtsquellen*, 2: 587, esp. n. 75.

[23] 12: 52-55.

[24] Ekkehard, pp. 290-292. Ekkehard participated in the synod of Guastalla (Schmale-Ott, "Untersuchungen," p. 409). His report was written shortly after his return and was part of the recension of his chronicle which he presented to Henry v early in 1107.

[25] On Donizo and the editions of his work see Rep. Font. 4 (forthcoming) 241-242; references in this study will be to the edition by L. Bethmann, MGH SS 12 (1856) 348-409. For Mathilda of Tuscany see A. Overmann, *Die Besitzungen der Grossgräfin Mathilde von Tuscien nebst Regesten* (Berlin 1893) and particularly idem, *Gräfin Mathilde von Tuscien, ihre Besitzungen: Geschichte ihres Gutes von 1115-1230 und ihre Regesten* (Innsbruck 1895); L. Simeoni, "Il contributo della contessa Matilde al papato nella lotta per le investiture," *Studi Gregoriani* 1 (1947) 353-372; F. Güterbock, "Possessi imperiali matildine tra Parma e Piacenza," *Archivio Storico Lombardo*, n.s. 1 (1936) 255-276; Gina Fasoli, "Rileggendo la 'Vita Matildis' di Donizone," *Studi Matildici: Atti e Memorie del II Convegno di Studi Matildici, Modena-Reggio E., 1-3 maggio 1970*, pp. 15-39. Deput. di Storia Patria per le Ant. Prov. Modenesi, Biblioteca, n.s. 16 (Modena 1971).

[26] Ed. P. Jaffé, MGH SS 12 (1856) 429-448. Relevant for the council of Guastalla is ch. 14 (ibid. 438). The treatise, narrating the quarrel between Abbot Egino (1109-1120) of S. Ulrich and Afra at Augsburg and Bishop Hermann of Augsburg (1096-1132), was written by Udalschalk, monk of the monastery and later its abbot (1124 - ca. 1150). It shows strong partisan sympathies on behalf of Egino whom Udalschalk had accompanied into exile at Rome. Cf. Wattenbach-Holtzmann, *Deutschlands Geschichtsquellen*, 2: 537-538.

[27] The codex will be discussed below pp. 47-50. Suffice it to say for the moment that it

Incorporated into Binius' second edition (1618)[28] of the *Concilia Generalia*,[29] the sources assembled by Baronius remained fundamental[30] for succeeding scholars.[31] The Jesuits Labbe and Cossart took the trouble to collate and publish the complete text of Baronius' canons from what they believed was Baronius' manuscript.[32] Coleti[33] is responsible for the chaotic

---

is probably not Cossart's Codex Censii, containing canons from Urban's council of Clermont, searched for by F. Gossman (*Urban II and Canon Law* [Washington 1960] 5 n. 13) and R. Somerville (*Decreta Claromontensia*, p. 119).

[28] The first edition of the work of Binius (1606; 3/2: 1307-1308) contained only the passage from Ekkehard of Aura (above n. 24) and a reference to the work of the Italian humanist scholars Platina (Bartholomew Platina [1421-1481], cf. Duchesne, *Liber Pontificalis* 2.1v) and Biondo (Flavio Biondo or Blondus [1392-1463], see R. Fubini, *Dizionario biografico degli Italiani* 10 [1968] 536-559): "De eadem [Guastalla] synodo haec Blondus et Platina recentiores: In Cisalpina Gallia seu Lombardia Paschalis ad Guardesallum Synodum agit de homagijs, de feudis, de sacramentis Episcoporum laicis antea exhibitis vel exhibendis. Decernit quoque ne Aemiliae urbes Placentia, Parma, Regium, Mutina, Bononia amplius Ravennati metropoli subessent; sed Pontifici immediate parerent." The passage, based on the *Liber Pontificalis*, was dropped in Binius' second edition.

[29] Binius, 2nd ed., 3/2: 440-441) corresponds to Baronius, *Annales* 12: 52-55. It should be noted that Binius did not completely transcribe the passage from Udalschalk's *De Eginone*, omitting the letters JL 6103 and JL 6119, but included a reference to their location. The omission seems to have been accidental, since Binius already introduced the letters at the bottom of p. 440 with: "sed litteras ab eo hunc in modum se continentes accepit" (*sic*). At the top of the next page, however, follow instead of the letters "Galonis S.R.E. Cardinalis Constitutiones." Binius' omission was repaired by Labbe and Cossart who again included the epistles.

[30] Labbe and Cossart assumed that Binius had incorrectly added to the description of the council of Guastalla (cf. the previous note): "Gallonis cardinalis constitutiones, item et Guillelmi, Parisiensium episcoporum, hic collocaverat Binius; sed cur Gallonem ad an. mccviii. Guillelmum ad mcccxx rejecerimus, ibi caussam afferemus" (Labbe-Cossart 10:752). They were mistaken, however. Binius' manner of printing shows clearly that he linked neither the canons of Galo nor the additions of Archbishop William of Sens with the council of Guastalla although he did publish them under the date 1107. For the "constitutiones S.R.E. Cardinalis Gallonis," correctly identified by Labbe-Cossart as issued by Cardinal Galo who visited France as legate of Pope Innocent III, see Labbe-Cossart 11/1 (1671) 32-35. The second set of Binius canons, "Wilhelmi Parisiensis Episcopi Additiones," which appear under the date 1107 is as yet unidentified.

[31] *Collectio Regia* 26: 755-758; Labbe-Cossart 10: 748-752; Hardouin 6/2: 1881-1886; Coleti 12: 1127-1132; Mansi 20: 1209-1216.

[32] Labbe-Cossart 10: 748: "Ex Cencii Camerarii MS. codice Vaticano." This should be compared with Baronius' introduction, *Annales*, 12: 53. As will be seen Baronius and the scholars Labbe and Cossart used some Vatican MS of the *Liber Censuum* containing the recension of Nicholas Roselli, also known as Cardinal of Aragon (below pp. 47-50), for their publications, but whether they used the same codex is impossible to tell. Labbe and Cossart presumably added the *titutli canonum* which are printed in italics, a type reserved for editorial comments. The *tituli* were reproduced in all subsequent editions.

[33] Coleti 12: 1128-1129. In the *Amplissima collectio* Coleti's text is inserted between that of Labbe-Cossart and the "Concilii Guastallensis descriptio Biniana" as "Fragmentum Concilii."

appearance of the Guastalla material in Mansi (20: 1209-1216). Mistakenly, he continued the passages which had been published by Baronius and Labbe-Cossart from the Vatican codex "qui liber Censuum inscribitur," with two further excerpts from the same work, of which one certainly is not connected to the council of Guastalla. The "Cassatio Privilegii quod extorsit Imperator a Papa" (*Privilegium illud ... aliorum consilium*) is part of the *acta* of the Lateran council of 1112. The second item, the "Refutatio Investiturae Episcoporum" of King Coloman of Hungary (1095-1116) may or may not be related to the council of Guastalla. While it can be accepted that the king did renounce investiture during the pontificate of Paschal II, the date is uncertain since the fragment in the manuscripts of the Roselli redaction of the *Liber Censuum* is undated. Scholars who discuss Coloman's ecclesiastical policy usually[34] refer to the renunciation under the year 1106 in connection with the council of Guastalla, but their evidence in all cases is Mansi, in other words Coleti's compilation, and is therefore not acceptable.[35]

## The Participants

The interest in the council of Guastalla was great. For the first time in Paschal's pontificate participants came from Germany as well as from Italy and France. Known by name from among the attending laity are the Coun-

---

[34] I. Szentpétery and I. Borsa, *Regesta Regum Stirpis Arpadianae*, 1 (Budapest 1923) omitted the document; G. Pray, *Annales Regum Hungariae*, Pars 1 (Vienna 1763) 110, dates it 1111. Pray used Coleti as well as the late *Chronicon pontificum et imperatorem* of Martinus Polonus (see MGH SS 22: 435), the only chronicle source for the "refutatio." It should be noted that the *Tractatus de investitura episcoporum* from 1109 refers to Hungary as one of the countries where investiture was no longer practised at that time (MGH Libelli de lite 2: 500). The *Tractatus*, therefore, would support a date before 1109 for the renunciation. But the evidence is too slender by itself. P. von Váczy, *Die erste Epoche des ungarischen Königtums* (Pécs 1936) 116ff. omitted a reference to the date of the renunciation, a procedure which I follow.

[35] E.g. S. L. Endlicher, *Rerum hungaricarum monumenta Arpadiana* (St. Gall 1849) 375; B. Hóman, *Geschichte des ungarischen Mittelalters* 1 (Budapest 1935) 358; J. Deér, "Der Anspruch der Herrscher des 12. Jahrhunderts auf die apostolische Legation," *Archivum Historiae Pontificiae* 2 (1964) 117-186, p. 156; Kempf, *The Church in the Age of Feudalism*, p. 402; L. Mezey, "Ungarn und Europa im 12. Jahrhundert, Kirche und Kultur zwischen Ost und West," *Vorträge und Forschungen* 12, *Probleme des 12. Jahrhunderts*, pp. 255-272, Konstanzer Arbeitskreis für Mittelalterliche Geschichte (1968). Mezey is the current editor for the forthcoming *Hungarica Pontificia*. I am grateful to J. Sweeney and Z. J. Kosztolnyik for advice.

tess Mathilda of Tuscany[36] and Count Hermann of Reinhausen in Saxony.[37] Archbishop Bruno of Trier, who led an official delegation of other ecclesiastics and nobles sent by King Henry v,[38] was present, and so was Archbishop Konrad of Salzburg.[39] Archbishop Hugh of Lyons died at Susa near Turin on his way to the council.[40] The same fate befell Bishop Rupert of Würzburg.[41] Bishop Gebehard of Trent was consecrated at the council.[42] From among his episcopal colleagues, Otto of Bamberg, Wido of Chur, and Hermann of Augsburg together with Richard, cardinal of Albano, Paschal's legate to Germany, were present at Guastalla.[43] In the company of Archbishop Bruno of Trier was a canon Reinhard from Mainz who, a few months later on 31 March 1107 was consecrated bishop of Halberstadt by Rothard of Mainz in place of the deposed Frederick.[44] Frederick of Halberstadt might have been among the participants and possibly also Bishop

---

[36] *Vita Mathildis* (2, c. 17 = MGH SS 12: 400-401) of Donizo. The countess was Donizo's informant. Tangl, *Teilnehmer*, discussed participants of the Guastalla synod pp. 185-186.

[37] *Translatio S. Modoaldi*, p. 295; Knonau, *Jahrbücher*, 6: 26.

[38] The best source for the embassy is the *Translatio S. Modoaldi*, p. 295; Ekkehard's report is rather general (Ekkehard, p. 290).

[39] He was consecrated by Paschal at the council. See *Gesta archiepiscoporum Salisburgensium*, ed. W. Wattenbach, MGH SS 11: 41, c. 12 and Ekkehard, p. 290.

[40] W. Lühe, *Hugo von Die und Lyon, Legat von Gallien* (Breslau 1898) 118-119 with bibliography.

[41] *Annales Patherbrunnenses*, p. 116: "Ruobertus Herbipolensis et Lugdunensis episcopi in itinere moriuntur." Cf. *Chronica Regia Coloniensis*, ed. G. Waitz, Scriptores rerum germanicarum in usum scholarum (1880) 45.

[42] Ekkehard, p. 290; Brackmann, GP 1/1 (1910) 20, no. 47.

[43] JL 6143; Udalschalk, *De Eginone*, p. 438. For Otto of Bamberg see Erich Freiherr von Guttenberg, *Das Bistum Bamberg*, Germania Sacra, Abteilung 2, vol. 1, part 1 (Berlin and Leipzig 1937) 115-138, esp. pp. 120-122; G. Juritsch, *Geschichte des Bischofs Otto I. von Bamberg, des Pommern-Apostels (1102-1139)* (Gotha 1889) esp. pp. 72-87; A. Brackmann, GP 3: *Provincia Maguntinensis*, part 3: *Dioeceses Strassburgensis, Spirensis, Wormatiensis, Wirciburgensis, Bambergensis* (Berlin 1935) 261-265, esp. p. 263 no. 43 where a reference to JL 6143 should be added; idem, ed., *Studien und Vorarbeiten zur Germania Pontificia* 3: *Die Bistümer Würzburg und Bamberg in ihrer wirtschaftlichen Bedeutung für die Geschichte des deutschen Ostens*, part 2, ed. Heinrich Büttner: *Bamberg* (Berlin 1937) esp. pp. 246-319; Hermann Jakobs, *Die Hirsauer: Ihre Ausbreitung und Rechtsstellung im Zeitalter des Investiturstreites*, Kölner historische Abhandlungen 4 (Cologne 1961) 140-145. Hermann of Augsburg and Richard of Albano are mentioned by Udalschalk, *De Eginone*, MGH SS 12: 438. For Richard see Schumann, *Päpstliche Legaten*, pp. 79-86.

[44] *Annalista Saxo*, ed. G. Waitz, MGH SS 6: 745; Jaffé, *Monumenta Moguntina*, pp. 381-382, nos. 34 and 35; Karlotto Bogumil, *Das Bistum Halberstadt im 12. Jahrhundert: Studien zur Reichs- und Reformpolitik des Bischofs Reinhard und zum Wirken der Augustiner-Chorherren*, Mitteldeutsche Forschungen 69 (Cologne 1972); Henking, *Gebhard*, p. 94; see also Jaffé, *Monumenta Bambergensia*, p. 510.

Henry of Paderborn.[45] Another member of the royal delegation was Adelgot who, also in 1107, became archbishop of Magdeburg (1107-1119).[46] Bishop Gebhard of Constance was very likely also present. Gebhard had been a member of the embassy which Henry v had sent across the Alps in January 1106, but did not share its misfortunes at Trent.[47] He continued on to Italy, where he was at the court of Mathilda of Tuscany early in March 1106 in the company of Bishop Wido of Chur.[48] Henking, who wrote the still authoritative biography of Gebhard, concluded: "Es ist sehr wahrscheinlich, dass Gebhard den ganzen ersten Theil des Jahres 1106 bis zum Concile von Guastalla, an welchem wir ihm wieder begegnen, in Italien zubrachte. Es fehlen uns aus dieser Zeit über ihn jede Nachrichten."[49] A brief entry in Udalschalk's *De Eginone et Herimanno* has traditionally been accepted as evidence for his attendance.[50] No other trace of Gebhard's activity at Guastalla remains, although his intervention on behalf of Bishop Her-

---

[45] Frederick was deposed at Guastalla as requested by the canons of Halberstadt who were present (below pp. 71-72; Bogumil, *Das Bistum Halberstadt*, p. 16). Tangl, *Teilnehmer*, p. 185, assumed that a paragraph in the *Annales Patherbrunnenses* as reconstituted by Scheffer-Boichorst ("Heinricus episcopus Patherbrunnensis, profectus Romam, aecclesia mediante sui restitutionem obtinuit. Frithericus Halverstadensis sine officio revertitur" — p. 113) referred to activity at the council of Guastalla. This, however, is only one among several possible interpretations of the passage (cf. *Annales Patherbrunnenses*, p. 113 n. 7) and the date of the Rome journey of Henry and Frederick seems uncertain. It should be noted, however, that Bogumil, *Das Bistum Halberstadt*, p. 16, accepts the presence at Guastalla of Frederick and Henry without discussion.

[46] See Dietrich Claude, *Geschichte des Erzbistums Magdeburg bis in das 12. Jahrhundert*, Teil 1, Mitteldeutsche Forschungen 67/1 (Cologne 1972) 392-393.

[47] Paul Ladewig and Theodor Müller, eds., *Regesta episcoporum Constantiensium: Regesten zur Geschichte der Bischöfe von Constanz*, vol. 1 (Innsbruck 1895) pp. 79-80, nos. 632-633. Henking, *Gebhard*, especially p. 93, but see also pp. 90-91 and p. 95; Knonau, *Jahrbücher* 6: 26 n. 40. A full account of the capture of the embassy with source references is found ibid. 5: 294-296. Ursula-Renate Weiss, *Die Konstanzer Bischöfe im 12. Jahrhundert*, Konstanzer Geschichts- und Rechtsquellen 20 (Sigmaringen 1975) does not include a discussion of Bishop Gebhard. She refers the reader to Henking's biography.

[48] Gebhard and Wido were witnesses to a donation of the countess and signed a charter. The regest and further references are found in Overmann, *Grossgräfin Mathilde*, p. 74 (date 10 March 1106); see also Knonau 5: 296, n. 29.

[49] Henking, *Gebhard*, p. 92. Ladewig-Müller, *Regesta episcoporum Constantiensium*, 1: 79-80, no. 634.

[50] "Synodus colligitur Warstallensis; assunt cum suo episcopo nuntii ecclesiae Augustensis; refert legatus (Richard of Albano) quae audierit, qualiterve audita distulerit; ideonea iteratur accusatio; nulla praetenditur excusatio; facile ab omnibus concordatur, ut talis episcopus deponatur. Quod et factum fuisset, si non Gebehardus Constantiensis in ipsa Augustensi ecclesia hoc faciendum persuasisset. Eo namque tempore domnus papa Theutonicum adire proposuerat regnum" (MGH SS 12: 438, ch. 14; a regest is found in Brackmann, GP 2/1: 34, no. 23). See also Ladewig-Müller, *Regesta episcoporum Constantiensium*, 1: 80, no. 636 and Henking, *Gebhard*, p. 95.

mann of Augsburg apparently made a favorable impression. Gebhard's suggestion to examine the case of Bishop Hermann at Augsburg in Germany must lie behind the expectation expressed by Ekkehard of Aura that Paschal would celebrate Christmas 1106 in Augsburg.[51]

Seven abbots are known to have attended the synod of Guastalla: Thietmar of Helmarshausen,[52] Gonter of the monastery of St. Lambert at Liessies (Avesnes-sur-Helpe [Nord]) (JL 6093), Abbot Hartmann of Göttweig,[53] Gerbert of the monastery of St. Vannes at Verdun,[54] Seher from the Lotharingian monastery of Chaumouzey in the diocese of Toul,[55] Abbot Radulf from Saint-Quentin, and Bernard, abbot of Vallombrosa in his capacity as cardinal of S. Crisogono and bishop-elect of Parma.[56] Ekkehard, who in 1108 became abbot of the monastery of Aura, was also there.[57] The canons of Halberstadt, or rather representatives of one faction of the Halberstadt canons,[58] arrived as did Augsburg canons,[59] either accusing or supporting their bishop before pope and council. An embassy, sent by Bishop Otbert of Liège (JL 6099) arrived shortly after the council, while representatives of Bishop Richer of Verdun (1089-1107) had reached Guastalla in time. The business of Abbot Gerbert of St. Vannes and the Chanter Azelin, however, had more to do with Countess Mathilda of Tuscany than with the assembly.[60]

---

[51] See above n. 11.

[52] *Translatio S. Modoaldi*, p. 295. It is said that the abbot was accompanied by a monk. None of the dignitaries, whose names are known, would have come alone, but this fact is seldom mentioned in the sources.

[53] Udalschalk, *De Eginone*, p. 438.

[54] Below n. 60.

[55] *Primordia Calmosiacensia* (MGH SS 12: 336-337). The chronicle includes the text of JL 6097 obtained by the abbot to settle his quarrel with Abbess Gisla of Remiremont, who, however, was not present at Guastalla. See E. Hlawitschka, *Studien zur Äbtissinnenreihe von Remiremont* (Saarbrücken 1963) 72-85 and especially pp. 79-81; A. Didier-Laurent, "L'Abbaye de Remiremont," *Mémoires de la Société d'Archéologie Lorraine et du Musée Historique Lorraine* 47 (3ᵉ sér. vol. 25) 1897, 259-498, p. 403 n. 2. Cf. Knonau, *Jahrbücher* 5: 254 and 6: 26 n. 40.

[56] Dr. Dietrich Lohrmann, Paris, kindly informed me that vol. 7 of *Papsturkunden in Frankreich* (forthcoming) will contain a privilege granted by Paschal to Abbot Radulf for the canons of Saint-Quentin-les-Beauvais. For Bernard see (in addition to the bibliography in the *Diz. Biogr. degli Italiani* 9: 292-300) Kehr, IP 5: 394, no. 5. Cf. Ganzer, *Auswärtiges Kardinalat*, p. 54.

[57] See above n. 15.

[58] *Annales Patherbrunnenses*, p. 116; Bogumil, *Das Bistum Halberstadt*, p. 16.

[59] Udalschalk, *De Eginone*, p. 438.

[60] *Laurentii de Leodio gesta episcoporum Virdunensium*, ed. G. Waitz, MGH SS 10: 486-525, 498. The *Gesta* were written around 1144 at the request of Hugh, monk of the monastery of St. Vannes at Verdun (ibid. pp. 486-487). See also Potthast, *Wegweiser* 1: 713. The *Gesta* report: "... Cumque ipsa alodia [Mosacum (Mousay near Stenay) and Satha-

It is notable that in contrast to the relatively copious information preserved concerning German participants, almost nothing is known about French and Italian bishops at the council.[61] Archbishop Hugh of Lyons was mentioned earlier,[62] and he was probably not the only one to undertake the journey to Guastalla.[63] JL 6095 shows that letters from bishops John of Thérouanne (1099-1130) and Godfrey of Amiens (1104-1115) were presented to the pope, who confirmed at the council these bishops' decision in favor of the monastery of Corbie against the claims of the chapter of Bruges.[64] It is, however, not known by whom the letters were brought. The names of some of the Italian participants can perhaps be deduced indirectly. It is probable that the Italian ecclesiastics who accompanied the pontiff to France, particularly if they were Romans, had left the eternal city with him and consequently were also at the council of Guastalla.[65] A judgment from the synod shows Abbess Berta of the monastery of S. Maria Theodatae as plaintiff before the Italian council,[66] and the presence of Bishop Bruno of Segni can possibly be assumed on the basis of a privilege for Abbot Hugh of St. Gilles in Nîmes,[67] dated Parma, 2 November 1106 and signed by Paschal II, Bruno and Cardinal Landulf.[68]

---

nacum (Stenay)] Mathildis marchisa, relicta ducis Godefridi Gibbosi, ut sibi a patribus hereditaria reclamaret, iterum praesul [Richer] eadem ab ipsa matrona multo pretio in Walestatensi sinodo per legatos suos Gerbertum abbatem et Azelinum cantorem redemit, et ab omni exactionis et reclamationis nodo libera Paschalis papa in eadem sinodo sub anathemate ... ea Virdunensi ecclesiae in perpetuum confirmaverunt." The text is quoted at length since the passage has caused Coleti (12: 1110) to credit Paschal with a synod held at Estinnes-au-Mont, near Binche (Belgium) in 1107. (See Graesse, *Orbis Latinus* 2: 380 s.v. Lestinae in Monte.) The passage was reprinted by Mansi (20: 1225). Paschal's charter from Estinnes-au-Mont, however, merely confirmed the decision made at Guastalla almost half a year earlier. See MGH SS 10: 498 n. 77 and Knonau, *Jahrbücher* 5: 287 and 6: 49 n. 26. On the history of Mousay and Stenay see Overmann, *Gräfin Mathilde*, pp. 193-210 and for the arrangements made at Guastalla ibid. p. 209.

[61] See, however, the inscription of one of the manuscripts reporting c. 4 of the council of Guastalla "ubi episcopi et abbates tam Galliarum quam et Langobardie et Tuscie necnon Germanie et Saxonie conuenerunt" (below p. 55).

[62] See n. 42 above.

[63] Ekkehard of Aura (p. 290) speaks of a multitude of clerics and laymen "qui de diversorum regnorum aeclesiis convenerant." The *Annales Patherbrunnenses* (p. 116) are only a little less imprecise: "Paschalis papa sinodum in vico Warestal agit, ad quam episcopi, duces, comites tam Italiae, quam Germaniae conveniunt."

[64] Pflugk-Harttung, *Acta pontificum Romanorum* 1: 88, no. 95.

[65] They are Cardinals Riso, Landulf, Diviso, John and Berardo; also mentioned are Equitius and Bishop Aldo of Piacenza (see below p. 79). For Berardo see Ganzer, *Auswärtiges Kardinalat*, pp. 67-69.

[66] Kehr, IP 6/1: 180 n. 30 and ibid. p. 212 n. 1. Kehr includes a bibliography.

[67] JL 6098. See E. Goiffon, *Bullaire de l'Abbaye de Saint-Gilles* (Nîmes 1882) 41.

[68] Grégoire, *Bruno de Segni*, p. 48, indicates that Bruno signed the privilege but does not

## The Canons

*Previous Editions and their Manuscripts*

### The *Liber Pontificalis*

A renewed interest in papal history and the old *Liber Pontificalis* was one of the varied manifestations of the Gregorian reform. In the first half of the twelfth century a continuation was written, ending with the life of Pope Honorius II (d. 1130), that included a vita of Pope Paschal II.[69] The identity of the author of Paschal's Life in this *Chronica Romanorum Pontificum* is still being discussed.[70] It hinges essentially on the interpretation of the following passage in the vita: "'Vade P. et tu, Const. et ex omnibus que ad prefecturam pertinent, ad curie commodum in testimonio venerabilis huius nostri diaconi te investias.' Parui iussis...."[71] Duchesne sought the author behind the abbreviation P., rejecting, however, the identification of P. with Petrus Pisanus as maintained amongst others by Watterich.[72] J. M. March, on the other hand, argued that the author is hidden under the abbreviation Const. = Constabulus or Comestabulus whom he tentatively identified with Petrus, son of Petrus Leonis, later Anaclete II and benefactor of the author of later lives in the series, Pandulf.[73] Whoever the author of Paschal's oldest vita was, he summarized the Guastalla legislation briefly:[74]

> In Langobardia apud Guardastallum celebravit concilium, in quo quidem de investituris, de hominiis et sacramentis episcoporum laicis exhibitis exhibendisque certis capitulis statutum est.

The passage was never used for the interpretation of the council with the exception of Binius' first edition where it was quoted from the writings of Platina and Biondo.[75]

---

mention the synod of Guastalla. Cardinal Landulf is probably identical with the archbishop of Benevento of the same name. See Ganzer, *Auswärtiges Kardinalat*, pp. 63-66 with further references.

[69] Ed. L. Duchesne, *Le Liber Pontificalis*, Bibliothèque des Écoles Françaises d'Athènes et de Rome, 2 (repr. Paris 1955) 199-328; Paschal's vita is found ibid. 296-310. See also the edition by J. M. March, *Liber Pontificalis prout exstat in codice manuscripto Dertusensi* (Barcelona 1925). C. Vogel who is responsible for vol. 3 (Paris 1957) of Duchesne's edition of the *Liber Pontificalis* (subsequently cited LP) published a collation of Duchesne's Vatican manuscript and the codex discovered by March at Tortosa (LP 3: 143-156).

[70] Vogel, LP 3: 17f. evaluated the debate.

[71] LP 3: 151.

[72] *Pontificum Romanorum Vitae* (Leipzig 1862) 1: liv; Duchesne, LP 2: xxxivf.

[73] LP ed. March, especially pp. 46-60.

[74] LP 2: 299; LP 3: 147; LP ed. March, p. 138.

[75] See above n. 28.

The text of at least some of the capitula thus adumbrated in Paschal's earliest vita was preserved in a later continuation of the *Liber Pontificalis*, composed in the second half of the twelfth century by Cardinal Boso.[76] Duchesne published Boso's work on the basis of MS Florence, Riccardianus 228, a thirteenth-century copy of the *Liber Censuum*[77] with several additional quaternions.[78] The series of papal lives is among these additions. The pages dedicated to Paschal II, however, do not represent a vita in the usual meaning of the word, but contain instead a series of Paschalian documents. Most of them are probably from the registers. Duchesne notes with surprise that they were nonetheless apparently haphazardly accumulated.[79] Boso's text for the council of Guastalla seems to fall into two distinct sections:[80] (1) "Aliud quoque concilium ... vita scientiaque commendat," and (2) "Aliud capitulum. Iamdiu ... periculum patiatur." A letter of Cardinal Pietro Diani to his fellow citizens of Piacenza indicates that the first part[81] at least was copied from Paschal's register: "Nos vero ... registra summorum pontificum diligenti indagatione perquisivimus, et in registro beatissimi Paschalis II decretum exemptionis civitatis nostrae a jugo Ravennae invenimus.... In hoc concilio constitutum est...."[82] The second part of Boso's text appears to be a random selection of two individual items from several other canons promulgated at Guastalla.

The interpretation of the Boso material for Guastalla would be greatly facilitated if it were possible to discern the principle behind the selection process. At least a tentative suggestion can be made. Boso, or his anony-

---

[76] Boso is often thought to have been an Englishman who came to Rome at the time of Pope Hadrian IV, e.g. LP 2: xxxvii-xliv. Fritz Geisthardt, *Der Kämmerer Boso*, Historische Studien 293 (Berlin 1936), especially pp. 37-40, argued that Boso was an Italian. His arguments seem convincing with the exception of the references to either Lucca or Pisa as Boso's place of birth. On Boso in general see, in addition to Duchesne and Geisthardt, Rep. Font. 2: 566 and P. Munz, *Boso's Life of Alexander III* (Totowa N.J. 1973) 1-39.

[77] See Duchesne, LP 2: xxxvii-viii for the relationship between MS Vat. lat. 8486, the original *Liber Censuum*, and MS Florence, Riccardianus 228.

[78] LP 2: 351-446. For a description of the codex see ibid. pp. xxxvii-viii, and Paul Fabre, *Etude sur le Liber Censuum*, pp. 180-184. See also Paul Fabre, "Les vies de papes dans les manuscrits du Liber Censuum," *Extraits des Mélanges d'Archéologie et d'Histoire*, Ecole Française de Rome 6 (1889).

[79] LP 2: xli: "... on doit s'étonner que, disposant d'une série ordonnée chronologiquement comme étaient les registres pontificaux, Boson n'ait pas mis plus d'ordre dans ses extraits ...."

[80] Also noted by Weiland, who edited the council of Guastalla for the MGH, Const. 1: 564-566, p. 564.

[81] Canons 1 and 2 as enumerated by Weiland (ibid., 565).

[82] See P. M. Campi, *Dell'Historia ecclesiastica di Piacenza*, 2 (Piacenza 1651) document 38, pp. 369-370; see also *Le Liber Censuum*, ed. Fabre-Duchesne, 1: 115, n. 2, col. a.

mous predecessor if Boso did not work directly from the sources, did not proceed chronologically when he composed the 'life'. The introductory passage and the final two paragraphs, written by Boso in order to adapt the collection to the requirements of the *Liber Pontificalis*, need not be considered in the present context. What remains is essentially a cluster of 1111-1112 materials, even though not all of Boso's documents can be dated with the desired clarity. Recorded first are the events of the spring of 1111. This account, very similar to the report in MS Vat. lat. 1984,[83] is followed by:

1. JL 6301, dated 5 July 1111[84]
2. JL 6252, dated 1101-1110[85]
3. an account of the Lateran council of 1112 under the wrong date 1113
4. Guastalla material (1106)
5. JL 5971, dated 1104 or 1101[86]
6. Refutacio regis Ungarie[87]
7. JL 6325, dated 19 June 1112
8. a letter of Archbishop Guy of Vienne to Paschal, "Sancte pietatis vestre," probable date 1112[88]
9. JL 6570, dated 1099-1118.[89]

All the documents seem at least indirectly related to the investiture problem, including JL 6570 found in Boso's vita addressed to an archbishop of Poland, a remarkable inscription, perhaps explained by the whole tenor of the collection that illuminates issues which divided the Apostolic See and the Holy Roman Empire. Eastern Europe is apparently regarded as part of the German sphere of influence. The odd inscription "Iuramentum de regno Teutonicorum" for JL 5971, if it is not an outright mistake, might be interpreted along similar lines. The selected Guastalla canons find their place naturally in this collection since they deal with investiture. The relationship between the legislation of 1112 and the earlier legislation of 1106 was

---

[83] Published by Louis Duchesne in the so-called "Annales Romani," LP 2: 338-343.
[84] Knonau, *Jahrbücher* 6: 222-223.
[85] Brackmann, GP 2/1: 135, no. 45; cf. Jaffé's *Regesta* under JL 6252.
[86] Brackmann, GP 1: 170, no. 38 with the date 1104; the date 1101 is suggested by Henking, *Gebhard*, pp. 64-65.
[87] It cannot be dated since the only manuscript evidence is Boso's Paschalian collection. See above nn. 34 and 35.
[88] The sequence of the letters exchanged between Paschal and Guy of Vienne is still being debated.
[89] See the earlier references, ch. 1, nn. 37, 39 and 40.

close. The Guastalla decrees were very likely repeated in 1112 as Bruno of Segni, one of Paschal's fiercest opponents at the time, had demanded.[90] Evidence for this is found in the *Breviarium Gestorum*, published by Ludwig Weiland, for the Lateran council of 1112.[91] It contains as the final item a canon from Guastalla: "Item aliud capitulum. Nullus abbas ... periculum patiatur." Although the inscription is the same as that found in Boso, the *Breviarium Gestorum* seems to present an otherwise independent textual tradition earlier in date.[92]

The evidence just discussed is scanty, but suggests nevertheless that the Guastalla canons in the Boso selection were chosen to illustrate Paschal's attitude towards Germany in connection with the events of 1111 and 1112. As Bresslau remarked long ago with regard to the register volumes of the late twelfth century, chronological organization exists side by side with a topical arrangement of certain documents that might even be separately bound.[93] Boso's treatise on the pontificate of Paschal II is conceivably an indication that such a topical organization of the registers goes back to the reform papacy. The extremely selective character of the Boso material

---

[90] See Bruno's ep. 2, MGH Libelli de lite 2: 564.

[91] MGH Const. 1: 573-574, no. 400.

[92] Weiland edited the text from two manuscripts, MS Barb. lat. 538, s. 12 first half, and MS Schaffhausen, Ministerialbibliothek 46 (see below p. 57). It should be pointed out that in two of the *Liber Censuum* manuscripts examined the Guastalla material is transposed. Codex Miscell. Arm. XV 1, Archivio Segreto, Biblioteca Apostolica Vaticana, fol. 291v-292r, shows a different sequence of documents from that found in MS Riccardianus 228. Bishop Gerard of Angoulême's reading of the document known as the "Cassatio" of the agreement of Ponte Mammolo (see LP 2: 370, line 31 - p. 371, line 17) is preceded by the excerpts from Guastalla, JL 5971 and the "Refutacio" (LP 2: 371, line 19 - p. 373, line 7). The "Cassatio" is then followed by the correspondence with Guy of Vienne and JL 6570. This transposition of material is found as well in a further *Liber Censuum* codex of the Archivio Segreto, Miscell. Arm. XXXV 18 (cf. LP 2: xxxviii), and in apparently similar form in a Vatican codex of the Correctores Romani (see MS Barb. lat. 860, fol. 75r). According to Duchesne, however, Riccardianus 228 has to be considered the parent of all later *Liber Censuum* manuscripts containing the papal *vitae* (LP 2, nos. 28-30). The transposition, therefore, has to be dismissed as an insignificant variant. For codex Miscell. Arm. XV 1 cf. Reinhard Elze, *Die Ordines für die Weihe und Krönung des Kaisers und der Kaiserin*, Fontes iuris germanici antiqui in usum scholarum ... editi 9 (Hanover 1960) 22.

[93] Harry Bresslau, *Handbuch der Urkundenlehre*, 3rd ed., vol. 1 (Berlin 1958) 113-114; E. Stevenson, "Osservazioni sulla Collectio Canonum di Deusdedit," *Archivio della R. Società Romana di Storia Patria* 8 (1885) 305-398, p. 373 n. 2. Cf. the Regestum super negotio imperii of Pope Innocent III, facsimile ed. by W. M. Peitz, *Regestum domni Innocentii tertii pape super negotio Romani imperi...*, Codices e Vaticanis selecti 16 (Rome 1927) and the partial publication *Das Register Papst Innocenz' III. über den deutschen Thronstreit: Regestum domni Innocentii tertii pape...*, ed. Walther Holtzmann, 2 vols., Bonn 1947-48. Cf. Erich Caspar, "Studien zum Register Gregors VII.," *Neues Archiv* 38 (1913) 143-226.

should at any rate be kept in mind during the further discussion of Guastalla decrees.

The *Liber Censuum* manuscript with the Boso additions in Florence, Riccardianus 228, was used by Nicholas Roselli (d. 1362), also known as the cardinal of Aragon,[94] who compiled a new redaction of the *Liber Censuum* in the fourteenth century.[95] "En ce qui regarde les vies des papes, le texte du cardinal d'Aragon ne diffère du précédent [MS Ricc. 228] que par des retouches de style et par quelques suppressions .... Il est évident que ce texte dérivé n'a aucune valeur critique," remarked Duchesne.[96] It is through this derivative version that the text of Cardinal Boso became primarily known to scholars, including the Correctores Romani.

\* \* \*

The Correctores Romani[97]

Among the notes of the Correctores Romani we find material which they had derived "ex Pontificale Iohannis de Aragonia." The Guastalla canons from this source are found on fols. 41r-42v in MS Vallicellianus C.24,[98] and

---

[94] A bibliography for Cardinal Nicholas Roselli is given by J. Quétif and J. Echard, *Scriptores ordinis praedicatorum recensiti*, 2 vols. in 4, Paris 1719-1721, 1/2: 649-651 and by L. Gasparri, "Osservazioni sul codice Vallicelliano C.24," *Studi Gregoriani* 9 (1972) 467-513, p. 507 n. 1.

[95] Duchesne, LP 2: xxxviii, no. 29. Duchesne discussed ibid. some of the numerous manuscripts of this recension. See below n. 108.

[96] LP 2: xxxix.

[97] The Correctores were appointed by the papacy in the mid-sixteenth century to prepare an emended edition of Gratian's *Decretum*. This edition, known as "Editio Romana," appeared in 1582. See Friedberg's introduction to his edition of the *Decretum*, p. lxxviff.; van Hove, *Prolegomena*, p. 347; Somerville, *Decreta Claromontensia*, p. 22; Karl Schellhass, "Wissenschaftliche Forschungen unter Gregor XIII. für die Neuausgabe des Gratianischen Dekrets," *Papsttum und Kaisertum, Forschungen zur politischen Geschichte und Geisteskultur des Mittelalters Paul Kehr zum 65. Geburtstag dargebracht* (Munich 1926) 674-690; idem, "Deutsche und Kuriale Gelehrte im Dienste der Gegenreformation," QFIAB 14 (1911) 287-314, especially p. 289; Johanna Petersmann, "Die kanonistische Überlieferung des Constitutum Constantini bis zum Dekret Gratians," DA 30 (1974) 356-449, especially pp. 406ff. Several of the Correctores were involved in work on the "Editio Romana" of the ecumenical councils as well. Cf. Claudio Leonardi, "Per una storia dell'edizione romana dei concili ecumenici (1608-1612) da Antonio Agustín a Francesco Aduarte," *Studi e Testi* 236, *Mélanges Eugène Tisserant* 6 (1964) 583-637; Vittorio Peri, "Due Protagonisti dell'editio romana dei concili ecumenici: Petro Marin ed Antonio d'Aquino," *Studi e Testi* 237, *Mélanges Eugène Tisserant* 7 (1964) 131-239; S. Kuttner, "L'Édition Romaine des conciles généraux et les actes du premier concile de Lyon," in *Miscellanea historiae pontificiae* 3.5 (Rome 1940) 3-40.

[98] For a description of this manuscript see Gasparri, "Osservazioni," pp. 467-513; Somerville, *Decreta Claromontensia*, pp. 46-47 and n. 5, and p. 70f. I am much obliged to Professor S. Kuttner for further information. The whole quire fol. 41-48 belongs to the

were copied from these folios onto fols. 28r-30v of the same manuscript. Sections of the codex once belonged to Antonio Agustín, a collaborator of the Correctores.[99] One of the manuscripts given to the Vatican library after Agustín's death was described in the *Index librorum ex Bibliotheca Antonii Augustini* as "Pontificale Joannis Aragonii cardinalis a Leone ix ad Alexandrum iii."[100] This description corresponds to item 213 in the catalogue of Agustín's library.[101] Unfortunately, the manuscript can no longer be identified. Signora Gasparri examined MS Vallicellianus C.25 which contains the Nicholas of Aragon version of Boso's work[102] and pointed out that Vall. C.25 gives the author's name as "Joannes, cardinal Aragonii." A marginal note corrected this into "Nicolas." Nevertheless she had to conclude that Vall. C.25 was not Agustín's manuscript.[103] Still, its existence lends considerable support to the hypothesis that Nicolas and Joannes are as identical as are apparently their writings. The notes of the Correctores Romani in MS Vallicellianus C.24 "ex Pontificale Johannis de Aragonia" will therefore be considered here as belonging to the Nicholas Roselli recension of Boso's Guastalla material.

*  *
*

Baronius and the Conciliar Editors

Baronius edited canons for Guastalla which he had discovered in "Vaticano codice, qui liber Censuum inscribitur, a Cencio Camerali collecto."[104] Duchesne concluded that what Baronius had used was the Roselli recension of the *Liber Censuum*.[105] In the absence of almost all dis-

---

papers which Antonio Agustín, archbishop of Tarragona and collaborator of the Correctores (1517-1586; see the references in n. 97 above and K. Weinzierl, LThK 1 [1957] 211) had from Michael Thomasius Taxaquet (d. 1578). Thomasius was Agustín's successor as bishop of Lérida (see Friedberg, *Decretum*, p. lxxvi n. 41; Eubel, *Hierarchia Catholica* 3: 229; Somerville, *Decreta Claromontensia*, pp. 48-49). Professor Kuttner also pointed out that the quire is misbound and that the sequence ought to be changed to: fol. 43r-48r, 41r-42r. MS Vallicellianus C.24 was known to Weiland through the description given of it by Pflugk-Harttung, *Iter Italicum* 1 (Stuttgart 1883) 105-106; see also ibid. 2: 197-198 and Weiland, MGH Const. 1: 565 n. 1.

[99] See the previous note.
[100] This index was published from MS Vat. lat. 3958 by Leonardi, "Per la storia dell'edizione romana dei concili ecumenici," pp. 609-626.
[101] "Joannis cardinalis Aragonii Pontificum historia a Leone ix exordiens anno MD. Liber in charta recenter descriptus forma folii' (ibid. p. 621 n. 239); see also Gasparri, "Osservazioni," p. 506.
[102] LP ed. Duchesne 2: xxx and xxxviii.
[103] Gasparri, "Osservazioni," pp. 506-507.
[104] Baronius, *Annales* 12: 53.
[105] LP ed. Duchesne 2: xxxix n. 4 col. a.

tinctions between the Boso and Roselli texts,[106] particularly with regard to the Guastalla material, little can be added here to support Duchesne. The last item transcribed by Baronius from the Vatican codex was JL 5971: "Hactenus de huius concilij canonibus in dicto codice repertis: quibus haec quae sequitur epistola eiusdem Paschalis subscripta legitur: Paschalis ...." This letter is introduced by Boso with the inscription "Iuramentum de regno Teutonicorum" and by Roselli with "Item aliud Capitulum Concilii." Baronius and with him Labbe-Cossart used neither inscription, but simply referred to a letter of Paschal. The fact, however, that they published the letter together with other Guastalla material indicates that what they had in front of them was a copy of the Roselli redaction, listing the letter as "aliud capitulum concilii." It can be further remarked that Labbe-Cossart did not divide the first section of the Guastalla text "Aliud quoque ... institutum est" into paragraphs.[107] This characteristic, if it can be called such, is proper to Nicholas Roselli.[108] According to Duchesne's edition Boso divided the same text into three paragraphs.[109]

With regard to Coleti's changes we are fortunately on sure ground. Coleti included as "Fragmentum concilii Guastallensis,"[110] a text which had been edited by E. Martène (1654-1739) in the *Thesaurus novus anecdotorum*[111] from a manuscript of the monastery of St. Vincent at Besançon: "In MS S. Vincentii Bisuntini post concilii canones et epistolam Paschalis in eo conscriptam ad Hebebardum [*sic*] Constantiensem episcopum et alios Teutonicos [JL 5971] in editione Labbeana relatum, haec sequuntur." The excerpts which follow — "Refutatio investiturae episcoporum, quam fecit rex Hungariae ad mandatum papae" and "Cassatio Privilegii quod extorsit imperator a papa" — are found in the same sequence and with the same in-

---

[106] LP 2: xxxix; Duchesne cited the following omissions as characteristic of the Roselli version: "1° Le début *Dicam breviter* et la notice de Jean XII, de sorte qu'il commence par la vie de Léon IX; 2° la vie de Victor II; 3° un passage de la vie de Grégoire VII, *In Calcedonensi namque concilio — ordinem quem incepimus prosequamur*; 4° un passage de la vie d'Alexandre III, *In nomine Domini — pro viribus laboravit.*"

[107] Baronius, *Annales* 12: 53. Labbe-Cossart 10: 748. At least in the case of Labbe-Cossart this cannot be considered accidental, because they divided the text wherever possible into chapters providing elaborate *tituli canonum*.

[108] *Vitae nonnullorum pontificum Romanorum a Nicolao Aragonii S.R.E. cardinali conscriptae*, ed. N. Aloisia, Rerum Italicarum Scriptores 3/1 (ed. Muratori), Milan 1723, pp. 274-587, p. 364.

[109] LP ed. Duchesne 2: 371.

[110] Coleti 12: 1128-1129.

[111] Ed. E. Martène and U. Durand, 4 (1717) 127-128.

scriptions in the *Vitae pontificum romanorum* of Roselli,[112] and differ in sequence and inscription in MS Ricc. 228 with Boso's version. Martène's MS "S. Vincentii Bisuntini" is perhaps MS 398 of the Bibliothèque municipale in Besançon.[113] Coleti also added variants to Martène's text from a manuscript which he himself had in front of him: "ex codice Lucensi nostri." While this may have been MS Lucca 545, a sixteenth-century copy of Roselli,[114] a detailed examination would be needed to prove that it was indeed Coleti's codex.

* * *

The Edition of Ludwig Weiland

Weiland's 1893 edition of the Guastalla canons[115] is the most recent scholarly attempt to provide a critical edition of the legislation from Paschal's 1106 synod. As the preceding analysis shows, earlier editors from the Correctores Romani to Baronius and Mansi depended on the *Liber Censuum* redaction of Nicholas Roselli, cardinal of Aragon. They used, therefore, a secondary rather than a primary source. Weiland broke with this tradition by returning to the original Boso text for which he used the edition by Duchesne. Weiland did not, however, identify the Roselli-Baronius-Mansi sequence and failed to recognize that c.4 also existed in an independent transmission in two redactions. The Udalricus text (redaction 2) of c.4 appears, indeed, in distinct type-face, but variants of redaction 1 of c.4 were incorporated into Duchesne's edition of the Boso text. Since several codices can now be added to both redaction 1, represented in Weiland by Vatican MS Palat. lat. 587 and Munich MS Clm. 3739 (August. eccl. 39), and redaction 2, represented hitherto only by the Codex Udalrici, it appears certain that the lone c.4 was circulated separately in Germany.[116] Considerable efforts must have been made, probably by participants as well as the papacy, to bring this conciliatory decree concerning the schismatic German clergy to their attention. C.2 also exists in an independent paraphrase in two sixteenth-century manuscripts, Rome, Biblioteca Vallicellia-

---

[112] *Vitae pontificum Romanorum*, 3/1: 364-365. Cardinal Boso included the "Refutatio," but with a different inscription: "Refutacio regis Ungarie" (LP ed. Duchesne 2: 373). The pravilegium is introduced simply by "Cassatio illius privilegii" (ibid. p. 370 and n. 31).

[113] *Catalogue général*, Octavo series, XXXII/1, no. 398, pp. 234-235. The codex was not seen. According to the catalogue it was written in the sixteenth and seventeenth centuries; the Roselli text covers fols. 50r-201v.

[114] LP ed. Duchesne 2: xxxviii. MS not seen.

[115] MGH Const. 1: 564-566, no. 395.

[116] I am particularly grateful to Dr. M. Bertram, Berlin, who brought this fact to my attention.

na, C.16, and Madrid, Biblioteca Nacional, 4207.[117] The dismemberment of the archdiocese of Ravenna,[118] although of short duration,[119] kept memories of Guastalla alive. Yet another section of Weiland's material, c.6, is preserved separate from the usual body of Guastalla canons as the last item of what was edited by Weiland elsewhere as a *breviarium* of the Lateran council of 1112.[120] In the light of these remarks and the new manuscript material, as well as for the sake of completeness and the addition of an apparatus fontium, Weiland's Guastalla material is here reedited.

The following distinctions are maintained:

1. the Boso tradition, MS Ricc. 228
2. the paraphrase of c.2
3. the independent tradition of c.4, redaction 1
4. the independent tradition of c.4, redaction 2
5. c.6 as transmitted with the *breviarium* of the Lateran council of 1112.

\* \* \*

The Boso Tradition

The relevant section of Boso's life of Paschal II, preserved in MS Florence, Riccardianus 228, will be reproduced from the edition by L. Duchesne, *Le Liber Pontificalis* (Bibliothèque des Ecoles Françaises d'Athènes et de Rome) 2 [1892] 371-372. The author and the manuscript tradition for his work are examined in detail ibid. xxxvii-xliv.

## Concilium apud Guardastallam[121]

**1.** Aliud quoque concilium idem domnus papa Paschalis celebravit intra Lombardiam, apud villam frequentissimam Guardastallum, anno dominice incarnationis MCVI, XI kalendas novembris, cum episcopis diversarum provinciarum sive ultra sive citra montes.

---

[117] In a note Weiland referred to the Madrid codex: "quaedam de concilio nostro insunt ... codici Matritensi P.95 saec. XVI" (MGH Const. 1: 565n.).

[118] Kehr IP 5: 57, no. 188 with bibliography.

[119] Gelasius II had already rescinded Paschal's decision in JL 6647. See Kehr IP 5: 57, no. 189. Piacenza, however, continued to fight against the claims of Ravenna until the late twelfth century. (See *Liber Censuum* 1: 115, col. a, n. 2.)

[120] MGH Const. 1: 573-574, no. 400.

[121] For the sake of convenience Weiland's numbering of Duchesne's paragraphs is maintained.

**2.** In hoc concilio constitutum est ut Emilia tota cum suis urbibus, id est Placentia, Parma, Regio, Mutina, Bononia, numquam ulterius Ravennati metropoli subiacerent. Hec enim metropolis per annos iam pene centum adversus sedem apostolicam erexerat se, nec solum eius predia usurpaverat, set ipsam aliquando Romanam invasit ecclesiam Guibertus eiusdem metropolis incubator.

**3.** Circa solutionem vero concilii lecta sunt de reconciliandis qui extra Ecclesiam catholicam ordinati sunt sanctorum Patrum capitula, Agustini ex epistola ad Bonifatium,[1] Leonis primi ex epistola ad episcopos Mauritanos,[2] Cartaginensis concilii quarti capitulum tertium, cuius initium est: *Placuit ut littere mittantur ad fratres et coepiscopos nostros et maxime ad sedem apostolicam.*[3] Novum vero in hec verba capitulum institutum est:

[1] Augustine ep. 185, *De Correctione Donatistarum Liber*, probably cap. 47, CSEL 57: 40-41, especially 41, line 2-8: "hoc erga istos ab initio seruauit Africana catholica ex episcoporum sententia, qui in ecclesia Romana inter Caecilianum et partem Donati iudicauerunt damnatoque uno quodam Donato, qui auctor schismatis fuisse manifestatus est, ceteros correctos, etiamsi extra ecclesiam ordinati essent, in suis honoribus suscipiendos esse censuerunt ...." An excerpt from ep. 185 including the above passage is found in MS Vat. lat. 1346 as the final addition on fol. 192r. The codex, containing the *Collection in Seven Books*, was composed in Rome or in the vicinity during the pontificate of Paschal. The same text as in Vat. lat. 1346 was found in MS San Daniele 203: "Qui a corporis compage diuisi extra ecclesiam et contra aecclesiam aecclesiae sacramenta tenuerunt ueniant; non se extollant aduersus maternam sollicitudinem, non referant ad elationis malum, quod facit ipsa propter pacis bonum. Sic multitudinibus per scismata et hereses pereuntibus subuenire consueuit. Hoc erga istos ab initio seruauit africana catholica qui in ecclesia romana inter Cecilianum et partem Donati iudicauerunt, dampnatoque uno quodam Donato qui auctor scismatis fuisse manifestatus est, ceteros correptos, etiamsi extra ordinati essent, in suis honoribus suscipiendos esse censuerunt. Et quos in sacrilego, sicut concilium eorum indicat scismate dampnauerant et in quorum iam locum alios ordinauerant postquam uiderunt ab eis populos non recedere, ne omnes perderent, in suis honoribus receperunt" (ex MS San Daniele 203, fol. 48r, cf. Blumenthal, "Codex Guarnerius 203," *Bulletin of Medieval Canon Law*, n.s. 5 (1975) 11-33). The index of the three volumes of the *Libelli de lite* documents the frequent use at the turn of the twelfth century of this particular letter of Augustine. Pope Urban II, for instance, referrred to it in a canon at the council of Piacenza held in 1095: "... Ubi enim multorum strages iacet subtrahendum est aliquid seueritati, ut addatur amplius caritati" (c. 12, MGH Const. 1: 563, no. 393). The *Prologue* of Ivo of Chartres referred to the very same excerpt (PL 161: 52; for Ivo's canonical writings and their complicated relationship with each other see van Hove, *Prolegomena*, pp. 330-332 and the references given there; the most recent discussion is found in Fuhrmann, *Einfluss und Verbreitung*, 2: 542-562, esp. n. 323). Paschal's decree leaves the question unanswered which section of Augustine's epistle was read. The indications in the following c. 4 imply that the excerpts presented to the assembly perhaps included the passage that attracted the attention of Urban and Ivo of Chartres (Augustinus, ep. 185, cap. 45 in fine, CSEL 57: 39-40: "uerum in huius modi causis, ubi per graues dissensionum scissuras non huius aut illius hominis est periculum, sed populorum strages iacent, detrahendum est aliquid seueritati, ut maioribus malis sanandis caritas sincera subueniat"). It will be remembered that Paschal suggested the decrees of Piacenza as guidelines for the settlement with Germany, and it is therefore not certain

whether the reference to the "strages populorum" (see c. 4 below) is an allusion to Urban's decree or to Augustine. Conceivably, Paschal referred to both as well as possibly to Ivo. Cf. R. Somerville, "Miscellany: Two Notes on Scotland and the Medieval Papacy," *The Innes Review* 23.2 (1972) 149-151. For Urban II and Ivo of Chartres see S. Kuttner, "Urban II and the Doctrine of Interpretation: A Turning Point?" *Post Scripta, Essays on Medieval Law and the Emergence of the European State in Honor of Gaines Post* (Rome 1972) pp. 53-85.

[2] Leo M., ep. 12. 6 (JK 410), both recensions (PL 54, col. 653 and 662); cf. H 625, with the inscription *Leo uniuersis episcopis per Africam constitutis in domino salutem.* Cf. also Bernold of Constance, *Libellus* 10: *De excommunicatis vitandis...*, 18: "In heresi ordinatus, qui tamen in fide sanctae Trinitatis non erraverit, cum ordine recipi potest, si necesse fuerit, ut Novatiani et Donatistae" (ed. F. Thaner, MGH Lib. de lite, 2: 120, line 2-3).

[3] Conc. Carthag. a. 401, c. 68 vers. Dion. (Munier, *Concilia Africae*, p. 200; Bruns 1: 172f.; PL 67, col. 204) cf. Ans. 8.34 (MS Vat. lat. 1364, fol. 199r-199v) inscr. ex conc. Africano.

**4.** Per multos iam annos regni Teutonici latitudo ab apostolice sedis unitate divisa est. In quo nimirum scismate tantum periculum factum est ut, quod cum dolore dicimus, vix pauci sacerdotes aut clerici catholici in tanta terrarum latitudine reperiantur. Tot igitur filiis in hac strage iacentibus, christiane pacis necessitas exigit ut super hos materna Ecclesie viscera aperiantur. Patrum itaque nostrorum exemplis et scriptis instructi, qui diversis temporibus Novatianos, Donatistas et alios hereticos in suis ordinibus susceperunt,[1] prefati regni episcopos in *scismate ordinatos*, nisi aut invasores aut symoniaci aut criminosi comprobentur in officio episcopali *suscipimus*; id ipsum de clericis cuiuscumque ordinis constituimus, quos *vita scientiaque commendat.*[2]

[1] Cf. the annotations to c. 3 above.
[2] Cf. Conc. Placent. a. 1095, c. 10: "Qui vero ab episcopis quondam quidem catholice ordinatis sed in hoc scismate a Romana aecclesia separatis consecrati sunt, eos nimirum, cum ad aecclesiae unitatem redierint, servatis propriis ordinibus, misericorditer suscipi iubemus, si tamen vita eos et scientia commendat" (MGH Const. 1: 562).

**5.** Aliud capitulum.
Iamdiu a pravis hominibus tam clericis quam laicis catholica est Ecclesia conculcata; unde plura temporibus nostris schismata et hereses emerserunt. Nunc autem per Dei gratiam huius nequitie deficientibus auctoribus in ingenuam libertatem resurgit Ecclesia. Unde providendum est ut horum schismatum cause penitus abscidantur. Patrum ergo nostrorum constitutionibus consentientes, ecclesiarum investituras a laicis fieri omni modo prohibemus. Si quis autem decreti huius temerator extiterit, tanquam materne iniurie reus, clericus quidem ab eiusdem dignitatis consortio repellatur, laycus vero ab ecclesiae liminibus arceatur.

**6.** Aliud capitulum.

Nullus abbas, nullus archipresbiter, nullus prepositus ecclesie audeat possessiones ecclesie sue vendere, commutare, locare, vel in feudum dare, sine communi fratrum consensu vel episcopi proprie civitatis, alioquin ordinis sui periculum patiatur.

* * *

The Paraphrase of C. 2

    Manuscripts:

Ma: Madrid, Biblioteca Nacional MS 4207 (P.95) fol. 336v
    A partial description of the contents of this paper codex, s. 16, is given by P. Ewald, "Reise nach Spanien im Winter von 1878 auf 1879," *Neues Archiv* 6 (1881) 219-398, 310f. Cf. Weiland, MGH Const. 1: 565: "quaedam de concilio nostro insunt ... codici Matritensi P.95 saec. XVI."

Ra: Rome, Biblioteca Vallicelliana, MS C.16, fol. 146r
    Paper, s. 16, 268 fols. several of which are empty, 315 × 220 mm. The title of the manuscript according to the *Inventarium omnium codicum manuscriptorum Graecorum et Latinorum Bibliothecae Vallicelliana* (1749) 1: "Opuscula varia et antiqua diversi generis Monumenta," indicates the miscellaneous character of the excerpts collected in the volume. Sources are not indicated, and it proved impossible to determine the author. The relationship between Ma and C.16 is apparently close.

    Basic MS: Ra

    Text:

Anno postea domini millesimo centesimo sexto presidente Pascali secundo apostolico concilio apud Guardastallum habito, urbes[a] Emiliae, Parma scilicet, Placentia, Regium Lepidi, Mutina, Bononia a metropoli Ravenna propter superbiam in romanam sedem eximuntur[b] sed per Gelasium papam secundum ut hic[c] patet restituuntur. Gelasius episcopus servus servorum dei... (JL 6647).

    [a] urbis *Ra Ma*    [b] excommuntur *Ma*    [c] si *Ma*

* * *

C. 4 Redaction 1

    Manuscripts:

E: Ekkehard of Aura, Chronicle Ekkehard III
    Ekkehard's text is used on the basis of the edition and translation by Franz-Josef Schmale and Irene Schmale-Ott (Ausgewählte Quellen zur Deutschen Geschichte des Mittelalters, Freiherr vom Stein-Gedächtnisausgabe 15, Darm-

stadt 1972) p. 292; cf. *Ekkehardi Chronicon*, ed. G. Waitz, MGH SS 6: 240f.
Fb: Frankfurt am Main, Stadt- und Universitätsbibliothek, Barth. 50, fol. 5v
The late eleventh-century codex contains the canonical collection of Burchard of Worms. The capitulatio of book 1 of the collection is followed on fol. 5v by c. 4 of Guastalla which was entered in a tiny script from the first half of the twelfth century. The manuscript is of West-German or Middle-Rhenish origin. See *Kataloge der Stadt- und Universitätsbibliothek Frankfurt am Main*, ed. C. Köttelwesch, vol. 3: *Die Handschriften der Stadt- und Universitätsbibliothek Frankfurt am Main*, part 2: *Die Handschriften des Bartholomaeusstifts und des Karmeliterklosters in Frankfurt am Main*, beschrieben von Gerhardt Powitz und Herbert Buck (Frankfurt am Main 1974) pp. 104f. and ix.
Go: Göttweig, Stiftsbibliothek, 85 (8) fol. 2r
The codex was not seen, but microfilm printouts for fol. 2r were obtained from the Monastic Manuscript Microfilm Library, Collegeville, Minnesota. C. 4 from Guastalla is an addition to fol. 2r, directly following the canons from Urban II's council of Piacenza held in 1095. The Guastalla text, however, is written in a different hand. See J. F. Schulte, "Die Rechtshandschriften der Stiftsbibliotheken von Göttweig Ord. S. Bened., Heiligenkreuz ... Schotten in Wien Ord. S. Bened.," *Sitzungsberichte* Vienna 57 (1867) 559-616, esp. p. 560 and Weiland, MGH Const. 1: 561n, no. 393 (Piacenza).
M: Bayerische Staatsbibliothek Munich, Clm. 3739, fol. 7v
See below p. 90. C. 4 of Guastalla was entered in the lower margin of fol. 7v, probably simultaneously with the 1107 decrees. The codex was used by Weiland. C. 4 is incomplete.
Vp: Città del Vaticano, Biblioteca Apostolica Vaticana, Palat. lat. 587, fol. 108v
This twelfth-century manuscript contains the *Decretum* of Ivo of Chartres concluding with Paschal's c. 4 from the council of Guastalla. The decree is written in the same hand as the remainder of the text. The codex was used by Weiland.

Basic MS: Vp

Text:

Decretum domni Paschalis pape quod decreuit in sinodo que celebrata est apud Uuaristallam anno incarnationis domini MCVI, indictione xiiii, xi kalendas nouembris ubi episcopi et abbates tam Galliarum quam et Langobardie et Tuscie necnon Germanie et Saxonie conuenerunt.[a]

Per multos iam annos regni teutonici[b] latitudo ab apostolicae sedis[c] unitate divisa est. In quo nimirum scismate tantum[d] periculum factum est ut, quod cum dolore dicimus,[f] vix pauci sacerdotes[g] aut clerici catholici[h] in tanta terrarum latitudine reperiantur. Tot igitur filiis in hac strage iacentibus christianae[i] pacis necessitas exigit ut super hos materna[j] aecclesiae viscera[k] aperiantur.[l] Patrum[m] itaque nostrorum exemplis et scriptis instructi, qui diversis temporibus Novatianos, Donatistas et alios hereticos in suis[n] ordinibus susceperunt, prefati regni episcopos in scismate ordinatos, nisi aut invasores aut symoniaci aut criminoso conprobentur,[o] in officio episcopali suscipimus. Id ipsum de clericis cuiuscumque ordinis constituimus quos vita scientiaque commendat.[p] Amen.[q]

[a] Decretum-conuenerunt *om. E*     Ex concilio habito Guardastallia secundo Paschali *Fb*     Decretum Paschalis Pape *Go*     Capitulum beati Paschalis pape apud Warstal *M*     [b] teutonici regni *tr. M*     [c] apostolici sedis] aecclesiae *M*     [d] tantum-est *om. M*     [e] quod *om. M*     [f] dicamus *M*     [g] sacerdotes] episcopi *M*     [h] catholici clerici *tr. M*     [i] christianae-aecclesiae *om. M*     [j] maternae *Fb*     [k] viscera *om. Fb*     [l] aperiantur] Misericordiae *praem. M*     [m] Patrum-commendat *om. M ibidem finis inconsummatus legitur*: Sanctorum patrum instructi scripturis qui Novitianos et Donatistas in suis ordinibus susceperunt.     [n] temporibus *add. Fb*     [o] sint probati *E*     [p] commendant *Fb*     [q] Amen *om. cett.*

\* \* \*

## C. 4 Redaction 2

Manuscripts:

Bl:   Bamberg, Staatsbibliothek, Lit. 140 (Ed. II.16) fol. 81r-81v
C. 4 of Guastalla is transcribed at the end of Bernold's treatise *De Berengarii haeresiarchae damnatione multiplici* (PL 148, col. 1453-1460) covering fols. 75r-81r of the codex. The manuscript is described by F. Leitschuh, *Katalog der Handschriften der Königlichen Bibliothek zu Bamberg* 1, erste Abtheilung (Bamberg 1898) 288-291.

Bp:   Bamberg, Staatsbibliothek, Patr. 30 (B.III.25) fol. 125r
As in Bl, c. 4 of Guastalla follows the treatise against Berengar. See F. Leitschuh, *Katalog der Handschriften der Königlichen Bibliothek zu Bamberg* 1, erste Abtheilung (Bamberg 1903) 385-387.

U:   Udalricus
The text is included on the basis of the edition by Philip Jaffé, *Monumenta Bambergensia* (1869) 252, no. 135; cf. Weiland, MGH Const. 1: 565f.

V:   Vienna, Österreichische Nationalbibliothek, 1705, fol. 32r
This manuscript, too, contains c. 4 of Guastalla at the end of Bernold's *De Berengarii haeresiarchae*. See *Tabulae codicum manuscriptorum praeter graecos et orientales in Bibliotheca Palatina Vindobonensi asservatorum* 1 (Vienna 1864) 277.

Basic MS: Bl

Text:

Decretum pape Pascalis .ii. actum Warstallis.[a] Quoniam aecclesia in multis locis et maxime in teutonicis partibus diu laborauit sub heresi et scismate, et si omnia illa quae ab illis hereticis et scismatibus[b] ordinata sunt annullari deberent quaedam aecclesiae omnino nudari uiderentur suis clericis, nos sequentes decreta sanctorum patrum de his qui[c] sub Acatio et Bonosio et Donatistis ordinati sunt statuentes decernimus[d] ut episcopi qui sub ipso scismate ordinati sunt omnes in suis honoribus permaneant nisi sint inuasores aut criminosi. De ceteris uero ordinibus paenes episcopos potestas sit ut quorum uita probabilis uideatur in suo gradu consistant.

[a] Decretum-Warstallis *om.* U    [b] scismaticis U    [c] qui *scripsi cum* U    quae BlBpV    [d] Bonoso U    [e] decreuimus U

\* \* \*

## C. 6 as Part of the Breviarium Gestorum of 1112

Manuscripts:

Sm: Schaffhausen, Ministerialbibliothek, 46
    In addition to Weiland, MGH Const. 1: 573-574, see W. Wattenbach, "Aus Stuttgart und Schaffhausen," *Neues Archiv* 6 (1880) 447-451, especially pp. 448-449.

Vl: Città del Vaticano, Biblioteca Apostolica Vaticana, Barb. lat. 538 (XI.181)
    This miscellaneous manuscript of 59 fols., s. 11 and s. 12 in., is of Italian origin and contains several conciliar addenda. Among them, over an erased portion of the text, is found the *breviarium* of Paschal's Lateran council of 1112 (MGH Const. 1: 573f.) with c. 6 of the council of Guastalla held in 1106. Underneath this final item of the *breviarium* the two circles of a papal rota are drawn but left empty. The last item in the codex, fol. 59v, is Berengar's confession from the Roman Lenten synod of 1079. The possibility that the Guastalla canons were repromulgated at the Lateran council of 1112 was discussed earlier (above p. 46).

Basic MS: Vl

Text:

Item aliud capitulum.[a]
Nullus abbas, nullus archipresbiter, nullus prepositus ecclesie audeat possessiones ecclesie sue uendere, commutare, locare uel in feudum dare sine communi fratrum /// consensu et episcopi proprie ciuitatis,[b] alioquin ordinis sui periculum patiatur.

[a] inscr. *om.* Sm    [b] ciuitatis] uel aliquod spiritale a laicali manu accipere *add.* Sm

### New Guastalla Texts

The only canons known hitherto from the council of Guastalla were essentially[122] those transcribed by Cardinal Boso. During the manuscript

---

[122] But cf. the independent manuscript tradition for c. 2 and especially c. 4. The latter confirms the accuracy of Boso's text.

research for this study, a different group of canons was found which, it will be argued, was probably also part of the Guastalla legislation. This second set of canons is appended in several twelfth-century copies of the *Collectio canonum* of Anselm of Lucca[123] to the sixth book of the collection: *De electione et ordinatione ac de omni potestate sive statu episcoporum*, a very suitable location for the decrees, since all of them deal with different aspects of the episcopal office. They are also found as cap. 141 of book 6 in the related *Collection in Thirteen Books* of MS Vat. lat. 1361 (cited subsequently as 13L). There are six codices with the Guastalla additions:[124]

1. Graz, Universitätsbibliothek 351
2. Parma, Biblioteca Palatina, Fondo Parmense 976
3. Naples, Biblioteca Nazionale, XII A.37-39
4. Florence, Biblioteca Mediceo-Laurenziana, San Marco 499
5. Florence, Biblioteca Mediceo-Laurenziana, Ashburnham 53 (incomplete)
6. Città del Vaticano, Biblioteca Apostolica Vaticana, Vat. lat. 1361 (incomplete).

Not one of them identifies the canons as having been promulgated at the 1106 synod: four of them, Graz, Parma, Naples, and Vatican City, attribute them to a council held by Pope Paschal II; the Florentine manuscripts contain no inscription at all.

Fortunately, it is possible to tentatively identify the canons with the aid

---

[123] This canonical collection, compiled in the early 1080's, was partially edited by F. Thaner, *Anselmi Lucensis collectio canonum una cum collectione minore*, fasc. 1 and 2 in 1 (Innsbruck 1906-15). For the date of the collection see Stickler, *Historia*, pp. 170-172; van Hove, *Prolegomena*, pp. 323-324; Fournier-Le Bras, *Histoire des collections canoniques*, 2: 25-37; P. Fournier, "Observations sur diverses récensions de la Collection Canonique d'Anselme de Lucques," *Annales de l'Université de Grenoble* 13 (1901) 427-458; Fuhrmann, *Einfluss und Verbreitung der pseudoisidorischen Fälschungen*, 2: 509-522. To the manuscripts listed by Thaner, three should be added: MSS Cambridge, Corpus Christi College 269 (see Z. N. Brooke, *The English Church and the Papacy* [Cambridge 1952] 91 and 241), Florence, Biblioteca Mediceo-Laurenziana, San Marco 499 and Huesca, Biblioteca Provincial 20 (see S. Kuttner, "Some Roman manuscripts of canonical collections," *Bulletin of Medieval Canon Law*, n.s. 1 [1971] 1-29, p. 13 and for San Marco 499 also H. Mordek, "Handschriftenforschung in Italien," QFIAB 51 [1971] 626-651, p. 628 n. 6). The Huesca codex, a sixteenth-century copy of Anselm recension C, was not seen nor could a microfilm be obtained. It is not known, therefore, whether it preserves the Paschal canons or not.

[124] The manuscripts are described below pp. 65-68. With the exception of 13L and MS Ashburnham 53, the codices are either part of Thaner's recension A¹ or related to it (but see Kuttner, "Some Roman Manuscripts," p. 13). At the present stage of scholarship it is unfortunately not possible to give a stemma codicum for Anselm's collection.

of a manuscript known to the Correctores Romani. This codex, a fragment from Segni now lost, can be reconstructed with the help of their description given in a manuscript at the Biblioteca Apostolica Vaticana, Vat. lat. 4891.[125] Preserved among the annotations to Gratian, C.16 q.7 c.16ff. is the following entry (fol. 169v):

> Item Paschalis 2. In margine: in concilio generali apud Guardastalum habito anno Domini 1116 [sic] quod habetur in Bibliotheca Vaticana, et R.D. Eps. Signin. fragmentum adduxit in quo haec capita habeantur.

This note, preceding Gratian, C.16 q.7 c.16 (*Si qui clericus*), shows that the Correctores had two manuscripts at their disposal for the emendation of this section of the *Decretum*: (1) a manuscript from the Vatican and (2) a fragment given to them by the bishop of Segni, "Reverendissimus Dominus Episcopus Signinus."[126]

It appears that at least the fragment from Segni (subsequently referred to as S), but probably also the Vatican codex, contained 3 canons: Gratian, C.16 q.7 c.16, C.16 q.7 c.17, and C.16 q.7 c.18. The Correctores notes in MS Vat. lat. 4891 (fol. 169v-170r) read:

> Can. *Si quis clericus*      16
> Idem citato loco (Guastalla),
> perquiratur tamen apud Decretistas
>
> Can. *Constitutiones*      17
> Ab hac hora in antea, ex fragmento MS (S)
> De manu laica, ex fragmento MS (S)
> Idem in concilio prefato (Guastalla)
>
> Can. *Nullus laicorum*      18
> Idem in margine citato Concilio (Guastalla)

---

[125] Vat. lat. 4891 is one of the Vatican manuscripts preserving minutes of the working sessions of the Correctores group. See S. Kuttner, "Brief Notes," *Traditio* 24 (1968) 504-507, p. 505.

[126] The name of the bishop of Segni who provided the Correctores with the manuscript is not indicated. He must have been a contemporary of the Correctores who had donated the fragment to this commission (active under the pontificates of Pius IV [1559-1565], Pius V [1566-1572], and Gregory XIII [1572-1585]) at some point between 1559 and 24 April 1571, when the notes for this section of the *Decretum* were written. (Vat. lat. 4891, fol. 169v: Feria 3. Die 24. Aprilis 1571.) Since the 1571 note refers to the donor as a living person he can be identified as Joseph Pamfili, bishop of Segni from 1570-1581 (Eubel 3: 319). The Correctores solicited throughout Europe information which would aid them in their task. Concerning the Correctores and the council of Guastalla see Schellhass, "Wissenschaftliche Forschungen," p. 677; see also Somerville, *Decreta Claromontensia*, p. 49, for cooperation between the Correctores and Franciscus Richardotus, bishop of Arras.

The next canon, *Sicut Domini* (Gratian, C.16 q.7 c.19) is annotated: "Item Alex. Papa; nusquam invenitur neque apud Decretistas perquiratur diligentissime."[127] Clearly, references to Guastalla cease with the annotation to c. 18, *Nullus laicorum*. The reference to "haec capita" in the introductory note preceding Gratian, C.16 q.7 c.16, therefore, presumably covered canons 16 to 18 inclusively.

With the help of the *Decretum* and the variants noted by the Correctores the fragment S may be hypothetically reconstructed as follows although the sequence of the canons in S presumably differed from Gratian's:[128]

> Paschalis papa in concilio generali apud Guardastalum[129]
>
> Si quis clericus, abbas uel monachus per laicos ecclesias obtinuerit, secundum Apostolorum sanctorum canones et Antioceni capitulum concilii excommunicationi subiaceat.
>
> Constitutiones sanctorum canonum sequentes statuimus ut quicumque clericorum ab hac hora in antea inuestituram ecclesiae uel ecclesiasticae dignitatis de manu laica acceperit, et qui ei manum imposuerit, gradus sui periculo subiaceat, et communione priuetur.
>
> Nullus laicorum ecclesias uel ecclesiarum bona occupet uel disponat. Qui uero secus egerit iuxta beati Alexandri primi capitulum ab ecclesie liminibus arceatur.

Doubts that the manuscript donated by the bishop of Segni to the Correctores indeed transmitted the text just recorded are to some extent alleviated by notes in another manuscript at the Biblioteca Apostolica Vaticana, Barb. lat. 860, containing chiefly the papers of Antonio d'Aquino in preparation for the Roman edition of the General Councils.[130] In the margin of fol. 78r of this codex is found a note, unfortunately only partially legible, accompanied by a reference to Gratian, C.16 q.7 c.16 (*Si quis clericus*): "In notis

---

[127] The following marginal note was entered subsequently: "Invenitur in epist. Alexandri Secundi in libro manuscripto Achillis Statii." Achilles Statius was a member of the Correctores under Pope Gregory XIII. The canon *Sicut Domini* will be discussed in Appendix 2.

[128] Nothing can be said, of course, about the age of S. Since, however, Bishop Bruno of Segni may have participated in the synod of Guastalla (above n. 68) it is conceivable that he came back with a copy of the canons for his own use. In a letter written to Paschal after the pontiff had granted Henry V the right of investiture in May 1111, Bruno referred to the canons of Guastalla and demanded that they be repromulgated (ep. 2, MGH Libelli de lite 2: 564).

[129] MS Vat. lat. 4891 does not state whether the Correctores obtained the inscription from the Vatican codex, from the fragment S, or whether they themselves provided it.

[130] The *Collectio Romana* appeared in 4 volumes, Rome 1608-1612. For Antonio d'Aquino see S. Kuttner, "L'Édition Romaine," esp. p. 11; C. Leonardi, "Per una storia dell'edizione Romana"; V. Peri, "Due protagonisti," for MS Barb. lat. 860 esp. p. 180 and other locations indicated in the index ibid. p. 232.

sunt tres <canones> concilii apud Guardastallam." The emendation
"canones" is made on the assumption that d'Aquino referred to the Correctores note in MS Vat. lat. 4891.

The second manuscript at the disposal of the commission for the emendation of Gratian's *Decretum* is also identifiable through a comparison of notes written by the Correctores and d'Aquino respectively. The Correctores said of the codex only that it was in the Biblioteca Vaticana.[131] In d'Aquino's Barb. lat. 860 the Roselli series of Guastalla canons (fol. 72r-72v) and JL 5971[132] is followed on fol. 73r by:

> Ex alio codice
> Ut per laicum nullus clericus aliquo honore inuestiatur.
> Paschalis II Papa dixit
> Constitutiones sanctorum canonum sequentes statuimus ut quicumque clericorum ab hac hora in antea inuestituram ecclesiae uel ecclesiasticae dignitatis de manu laicali acceperit, et iste, et qui ei manum imposuerit gradus sui periculo subiaceat, et communione priuetur.[133]

On fol. 76r the same canon is accompanied by the note: "In Vat. in 4° numero 1882."[134] Additional references to this codex in quarto in MS Barb. lat. 860[135] show that it must be both the "other codex" mentioned by d'Aquino's secretary on fol. 73r and the Vatican manuscript used by the Correctores Romani in connection with Gratian, C.16 q.7 cc.16-18.

The notes of the Correctores in MS Vat. lat. 4891, however, are the only

---

[131] Above p. 59: "... in concilio generale apud Guardastalum ... quod habetur in Bibliotheca Vaticana."

[132] The source for these canons is given as "ex Cencio Camerario fol. 274."

[133] Since MS Barb. lat. 860 contains only this single canon from the Segni-Anselm of Lucca tradition, it will not be included in the edition below and the text is given here instead.

[134] Efforts to identify this manuscrit have not met with any success. The author would like to thank Msgr. Ruysschaert of the Biblioteca Apostolica Vaticana and Professor S. Kuttner for their kind assistance. MS Vat. lat. 6948, a work copy for the seventeenth-century catalogue of the Vatican library compiled by the brothers Rainaldi, replaced on fol. 26 the manuscript number 1882 with the new shelf mark "1339 Coll. can." While it is possible that 1882 was a canonical collection, it cannot have been the present manuscript Vat. lat. 1339 which contains the *Collection in Five Books*. The collection, dating from the early decades of the eleventh century and of Italian origin, was recently edited by M. Fornasari, *Collectio Canonum in v Libris* (Corpus Christianorum, Continuatio Mediaevalis 6, 1970). For the Rainaldi brothers see F. Ehrle, "Zur Geschichte der Katalogisierung der Vatikana," *Historisches Jahrbuch* 11 (1890) 718-727.

[135] Professor Kuttner kindly informed me that the same reference to MS 1882 in 4° also occurs in Vallicellianus C.24, fol. 227r, in a notice on Innocent II's council of 1139. The Vallicellianus note was copied for Antonio d'Aquino and is found in MS Barb. lat. 860 on fol. 91r.

source which identifies the canon *Constitutiones sanctorum* (Gratian, C.16 q.7 c.17) as a decree from Guastalla.[136] D'Aquino's Barberinus does not specifically attributed the decree to any particular synod. In Friedberg's edition of the *Decretum* the text is linked to the council of Troyes held in 1107.[137] The printed commentary of the Correctores which accompanies *Constitutiones sanctorum* in the *Editio Romana*, however, supports the Guastalla attribution: "Capitis huius [c.16 Si quis clericus] et sequentis [c.17 Constitutiones] sensus est in fragmento manuscripto concilii apud Guardastallum, a Paschali habito A.D. 1116 [*sic*] quod in bibliotheca Vaticana servatur."[138] Such support is also found in a list of books used by the Correctores which is reproduced in Friedberg's prolegomena. Under "Paschalis I" (*sic*) we read: "Epistolae et decreta, ex bibliotheca Ormanetti Episcopi Patavini,[139] et fragmentum concilii apud Guardastallum, ex Vaticana."[140] Even here a link to the entry in MS Vat. lat. 4891[141] is faintly discernible, for while the various Correctores references appear today obscure, they have one thing in common: each note insists that the *Decretum* contains legislation from Guastalla.[142]

In addition to Gratian, C.16 q.7 c.17, C.16 q.7 c.16 (*Si quis clericus*) and c.18 (*Nullus laicorum*) were also identified as Guastalla decrees in the Correctores' minutes. The latter two are also part of the Paschalian canons in certain Anselm of Lucca manuscripts and 13L.[143] It is suggested here that the remaining four canons in these codices were also among the decrees of

---

[136] The date 1116 in the note (above p. 59) is a mistake for 1106, the only year when Paschal held a council at Guastalla. His 1116 council was held in the Lateran.

[137] See Appendix 2. The canon was apparently repromulgated at Troyes in 1107 and at the Lateran council of 1110.

[138] Gratian, *Decretum* C.16 q.7 c.16 *Notatio Correctorum* in Friedberg's edition. It should be noted that the printed notes refer only to two canons whereas the manuscript refers to three. The connection between the handwritten and printed notes is nevertheless established through the references to *fragmentum* and the erroneous date 1116.

[139] The reference is to the Italian humanist Niccolò Ormanetto, bishop of Padua from 1570-1577. One of his manuscripts used by the Correctores is the "Liber Veronensis," but whether this is the codex referred to here under Paschalis I is an open question.

[140] *Decretum*, ed. Friedberg, p. lxxxviii.

[141] See above p. 59.

[142] Friedberg's edition does not identify a single one of them. See Appendix 2.

[143] Since 13L is largely based on the work of Anselm of Lucca with additional material taken especially from the Panormia of Ivo of Chartres (see the recent analysis by Kuttner, "Some Roman Manuscripts," pp. 9-13) and no copy of the Panormia that I examined contains Guastalla decrees, one may conclude that the Guastalla text in MS Vat. lat. 1361 was very likely derived from a manuscript of the *Collectio canonum* of Anselm of Lucca. As in all other cases the decrees are found in book 6. Therefore 13L will be treated in the present discussion as if it were one of the Anselm of Lucca codices. The fragment S and Barb. lat. 860 will be discussed separately.

1106. There is no proof for this hypothesis because it is not known by whom or exactly when this particular set of additions to Anselm's canonical collection was made. All six manuscripts date from the twelfth century,[144] and are probably of Italian origin with the possible exception of the Graz codex. It is safe to assume that the majority would be dated to the decades prior to 1140 if the scriptoria of origin were known. But this evidence is not available, and it is well, therefore, that the text itself of the series proves that we are not dealing with a compilation of Paschalian canons taken from Gratian's *Concordia discordantium canonum*. One of the canons, *Nullus episcopus*, was not included by Gratian. The others are scattered among the Causae with attribution to Pope Paschal I or II, but never with Guastalla in the inscription.[145]

The most common inscription accompanying the decrees is "Ex concilio Paschalis papae." The *Decretum* of Gratian confirms that the attribution to Paschal is authentic, and it is evident from the text that it can be understood to refer to Pope Paschal II. The second fact to be gleaned from the inscription is that the canons were promulgated by a single council, identified by the Correctores as Guastalla. It might be argued, though, that this interpretation places too much weight on an inscription since inscriptions in canonical collections are notoriously imprecise. Two points can be raised to support my hypothesis that nonetheless the Correctores' identification can be extended on the basis of the inscription to cover all of the decrees. (1) The manuscripts are at one with my contention. They treat the material "ex concilio Pascalis pape" as one block of text. Two among the six codices are incomplete, but even they (Florence, Ashburnham 53 and 13L) contain canons 3 and 4[146] and canons 2-4 respectively in the correct sequence without significant variants. 13L preserved as well the inscription "ex concilio Pascalis pape" although c. 2 follows instead of c. 1. The other manuscripts are complete. This fact is particularly striking whenever the Paschal text constitutes the final addition to book 6 as in the case of MSS Florence, San Marco 499, Graz UB 351, and Naples XII A.37-39. (2) No canon in the Anselm set appears among material associated with others of Paschal's councils.

To sum up, six manuscripts, including 13L, contain a series of six Paschalian decrees of which two certainly and four very likely were promulgated at the council of Guastalla in 1106. There is, however, a seventh

---

[144] I am much obliged to Professor J. Autenrieth for her kind assistance.
[145] See Appendix 2: The Guastalla canons and Gratian's *Decretum*.
[146] C. 4 in the Laurenzianus lacks the last subordinate clause. See the edition below.

canon, *Constitutiones*, that was also identified by the Correctores and probably in d'Aquino's Barb. lat. 860 as a decree from Guastalla. The Barberinus presents *Constitutiones* as a single addition to the Roselli text; the Correctores found the canon together with two from the Anselm series in a fragment from the library of the bishops of Segni. In this fragment, probably just a leaf from an old codex, *Constitutiones* is apparently sandwiched between c. *Si quis clericus* and c. *Nullus laicorum*, that is c. 6 and c. 3 of the Anselm text respectively, and in this order. The arrangement of S coincides with the sequence of canons 16, 17, 18 of Gratian's C.16 q.7. It is unlikely that S agreed to this extent with Gratian, and the notes of the Correctores should be interpreted only as indicating that the scholars had in front of them a manuscript fragment which contained Gratian, C.16 q.7 c.16, 17, and 18 as decrees from Guastalla but not necessarily in this order. Because the Correctores clearly identified *Constitutiones* the text will be included in the edition below although the decree is not part of the Anselm of Lucca series. It was promulgated two more times, at Troyes in 1107 and later at the Lateran council of 1110.

The arguments concerning the attribution of the new texts were presented in such detail because the decrees have nothing in common with Boso's canons, an enormous obstacle to their identification. One exception is conceivably the prohibition of lay investiture. Even here, though, the treatment differs completely. To facilitate a comparison, the four relevant decrees are presented here in parallel columns.

| Boso, *Liber Pontificalis* | Anselm of Lucca series c. 3 |
|---|---|
| Aliud capitulum.<br>Iamdiu a pravis hominibus tam clericis quam laicis catholica est ecclesia conculcata: unde plura temporibus nostris schismata et hereses emerserunt. Nunc autem per Dei gratiam huius nequitie deficientibus auctoribus in ingenuam libertatem resurgit ecclesia. Unde prouidendum est, ut horum schismatum cause penitus abscidantur. Patrum ergo nostrorum constitutionibus consentientes, ecclesiarum inuestituras a laicis fieri omnimodo prohibemus. Si quis autem decreti huius temerator extiterit tamquam materne iniurie reus, clericus quidem ab eiusdem dignitatis consortio re- | Nullus laicorum ecclesias uel ecclesiarum bona occupet uel disponat. Sicut enim beatus Stephanus papa martyr scribit, laici quamuis religiosi sint nulli tamen de ecclesiasticis facultatibus aliquid disponendi legitur umquam attributa facultas. Qui uero secus egerit iuxta beati Alexandri primi capitulum ab ecclesie liminibus arceatur. |

pellatur, laicus uero ab ecclesie liminibus arceatur.

| Anselm of Lucca series c. 6 | Segni fragment S |
|---|---|
| Si quis clericus, abbas uel monachus, per laicos ecclesias obtinuerit, secundum sanctorum apostolorum canones et Antiocheni concilii capitulum excommunicationi subiaceat. | Constitutiones sanctorum canonum sequentes statuimus ut quicumque clericorum ab hac hora in antea inuestituram ecclesiae uel ecclesiasticae dignitatis de manu laica acceperit, et qui ei manum imposuerit, gradus sui periculo subiaceat, et communione priuetur. |

Boso's version with its special characteristics and the authority of the papal registers behind it,[147] is rhetorically elaborate and less precise than any of the other decrees. Keeping in mind what little is known about conciliar procedures during this period,[148] and omitting c. *Constitutiones* for the moment, it can perhaps be said that the canons *Nullus laicorum* and *Si quis clericus* represent earlier stages in the drafting of the legislation, that they are *breviaria*. The decree *Iamdiu* of Boso, for example, only alludes to more ancient conciliar legislation: "... patrum ergo nostrorum constitutionibus consentientes ...." Both other canons directly name the precedents presumably found in the canonical collections that were used at the council of Guastalla. The ornate *Iamdiu* seems to be the later and final redaction made at the papal curia. It is surprising that it contradicts the decree *Si quis clericus*. *Iamdiu* refers only once to clerics, pointing out that in contrast to laymen clerics would not be excommunicated but would only lose their ecclesiastical rank. This softening is possibly a result of the deliberations at Guastalla, and if so a compromise with the German clergy. Finally, c. *Constitutiones*, more clearly than *Iamdiu*, is intellectually a contraction of the statements made in c. *Nullus laicorum* and c. *Si quis clericus*. C. *Constitutiones*, too, softens the punishment for accepting clergy to loss of rank for future infringement of the lay investiture prohibition.

Manuscripts[149]

Fa: Florence, Biblioteca Mediceo-Laurenziana, Ashburnham 53, fol. 85r
    Parchment, s. 12, 206 fols. in 2 cols., 345 × 212 mm, Italian, illuminated

---

[147] Above pp. 44-47.
[148] See above, Introduction, n. 28.
[149] Only those manuscripts are described in detail for which no description in print is available. Unless stated otherwise all manuscripts contain the *Collectio canonum* of Anselm of Lucca.

initials and rubrics; four modern paper fly-leaves in front and back. A provenance is indicated in a fifteenth-century hand on fly-leaf d: "Istum codicem habuimus a domino Ludovico de Interannis [Terni] qui etiam hanc bibliothecam edificavit." Later the codex was acquired by Libri during the sale of the library of Count Boutourlin[150] in 1839.[151] Subsequently acquired by Lord Ashburnham,[152] it was among the manuscripts bought back by the Italian government and turned over to the Biblioteca Mediceo-Laurenziana. On fol. 85r the manuscript contains cc. 3 and 4 of the set of 6 decrees found in other manuscripts of Anselm of Lucca's compilation. They are written in the same hand as the remainder of the codex.

Bibliography: L. Deslisle, "Notice sur des manuscrits du fonds Libri conservés à la Laurentienne," *Notices et Extraits des manuscrits de la Bibliothèque Nationale et autres bibliothèques* 32 (1886) part 1: 27-28; Ministero della Pubblica Istruzione (Indici e Cataloghi 8) *I Codici Ashburnhamiani della R. Bibl. Mediceo-Laurenziana* 1/1 (Rome 1887) 12, no. 9. *Catalogue of the Manuscripts at Ashburnham Place. Part the First, comprising a collection formed by Professor Libri* (London s.d.), see no. 53 and no. 984, both describing Fa. *Catalogue de la bibliothèque de feu M. le Comte D. Boutourlin dont la vente se fera le lundi 25 novembre 1839* (Paris 1839) 49, no. 414.

Fm: Florence, Biblioteca Mediceo-Laurenziana, San Marco 499, fol. 106r
Parchment, s. 12, 209 fols. in 2 cols., 310 × 205 mm, Italian, red capitals and inscriptions, occasionally initials, written by several hands. On the first parchment fly-leaf verso the provenance is indicated: "Conventus S. Marci de Florentia ordinis praedicatorum. De hereditate Nicolai Nicoli Florentini viri doctissimi."[153] The Guastalla canons were entered in the same hand as the main text.
Bibliography: Mordek, "Handschriftenforschungen," pp. 628-629 n. 6; Kuttner, "Some Roman manuscripts of Canonical Collections," *Bulletin of Medieval Canon Law*, n.s. 1 (1971) 7-29, p. 13.

Gu: Graz, Universitätsbibliothek 351, fol. 105r
Parchment, s. 12, second half. The codex was a gift of Gottschalk von Diernstein, who is mentioned in documents before 1184, to the Chorherrenstift of Seckau. The Guastalla canons are written by the same hand as the main body of text.

---

[150] Count Boutourlin was a Russian émigré who settled in Florence and acquired within 15 years a famous library. See *Catalogue de la bibliothèque de feu M. le Comte*, pp. 1-3.
[151] Delisle, *Notice*, p. 27n.
[152] *Catalogue of Ashburnham Place*, no. 53 and no. 984.
[153] 1363-1437. A biography and bibliography for the famous Florentine humanist Niccolò Niccoli is given by Cosenza, *Biographical and Bibliographical Dictionary of the Italian Humanists and of the World of Classical Scholarship in Italy, 1300-1800*, 3 (1962) 2462ff. See in particular now B. L. Ullman and P. A. Stadter, *The Public Library of Renaissance Florence: Niccolò Niccoli, Cosimo de' Medici and the Library of San Marco*, Padua 1972.

Bibliography: A. Kern, *Die Handschriften der Universitätsbibliothek Graz* (Verzeichnis der Handschriften im Deutschen Reich 2) 1 (1942) 208; Fournier, "Diverses récensions," pp. 430 and 434; A. Theiner, *Disquisitiones criticae* (Rome 1836) 338.

N: Naples, Biblioteca Nazionale, XII A.37-39, vol. A 38, fol. 62v-63r
This manuscript of the *Collectio canonum* of Anselm of Lucca is written in three parts by the same hand. (A.37 contains books 1-4, A.38 books 5-9, A.39 books 10-13.) XII A.38 consists of 131 parchment fols. in 2 col., s. 12, 300 × 195 mm, red and blue capitals, rubrics and occasional initials, Italian. The Guastalla material is found at the end of book 6 and is written in the same hand as the remainder of the text.
Bibliography: Fournier, "Diverses récensions," pp. 434-437 and especially Kuttner, "Some Roman manuscripts," p. 13 as well as Mordek, "Handschriftenforschungen," p. 628 n. 6. Both Kuttner and Mordek point out that the Naples Anselm of Lucca combines apparently the basic features of recension A with some of the interpolations and appendices characteristic of C. This was first indicated by Fournier, "Diverses récensions," p. 437.

P: Parma, Biblioteca Palatina, Fondo Parmense 976, page 231
Parchment, s. 12, second half, 447 pages in 2 cols., 310 × 205 mm, Italian, red inscriptions and initials. The original shelf mark HH. III. 9 was changed to 976 when the handwritten catalogue of the Fondo Parmense was prepared. With the exception of two former manuscript numbers on fol. 1: 855 and 1021, the codex contains no mark of ownership, provenance or origin. The lower margin of the first parchment flyleaf has been cut off, perhaps in order to delete an ex libris. An autograph note by the first librarian of the Biblioteca Palatina at Parma, Paolo M. Paciaudi, on paper flyleaf c, shows that P came to the library during his lifetime.[154] Paciaudi frequently acquired manuscripts from France[155] as well as from princely Italian families. According to the present director of the Biblioteca Palatina, A. Ciavarella, Paciaudi carefully deleted even in his personal notes all references to the provenance of the manuscripts which he obtained. The Guastalla canons are written in the same hand as the main text.
Bibliography: A. Ciavarella, *Notizie ... della Biblioteca Palatina di Parma* (Parma s.d.); F. Blume, *Iter Italicum* (Berlin and Stettin 1824-36), 4 vols. in 2; vol. 2: 1-6; Neigebaur, "Die Bibliotheken in Parma," *Serapeum* 23 (1858) 353-362.

---

[154] With the encouragement of Duke Philip of Bourbon (1749-1765), Paciaudi became the founder of the new library (the Farnese library had been taken to Naples in 1734) which was opened to the public in 1769.

[155] ".. Diese rechtswissenschaftlichen Handschriften und andere wurden von dem ersten Bibliothekar Paciaudi in Frankreich in der Zeit angekauft, als die Jesuiten ihr Eigentum zu verkaufen anfingen, da ihr Ende bevorstand." Neigebaur, "Bibliotheken," p. 356f.

S: Segni fragment, known to the Correctores Romani and hypothetically reconstructed, above p. 60

Ve: Città del Vaticano, Biblioteca Apostolica Vaticana, Vat. lat. 1361, fol. 147r
This manuscript of a *Collection in Thirteen Books* named after the codex was seen in microfilm at the Vatican Film Library of the Pius XII Memorial Library, Saint Louis University.
Bibliography: Kuttner, "Some Roman Manuscripts," pp. 9-13 where earlier literature is indicated.

## The Edition

For the sake of convenience, the sigla used in the edition of the canons of Guastalla in the Anselm of Lucca tradition are here summarized:

Fa  Florence, Biblioteca Mediceo-Laurenziana, Ashburnham 53
Fm  Florence, Biblioteca Mediceo-Laurenziana, San Marco 499
Gu  Graz, Universitätsbibliothek, 351
N   Naples, Biblioteca Nazionale, XII A.37-39
P   Parma, Biblioteca Palatina, Fondo Parmense 976
S   Segni fragment, reconstructed from MS Vatican City, Biblioteca Apostolica Vaticana, Vat. lat. 4891 and Gratian's *Decretum*, ed. E. Friedberg.
Ve  Città del Vaticano, Biblioteca Apostolica Vaticana, Vat. lat. 1361.

The basic manuscript is Gu. Gu has been chosen primarily on the basis of Thaner's conclusion that the codex belonged to class $A^1$, representing the *Collectio canonum* of Anselm of Lucca in its least corrupt state. P also is a manuscript of class $A^1$, but less carefully executed than Gu.

Notes on the presentation of the text have been given in the Introduction. The canons are divided in accordance with indications found in the manuscripts.

## Ex concilio Pascalis[a] pape[b]

[a] Paschalis *N*   [b] ex—pape] *om. Fa Fm*   Ex concilio papa Paschalis *P*   Paschalis papa in concilio generale apud Guardastalum *S*

1. Episcopi[a] lectioni et orationi uacent et *semper secum presbiteros et diaconos* aut alios *boni testimonii* clericos habeant ut secundum *apostolum*[1] et sanctorum patrum instituta possint inreprehensibiles inueniri.

[a] Episcopi—inueniri] *om. Fa S Ve*

---

Cf. Ps.-Lucius, ep. 1 [unica], 1 (H 175; JK †123; F 3: 872 no. 200). The direct source for the canon cannot be determined. Any collection mentioned by Fuhrmann with the exception of Deusd. 2.40 might have furnished the text. Cf. also "Benonis aliorumque cardinalium ... scripta," *Libelli de lite* 2: 370 lines 14-16.   — Grat. C.2 q.7 c.60.

---

[1] 1 Tim. 3: 7.

**2.** Nullus[a] episcopus in aliena parrochia[b] uel parrochiano alterius diuina quaelibet audeat[c] officia celebrare, quod qui presumpserit pena sacris[d] canonibus instituta mulctetur quia irrita erit huiusmodi celebratio et ipse periculo sui ordinis subiacebit.[1]

[a] Nullus—subiacebit] *om. Fa S*   [b] prouincia uel *praem. N*   [c] officia audeat *tr. Ve*   [d] canonibus sacris *tr. N*

---

[1] In spite of considerable changes the source might have been Ps.-Sixtus II, ep. 2, 6 (H 192, 28; JK †134; F 3: 898 no. 251) i.e. either 74T c. 195 or Ans. 6.113.

**3.** Nullus laicorum ecclesias uel ecclesiarum bona occupet uel disponat.[a] Sicut enim beatus *Stephanus papa martir* scribit, *laici, quamuis religiosi sint*,[b] *nulli* tamen *de ecclesiasticis facultatibus aliquid disponendi legitur umquam*[c] *attributa facultas*.[1] Qui uero secus egerit iuxta beati Alexandri primi capitulum ab ecclesiae liminibus arceatur.

[a] disponet *Fa*   [b] religiosi sint *om. P sed lacuna remansit*   [c] utraque *Fa*   nunquam *Fm*   [d] capituli *Fa*

---

[1] Ps.-Stephanus I, ep. 2.12 (H 186, lines 9-10; JK †131; F 3: 806 no. 43) Deusd. 3.47   Cf. 74T c. 260   Ans. 5.10   Deusd. 4.54   Grat. C.16 q.7 c.18 (cf. Appendix 2)

See JL 6145 and below p. 119 c. 4 of the Lateran council of 1110 with the accompanying remarks. The latter are equally applicable to this canon from Guastalla. The source in 1106, however, was not as in 1110, 74T c. 260, but the *Collectio canonum* of Deusdedit, unless, of course, an intermediate collection furnished Paschal's text.

**4.** Sicut domini uestimentum scissum non est sed de eo sortiti sunt[1] ita nec ecclesia scindi debet, quia[a] in unitate tota[b] consistit. In potestate ergo[c] proprii episcopi ecclesiae[d] reducantur et ab ipso sicut in sacris canonibus cautum est[2] ordinentur, alioquin[e] et ecclesiae ipsi[f] et clerici earundem diuinis destituantur officiis.[3]

[a] quia in unitate tota] sed tota in unitate *Fa*   [b] ecclesia *add. N*   [c] ergo] igitur *Fa*   [d] ecclesiae *om. Fa*   [e] alioquin—officiis *om. Fa*   [f] ipsae *P*   et ipsi clerici *tr. Ve*

---

[1] John 19: 23f.
[2] Cf. below p. 119, c. 2 and 3 of the Lateran council of 1110.
[3] Cf. Cyprian, *Liber de unitate ecclesiae*, cap. 7: "... De tunica autem quia de superiore parte non consutilis sed per totum textilis fuerat, dixerunt ad invicem: Non scindamus illam, sed sortiamur de ea cuius sit. Unitatem illa portabat de superiore parte venientem, id est de coelo et a patre venientem, quae ab accipiente ac possidente scindi omnino non poterat sed totam simul et solidam formitatem inseparabiliter obtinebat..." (Migne PL 4, col. 504-505).   — Grat. C.16 q.7 c.19.

**5.** Abbatibus[a] qui neque sub episcopo neque sub metropolitano neque sub primate neque sub patriarcha[b] sunt nullus prorsus[c] episcoporum episcopalia quelibet amministret. Cum enim se nulli omnino subesse profiteantur episcopo, consequens est ut nullus ipsorum[d] que sua sunt eis tamquam exteris largiatur.[1]

[a] Abbatibus—largiatur] *om. Fa S Ve*    [b] patriarchi *P*    [c] episcoporum prorsus *tr. Fm N*    [d] ipsorum] episcoporum *Fm*

---

[1] Cf. MS Paris BN lat. 4284, fol. 164r: "Decretum Urbani pp. Nemausensu concilio. Quia monachorum quidam ius suum auferre contendunt statuimus ne in parrochialibus ecclesiis quas tenent absque episcoporum concilio presbiteros collocent sed episcopi parrochie curam cum abbatum consensu sacerdoti committant ut eiusmodi sacerdotes de plebis quidem cura episcopo rationem reddant; abbati vero pro rebus temporalibus ad monasterium pertinentibus debitam subiectionem exibeant et sic cuique sua iura servatur." For this forgery see S. Kuttner and R. Somerville, "The So-Called Canons of Nîmes (1096)," *Tijdschrift voor Rechtsgeschiedenis* 38 (1970) 175-189, especially p. 178 and n. 18.    — Grat. C.18 q.2 c.18.

**6.** Si[a] quis clericus, abbas uel monachus per laicos ecclesias obtinuerit, secundum sanctorum[b] apostolorum[c] canones[1] et Antioceni concilii capitulum[2] excommunicationi subiaceat.[3]

[a] *Canones v et vi non separat Gu*    Si quis—subiaceat] *om. Fa Ve*    [b] apostolorum sanctorum canones *tr. S*    [c] canones apostolorum *tr. Fm*

---

[1] *Canones Apostolorum* c. 31 ( = Deusd. 4.19): "Si quis episcopus saecularibus potestatibus usus aecclesiam per ipsas optineat, deponatur et segregentur omnes, qui illi commonicant." The full text of the decree is quoted by Paschal in JL 6145 (see below p. 83) and was cited *ex* Deusd. 4.19. As in the case of Burch. 3.109, Ivo Decr. 3.85 and 5.119, Deusd. 4.19 uses the Isidorian version of the decree (H 29). For vers. Dion. see Turner 1/1: 20-21. Paschal's use of the *Collectio canonum* of Deusdedit can be assumed because it is only in this collection that Can. Apost. 31 is found in the vicinity of the decree to which Paschal refers as *capitulum* of the council of Antioch. See the following note.

[2] Paschal quotes the full text of the canon in JL 6145: "... Item ex concilio Antiocheno. Si quis presbyter uel diaconus per saecularem dignitatem ecclesiam Domini obtinuerit, et ipse et ordinator eius a communione modis omnibus segregentur, et sub anathemate sint, sicut Simon Magus de Petro apostolo..." = Can. Apost. 30 vers. Isidor. (H 29; cf. vers. Dion. 1 c. 29 and vers. Dion. 2 (3) c. 30 in Turner 1/1: 20-21) quoted *ex* Deusd. 4.22 (inscr. *Ex eodem cap. xii*). Ans. 7.191 (MS Vat. lat. 1364, fol. 187v) also attributes the decree to the council of Antioch.

[3] Cf. the Synodica generalis of Pope Nicolas II, c. 6: "Ut per laicos nullo modo quilibet clericus aut presbyter obtineat aecclesiam, nec gratis nec pretio" (MGH Const. 1: 547 no. 384) and the corresponding decree of Pope Urban II from the council of Clermont (Somerville, *Decreta Claromontensia*, p. 90, c. 2): "Episcopi, uel abbates, aut aliquis de clero, aliquam ecclesiasticam dignitatem de manu principum, uel quorumlibet laicorum, non accipiant." Cf. also below, p. 119, c. 1 of the 1110 council.    — Grat. C.16 q.7 c.16.

7. ⌜Constitutiones sanctorum canonum sequentes statuimus ut quicumque clericorum ab hac hora in antea inuestituram ecclesiae uel ecclesiasticae dignitatis de manu laica acceperit, et qui ei manum imposuerit, gradus sui periculo subiaceat, et communione priuetur.⌝[1]

Constitutiones—priuetur] om. Fa Fm Gu N P Ve

---

[1] Cf. below p. 93, c. 5 of the council of Troyes and below p. 119 for c. 1 of the Lateran council of 1110.  — Grat. C.16 q.7 c.17.

## OTHER NOTABLE DECISIONS OF THE COUNCIL

Ekkehard of Aura described papal activity at the synod: "monasteriis privilegia concessit, presentes ovium Christi pastores mellifluis alloquiis, absentes paternis commonitoriorum literis instruxerit."[156] A less amiable pontiff and a more militant synod is reflected in the *Annales Patherbrunnenses*: "Plures ibi episcopi Italiae dampnantur, quidam anathematizantur. Patriarcha Aquileiae anathematizatur; Fridericus Halverstadensis, accusantibus eum ecclesiae canonicis, honore episcopali privatur. Similis sententia de Withelone Mindensi habetur. Leodicensis et Cameracensis anathematizantur."[157] The only Italian bishop known to have been censured is Peter of Padua (1096-1106, d. 1119), who was deposed at Guastalla.[158] The city of Parma submitted to Paschal.[159] The excommunication of Udalric, patriarch of Aquileia, abbot of St. Gall[160] and inveterate foe of reformers and papacy can have surprised no one. In the case of Frederick of Halberstadt and Widelo of Minden, Paschal did little more than confirm the suspensions pronounced by the papale legate early in 1105.[161] Still, it is clear that the agenda laid down in Paschal's letter of November 1105 to

---

[156] Ekkehard, pp. 290-292; see also Somerville, *Decreta Claromontensia*, chapter 2, esp. pp. 33ff., where pastoral activities during councils are discussed. JL 6093, 6095-6097 illustrate Ekkehard's description.

[157] *Annales Patherbrunnenses*, p. 116.

[158] Kehr IP 7/1: 159 no. 7.

[159] Donizo, *Vita Mathildis*, MGH SS 12: 401. On St. Bernard of Parma see *Diz. Biogr. degli Ital.* 9 (1967) 292-300 (R. Volpini).

[160] Kehr IP 7/1: 34 no. 74 with further references. See also Knonau, *Jahrbücher* 5: 211 n. 4. The dismemberment of the archdiocese of Ravenna is a concomitant decision.

[161] Knonau, *Jahrbücher* 5: 223 and p. 227; ibid. 6: 45n. See also Bogumil, *Das Bistum Halberstadt*, pp. 12-13 and for the case of the bishop of Minden, E. Gisbert, "Bischöfe von Minden," *Mindener Jahrbuch* 5 (1930/31) pp. 5-80, esp. pp. 25-28 as well as Kurt Ortmanns, *Das Bistum Minden in seinen Beziehungen zu König, Papst und Herzog bis zum Ende des 12. Jahrhunderts*, Reihe der Forschungen im Schäuble Verlag 5 (Bensberg 1972) 55-59.

Archbishop Rothard of Mainz was adhered to,[162] and that the council dealt in detail with schismatic bishops, in other words bishops who had been invested by Emperor Henry IV. These were deposed at Guastalla — but usually only if they had not attended the synod and thus refused to be reconciled to the Roman church.

The dominant aspect of the synod was indeed a determined effort to overcome the schism and to coordinate once again the German and the Roman church.[163] Wherever possible this was done through reconciliation rather than excommunication. Schismatics who came to Guastalla, or who sent representatives to declare their submission to the Holy See,[164] were treated leniently. The figure of Archbishop Bruno of Trier is a case in point.[165] According to the *Gesta Treverorum* Bruno was deposed at the beginning of the synod because he had been invested with ring and staff by the emperor. Not only that, but he had also assumed his duties without having received the pallium.[166] Nevertheless, the council reinstated Bruno, who was presented with the pallium, only three days later. A very light penalty was enjoined: "Quociens in spacio trium proximorum annorum missarum solempnia celebraret, dalmatica non uteretur."[167] Bishop Hermann of Augsburg (1096-1132) was not quite so favorably received as Archbishop Bruno, but even he obtained a postponement of his case[168] that led eventually to his restoration.[169] The synod had just excommunicated Bishop Otbert of Liège, but only a few weeks later, in a letter dated November 1106, Paschal asked Bruno of Trier to reconcile Otbert, his clergy and his city with the Roman church. Otbert had sent a delegation which reached Paschal shortly after the council and "suppliciter consortium nostrae communionis expeciit."[170] Paschal responded unhesitatingly: "Nos,

---

[162] JL 6050: "Porro episcopos qui sub excommunicatione in eodem schismate manus impositionem susceperunt, ad concilii sententiam deferendos arbitramur; tantum enim tantarum personarum malum generaliter deliberatione aut curandum est aut detruncandum."

[163] Cf. above c. 4 of the Boso-*Liber Pontificalis* series.

[164] I.e. Otbert of Liège. See also above chapter 1, pp. 22-23.

[165] *Gesta Treverorum*, MGH SS 8: 192. In general cf. Schlechte, *Erzbischof Bruno*, pp. 35-38. Schlechte does not discuss Bruno's condemnation and immediate reconciliation.

[166] R. Benson, *Bishop-Elect*, pp. 169-173 (with further literature) discusses the significancxe of the pallium under Pope Paschal II.

[167] MGH SS 8: 192.

[168] Udalschalk, *De Eginone*, MGH SS 12: 438. The chronicle reports that he returned home as "semiepiscopus." Cf. JL 6103 and Brackmann, GP 2/1: 134 no. 43.

[169] Hermann's case is complicated; for his restitution see Paschal's letters JL 6548 and JL 6119 and especially a letter of ca. 1130, sent by the Cardinal Legate Gerhard or Gebehard to Abbot Udalschalk. See Jaffé, *Monumenta Moguntina*, p. 397 no. 48.

[170] JL 6099; see Jaffé, *Monumenta Bambergensia*, p. 508 no. 14.

scientes Domini voluntatem, qui omnes homines vult salvos fieri et neminem perire, nostras in hoc tibi vices committimus, ut scripto professionis accepto ... ipsum et Leodicensem clerum sive populum a vinculo excommunicationis absolvas et catholicae aecclesiae reconcilies."[171] With the submission of Liège Paschal also took a further step towards the solution of the long drawn-out conflict in Cambrai.[172] The excommunication reported in the *Annales Patherbrunnenses* refers to Walcher, or Gaucher, of Cambrai. Walcher, invested by Emperor Henry IV in 1093, had been deposed once before, by Urban II at the council of Clermont (1095), but refused to give way to Manasses, elected and confirmed at the same synod. In 1103 Paschal had to transfer Manasses, who could not gain a foothold in Cambrai, to the bishopric of Soissons. But this does not mean that the Cambrai reformers surrendered. In 1105 (25 June) they elected Abbot Odo of St. Martin of Tours as their next bishop. Odo was consecrated by his metropolitan, Archbishop Manasses of Reims, the uncle of Manasses of Soissons, a few days later (2 July). Paschal's support for Odo at Guastalla and Odo's reputation for saintliness together with his diplomatic skills rendered Walcher's position untenable. Otbert of Liège evidently withdrew his support, and the belated recognition for Walcher from Henry V late in 1107 was of no avail.[173]

Paschal's successes in 1106 were nonetheless only a small step towards the reconciliation of the German church. The archbishop of Trier was a skilled negotiator on behalf of Henry V[174] and managed to obtain with the aid of Countess Mathilda a kind of truce. Paschal and the synod compromised. They did not permit investiture as Bruno apparently demanded, but prohibited it again.[175] As a conciliatory gesture, however, they neither condemned Henry V nor the bishops whom he had invested since early 1105 in place of schismatic ecclesiastics who were deposed: Gottschalk of Minden, Udalrich of Regensburg, Gebhard of Speyer and Konrad of Salzburg. The latter came to Guastalla and was consecrated by Paschal.[176]

---

[171] JL 6099.

[172] For the diocese of Cambrai see M. Chartier, DHGE 11 (1949) 547-565, esp. p. 560 and A. Cauchie, *La querelle des investitures dans les diocèses de Liège et de Cambrai* (Paris 1890).

[173] Walcher retired into a monastery after an unsuccessful visit to Rome. See *Gesta episcoporum Cameracensium*, MGH SS 7: 505, c. 11.

[174] Donizo, *Vita Mathildis*, MGH SS 12: 400-401. Schlechte, *Erzbischof Bruno*, p. 35ff. Bruno's hand was surely strengthened by the fact that Henry IV had recently died (July 1106).

[175] See the canons above pp. 64-65.

[176] Guleke, *Kirchenpolitik*, pp. 113-114, nos. 1, 3, 4 and 5.

# 3

# The Council of Troyes, 23 May 1107

From Guastalla, Paschal continued his northward journey, but not to Germany as some parties there had hoped.¹ The pontiff, like two of his recent predecessors, made his way to France where he celebrated Christmas at Cluny.² His presence there is again documented for early February.³ At Easter Paschal and his entourage were guests of Bishop Ivo at Chartres.⁴

---

¹ German historians have frequently debated why and when Paschal decided not to hold a council in Germany as was perhaps envisioned at Guastalla, but the evidence is too scanty to allow a reply to the question. See Ekkehard, p. 294; W. Giesebrecht, *Geschichte der deutschen Kaiserzeit* 3: 775; Henking, *Gebhard*, pp. 92 and 94-95; Knonau, *Jahrbücher* 6: 30 n. 41.

² Ekkehard, p. 294: "... profectionem suam cum Hyspaniarum legatis per Burgundiam ad Gallias convertit et natalis dominici gaudium sua presentia Cluniacensibus multum ampliavit."

³ JL 6114-21; J. Mabillon, *Annales Ordinis Sancti Benedicti...* 5 (Lucca 1742) 499: "Postquam Paschalis natale Domini Cluniaci celebraverat, ibidem perstitit usque ad mensem Februarium anni sequentis, quo tempore Aymerico Casae-Dei abbati diploma concessit, quo, Gregorii vii et Urbani ii exemplo, omnia monasterii jura et bona confirmat." Paschal, however, must have left Cluny at least occasionally. He consecrated churches elsewhere. (See Jaffé, *Regesta* 1: 728.) For Paschal's journey to and through France in general see ibid. pp. 726-732; Kehr IP 6/1: 228 no. 1; Kehr IP 6/2: 209 no. 1. M. Giraud, *Essai historique sur l'abbaye de S. Barnard et sur la ville de Romans; première partie accompagnée de pièces justificatives inédites, entre autres du Cartulaire de Romans annoté* (Lyons 1856) 3: 16 no. 6bis and pp. 17-18 n. 2; cf. E. Albert, *Note sur un passage à Privas attribué au pape Pascal II (1099-1118)*, (Paris 1893). Many details can also be found in B. Monod, *Essai sur les rapports de Pascal II avec Philippe Ier (1099-1108)*, (Paris 1907).

⁴ See Ordericus Vitalis, *Historiae Ecclesiasticae libri tredecim*, ed. A. Le Prevost, vol. 4 (Paris 1852) 188 under the date 1103. A new edition by Marjorie Chibnall, *The Ecclesiastical History of Orderic Vitalis*, is appearing, but the relevant volume 1 is still in press. For Orderic and his work see ibid. 2 (Oxford 1969) xiii-xliii. See also a letter of Ivo of Chartres to Paschal (PL 162, ep. 175, cols. 177-178). For Ivo of Chartres in general see R. Sprandel, *Ivo von Chartres und seine Stellung in der Kirchengeschichte*, Pariser Historische Studien 1 (Stuttgart 1962); for Ivo and the solution of the investiture controversy especially

From Chartres he travelled to St. Denis for a conference with the French kings Philip I and Louis VI which was recorded three decades later by an eyewitness, Abbot Suger.[5] According to this account, the kings and Paschal discussed the state of the church in general in a very friendly manner, "familiariter," and the pontiff concluded the conversations with an entreaty that the French kings should continue the tradition of the great Charles and come to the aid of the successor of Peter against tyrants and enemies of the Church, especially Emperor Henry.[6] Royal support is reflected in King Philip's request that high French ecclesiastics and nobles accompany the pope to Châlons-sur-Marne, where Paschal met ambassadors of Henry V,[7] just prior to the opening of the council of Troyes on Ascension Day 1107 (May 23). The German embassy was again, as at Guastalla, led by Archbishop Bruno of Trier who apparently demanded on behalf of the king that Paschal recognize Henry's right to investiture with ring and staff as well as to the oath of fealty of those ecclesiastics he had invested.[8] The council of

---

H. Hoffmann, "Ivo von Chartres und die Lösung des Investiturproblems," DA 15 (1959) 393-440; A. Becker, *Studien zum Investiturproblem in Frankreich* (Saarbrücken 1955) especially pp. 99-104. For Paschal's Easter visit to Chartres see also Monod, *Essai*, p. 53 and n. 3.

[5] Suger, *Vita Ludovici grossi regis*, ed. and transl. H. Waquet, Les Classiques de l'histoire de France au moyen âge 11 (Paris 1929; repr. Paris 1964) 52-56; see Becker, *Investiturproblem*, pp. 121-122 and A. Luchaire, *Louis VI le Gros: Annales de sa vie et de son règne (1081-1137)*, (Paris 1890) 26 no. 47. Luchaire dated the interview 30 April - 3 May.

[6] Suger, *Vita Ludovici grossi*, p. 54: "... Cum quibus de statu ecclesie, ut sapiens sapienter agens, familiariter contulit, eosque blande demulcens, beato Petro sibique ejus vicario supplicat opem ferre, ecclesiam manutenere, et, sicut antecessorum regum Francorum Karoli Magni et aliorum mos inolevit, tyrannis et ecclesie hostibus et potissimum Henrico imperatori audacter resistere." See the analysis by Becker, *Investiturproblem*, pp. 121-122 and notes.

[7] Luchaire, *Louis VI le Gros*, p. 26 no. 48, suggests as date for the assembly of Châlons the days between 3 May (JL 6132) and 13 May (JL 6134). The account of the meeting is preserved by Suger, *Vita Ludovici grossi*, pp. 56-60 and in the *Annales Patherbrunnenses*, p. 117. Ekkehard of Aura inverted the sequence of the meeting at Châlons and the council of Troyes (Ekkehard, pp. 294-295). For Philip's request see Suger, *Vita Ludovici grossi*, pp. 54-56 as well as Luchaire, *Louis VI le Gros*, p. 26 no. 48.

[8] Suger, *Vita Ludovici grossi* c. 10, pp. 56-58: "Talis est (inquit) domini nostri imperatoris pro qua mittimur causa. Temporibus antecessorum nostrorum, sanctorum et apostolicorum virorum magni Gregorii et aliorum, hoc ad jus imperii pertinere dinoscitur, ut in omni electione hic ordo servetur: antequam electio in palam proferatur, ad aures domini imperatoris perferre, et si personam deceat, assensum ab eo ante factam electionem assumere; deinde in conventu, secundum canones, peticione populi, electione cleri, assensu honoratoris proferre, consecratum libere nec simoniace ad dominum imperatorem pro regalibus, ut anulo et virga investiatur, redire, fidelitatem et hominium facere. Nec mirum; civitates enim et castella, marchias, thelonea et queque imperatorie dignitatis nullo modo aliter debere occupare ...." On the difficulties of interpreting this passage see particularly Benson, *Bishop-Elect*, pp. 243-244 with nn. 52-54; Becker, *Investiturproblem*, pp. 121-122; J. Fried, "Der

Troyes, held immediately after the negotiations at Châlons-sur-Marne had been broken off on a note of great hostility, is Paschal's reply to Henry's demands. This was already noted by contemporaries.[9] It is no wonder that the synod excited the interest of both French and German chroniclers.[10]

## The Sources and Previous Scholarship

Baronius published in the *Annales Ecclesiastici*[11] under the year 1107 for Paschal's council of Troyes a passage from the chronicle of Ekkehard of Aura[12] and two letters written by Ivo of Chartres to Paschal and the clergy of Dol, respectively.[13] Binius' first edition (1606) included Ekkehard's report and a reference to Suger[14] as well as to Johannes Trithemius (1462-1516).[15] In the second edition of the *Concilia Generalia* Binius replaced his remarks about the chronicler and the abbot of Sponheim by a reference to one of Ivo's letters that had been published by Baronius.[16] This new Binius text is found unchanged in the *Collectio Regia*.[17] G. Cossart made the first

---

Regalienbegriff im 11. und 12. Jahrhundert," DA 29 (1973) 450-528, p. 468 n. 57. All three contributions discuss and indicate eaarlier literature. For the role of Bruno of Trier see Schlechte, *Bruno von Trier*, pp. 39-44. The most recent discussions are F. Hausmann, *Reichskanzlei und Hofkapelle unter Heinrich v. und Konrad III.*, MGH Schriften 14 (Stuttgart 1956) 13-14 and particularly Bogumil, *Das Bistum Halberstadt*, pp. 21-22.

[9] *Annales Patherbrunnenses*, p. 117: "Domnus papa ... sinodum apud Trecas tractat. Ibi causae, super qua ipse et rex conventuri erant, inducias ad Romanam sedem ponit, ut super ea canonice agatur."

[10] Most chronicles are listed by Knonau, *Jahrbücher* 6: 54 n. 30. Chronicles which only mention the council but do not contain useful specific information are: *Annales Besuenses* (MGH SS 2: 250); *Annales S. Benigni Divionensis* (MGH SS 5: 43); *Annales Elnonenses maiores* (MGH SS 5: 14) and the *Chronicon S. Andreae* (MGH SS 7: 545).

[11] Vol. 12, pp. 59-60.

[12] Ekkehard, p. 294.

[13] PL 162, ep. 176 (col. 178-179) and ep. 178 ibid. (col. 180).

[14] See vol. 3/2: 1308. "Hanc synodum Sugerius Abbas in vita Ludovici Grossi Francorum Regis universale Concilium nominat." See Suger, *Vita Ludovici grossi*, p. 60.

[15] Binius 3/2: 1308. For Johannes Trithemius, abbot of Sponheim and the Schottenkloster at Würzburg see K. Arnold, *Johannes Trithemius (1462-1516)*, (Würzburg 1971) esp. pp. 144-157; C. Steffen, "Untersuchungen zum 'Liber de scriptoribus ecclesiasticis' des Johannes Trithemius," *Archiv für Geschichte des Buchwesens* 10 (1970) cols. 1247-1354; R. Behrendt, "Abbot John Trithemius (1462-1516), Monk and Humanist," *Revue Bénédictine* 84 (1974) 212-229, where other recent Trithemius contributions are evaluated. Also very helpful is Paul Oskar Kristeller, "The Contribution of Religious Orders to Renaissance Thought and Learning," first published in the *American Benedictine Review* 21 (1970) 1-55 and now printed in P. O. Kristeller, *Medieval Aspects of Renaissance Learning*, ed. and transl. by Edward P. Mahoney (Durham 1974) 95-158. For Trithemius see especially the bibliography ibid. p. 156.

[16] Vol. 3/2, p. 442 (2nd ed.)

[17] Vol. 26, pp. 764-765.

major additions. Having reintroduced the reference in Suger to the council as "universale concilium," he cited several chronicles as relevant: the *Chronicon Sancti-Petri-Vivi Senonensis*,[18] the *Chronicon Malleacense*,[19] and the *Annales Patherbrunnenses*. Cossart also drew attention to letters of Richard, cardinal of Albano, legate. The work of Labbe-Cossart was not altered by Hardouin,[20] but Coleti appended to the "additio" of Cossart a passage that can be identified as from the *Ecclesiastica historia* of Albert Krantz:[21]

> Crantzius denique libro 5 cap. 33 de hoc concilio ait: Paschalis autem Pontifex tum in Galliis apud Trecas habuit generale concilium. In quo inter alia decretum est, quod nemo investituram alicujus beneficii aut ecclesiasticae dignitatis a manu laica excipiat, quoadusque haec questio inter Papam et Regem synodaliter terminaretur; et restituit Papa omnibus Ecclesiis libertatem suam, ut secundum praecepta Canonum Praelatos sibi eligerent, quos dignos judicarent. Quo tempore ex eisdem causis Patriarcha Aquilejensis, Leodiensis, et Cameracensis episcopi anathematizantur; Mindensis quoque, et Halberstadiensis privantur; Coloniensis et sui suffraganei ab officio suspenduntur, quia aberant Concilio generali; Archiepiscopus Moguntinus, et Episcopus Constantiensis suspenduntur, quia aliquos contra Canonum statuta electos instituerunt.[22]

Berardi, too, published this description of the council.[23] Krantz' source were the *Annales Patherbrunnenses* under the year 1107 except for one phrase, "Quo tempore ... Cameracensis episcopi anathematizantur," which refers to events that had occurred at the council of Guastalla. The *Annales* report Guastalla in a paragraph that immediately precedes the entries for 1107.[24] The material for the two councils appears intermingled in Krantz' note, but

---

[18] Clarius of Sens, *Chronicon Sancti-Petri-Vivi Senonensis*, ed. L. M. Duru, Bibliothèque historique de l'Yonne 2 (Auxerre 1863) 451-597, p. 515.

[19] *Chronicon sancti Maxentii Pictavense (vulgo dicitur Malleacense)*, [Chronicon of Maillezais], ed. Marchegay-Mabille, Chroniques des Eglises d'Anjou (Paris 1869) 349-433.

[20] 6/2: 1887-1888.

[21] *Alberti Krantzii rerum germanicarum historici clarissimi ecclesiastici historia, sive metropolis...*, ed. Johannes Wolf (Frankfurt 1567) liber 5, cap. 33, p. 140. For Krantz see H. Reincke, "Albert Krantz als Geschichtsschreiber und Geschichtsforscher," in *Festschrift der Hamburgischen Universität für W. von Melle* (1933), pp. 3ff. and Max Grobecker, *Studien zur Geschichtsschreibung des Albert Krantz* (Hamburg 1964).

[22] Coleti 12: 1133-1136 = Mansi 20: 1218.

[23] C. S. Berardi, *Gratiani Canones Genuini ab Apocryphis Discreti* (Venice 1777) 2/2: 386.

[24] See *Annales Patherbrunnenses* in the reconstruction of Scheffer-Boichorst in the sequence p. 118, pp. 117-118.

the scholar's dependence on the *Annales Patherbrunnenses* seems clearly established.

Thanks to the researches of E. Martène (1654-1739), Mansi was able to add new material. His first supplement contained a relevant passage from the Annalista Saxo,[25] which Martène had originally published from the chronicler's autograph, MS Paris, BN lat. 11851, together with JL 6145, 6144 and 6173.[26] These letters were marginal additions to the codex. So was a set of four canons which Martène published in volume seven of the *Veterum scriptorum amplissima collectio*.[27] They were included in Mansi's second supplement.[28] Mansi himself added information concerning one of the canons promulgated at Troyes which was described by Paschal in one of his letters (JL 6158).[29]

Weiland's edition of the Troyes canons contributed further canonical material from two additional manuscripts: MS Göttweig 53 (56) and Munich, Bayerische Staatsbibliothek Clm. 3739.[30] The Göttweig manuscript contains, in addition to the canons published by Martène, an initial canon, and provides variant readings for the remainder.[31] The Munich codex, on the other hand, represents a different tradition. This was acknowledged by Weiland who published the Munich text as version b.

## The Participants

"Domnus papa copioso episcoporum et abbatum aliorumque catholicorum conventu sinodum apud Trecas tractat," report the *Annales Pather-*

---

[25] His chronicle, closely related to the chronicle of Ekkehard of Aura for our period, is edited by G. Waitz, MGH SS 6: 542-777. Mansi's passage is found ibid. p. 745, lines 48-55 followed immediately by the text on p. 746, lines 6-8. The canons from Troyes had been omitted in Mansi's first supplement.

[26] E. Martène and U. Durand, *Veterum scriptorum et monumentorum historicorum ... amplissima collectio* 1 (1724) 616-620.

[27] Ibid. 7 (Paris 1733) 67. The nine volumes of the *Veterum scriptorum collectio* are divided according to subject matter. Vol. 1 contains "Miscellanea epistolarum et diplomatum," vol. 7 "Varia concilia" and "statuta synodalia." For this reason the marginalia from MS BN lat. 11851 were separated and appeared in different volumes.

[28] Mansi 20: 1219-1224. Mansi included Martène's prefatory remarks concerning BN lat. 11851 (vol. 1 p. xxi) as a footnote (Mansi 20: 1218 n. 1) as well as in the text (ibid. p. 1219).

[29] Mansi referred also to the judicial decision preserved in JL 6154 and to a letter of Lambert of Arras (20: 1223-1224). See below n. 47.

[30] MGH Const. 1: 566-567, no. 396.

[31] Weiland, just as Martène, enumerated four canons, but Weiland combined Martène's canons 2 and 3 to form c. 3 of his edition.

*brunnenses.*[32] Privileges for several French monasteries were issued at the council, and provide evidence for some of the "abbots and other catholics" who had come to Troyes.[33] Among them were Prior Cono of the cathedral church of Arrouaise (JL 6136),[34] Abbot Hugh of St. Aman (JL 6137), Abbot Theodoric of St. Trond (JL 6138), Abbot Hermet of Bergues-Saint-Winoc (JL 6138a), Abbot Bernier of Bonneval (JL 6139), Abbot Rudolf of Montier-la-Celle (JL 6141), and the Deacon Guarin of the cathedral church St. Etienne at Châlons-sur-Marne (JL 6142). The same can be said for Abbot Rudolf of the monastery of St. Etienne in Fesmy.[35] The privileges of the monastery of Saint-Fuscien-au-Bois in the diocese of Amiens were entrusted to its Abbot Radulf: "Tuis igitur, fili in Christo karissime, precibus annuentes, beati Fusciani martiris monasterium cui Deo auctore presides, presentis decreti assertione munimus."[36]

Documents embodying synodal or papal judicial decisions are primarily a source for the names of episcopal participants and for members of Paschal's entourage. A judgment from Langres (JL 6125), dated 24 February 1107, was signed by Richard cardinal of Albano,[37] Bishop Aldo of Piacenza,[38] Bishop Odo of Cambrai (1105-1113), the Roman cardinal priests Riso of S. Damaso, Landulf of S. Lorenzo in Lucina, Diviso of S. Martino, the cardinal deacons John of S. Maria in Cosmedin and Berardo of S. Angelo.[39]

---

[32] P. 117.

[33] JL 6136-42. JL 6140 implies the presence of a Spanish delegation. Cf. the scanty treatment of the synod in Tangl, *Teilnehmer*, pp. 186-187.

[34] A chronicle, *Fundatio monasterii Arroasiensis auctore Galtero abbate*, ed. O. Holder-Egger (MGH SS 15/2: 1888, 1117-1125), reports that Cono, later cardinal of Palestrina (see Klewitz, "Kardinalskollegium," p. 211 no. 10 with bibliography), one of the founders of the monastery of Arrouaise, encountered Paschal at the council of Troyes. According to the chronicle, it was there that the pontiff induced him to come to Rome (MGH SS 15/2: 1120 c. 5). For some of Cono's later activity see R. Hiestand, "Legat, Kaiser und Basileus; Bischof Kuno von Praeneste und die Krise des Papsttums von 1111/1112," in *Aus Reichsgeschichte und Nordischer Geschichte, Festschrift Karl Jordan*, Kieler Historische Studien 16 (Stuttgart 1972) 141-152; Somerville, "Beauvais," pp. 493-503 and R. Hüls, "Das Kardinalskollegium in seiner Entstehungszeit," Ph.D. diss. Göttingen 1975 (not seen). See now also A. Cadderi, *Conone di Preneste* (Rome 1974).

[35] The privilege for this new foundation in the diocese of Cambrai was published by J. Ramackers, *Papsturkunden in den Niederlanden*, Abhandlungen Göttingen, 3. Folge, 9 (1934) 96 no. 8 with bibliography.

[36] Ramackers, *Papsturkunden in Frankreich*, Neue Folge 4, Abhandlungen Göttingen, 3. Folge, 27 (1942) no. 7, pp. 70-72.

[37] See below n. 76.

[38] Aldo spoke for the pope at the meeting at Châlons-sur-Marne (Suger, *Vita Ludovici grossi*, p. 58).

[39] For the cardinals see Klewitz, "Kardinalskollegium," pp. 210-221.

The document finally also refers to the presence of Prior Radulf of Reims and two representatives of the church of Toul who witnessed the decision as well as prominent French noblemen. Without further evidence, however, it would be hasty to conclude that the French signatories in every case accompanied Paschal to the council. The presence at the synod is certain only for Radulf of Reims and four members of the papal entourage who were mentioned in JL 6125. The datum clause in several privileges from Troyes is evidence for the chancellor's presence. The cardinal of Albano stressed his participation in a letter he wrote three years later.[40] Two other members of the curia are mentioned in a privilege issued by Paschal 6 June 1107 (JL 6154), in favor of the monastery of Cluny, that confirmed a corresponding decision, now lost, from the synod at Troyes. According to this letter Abbot William of St. Peter's Abbey at Chartres had accused the monks of Cluny, "nobis in Trecensi concilio praesidentibus," and Paschal decided the case in the presence of several high ecclesiastics: "sane huic nobiscum judicio affuerunt venerabiles episcopi, Leodegarus Bituricensis, Aldo Placentinus, Girardus Engolismensis, Ildebertus Cenomanensis et nostrae sanctae Romanae ecclesiae cardinalis Landulfus, de titulo S. Laurentii, qui dicitur in Lucina."[41] In addition to the Italians Aldo of Piacenza and Cardinal Landulf JL 6154 mentions the presence of the abbot of St. Peter's at Chartres, a delegation from Cluny, and of three French bishops: Leodegar of Bourges (1097-1120), Gerard of Angoulême (1101-1136),[42] and Hildebert of Lavardin or Le Mans.[43] Four other French bishops at Troyes witnessed a decision issued at the council that terminated the quarrel between the canons of the church of Ste. Marie at Arras and the abbot of St. Vaast concerning the chapel of St. Mauritius.[44] They were John of Thérouanne,[45] Godfrey of Amiens (1104-1115), Galo of Paris (1104-1116)[46] and Lambert of Arras (1093-1115) who attached his seal to the document. Abbot

[40] See below n. 76.
[41] Mansi 20: 1041.
[42] For this important ecclesiastic see Schieffer, *Päpstliche Legaten*, pp. 184-194 and pp. 218-223; cf. in general J. de La Martinière, DHGE 3 (1924) 248.
[43] His dates are 1056-1134, when he died as archbishop of Tours. See A. Hamman, LThK 5 (1960) 340 for a brief biography and a bibliography. Particularly important is Peter von Moos, *Hildebert von Lavardin, 1056-1133: Humanitas an der Schwelle des Höfischen Zeitalters*, Pariser Historische Studien 3 (Stuttgart 1965).
[44] It is dated May 23, 1107 and published by Ramackers, *Papsturkunden in Frankreich* 3: 46-47 no. 10.
[45] John of Mont-St. Eloy, a former archdeacon at Arras, was confirmed as bishop of Thérouanne by Pope Urban ii in 1099. He died in 1130. See Somerville, *Decreta Claromontensia*, pp. 56-57 and the references given ibid. nn. 45-50.
[46] 1104-1116. For the career and the close connection between this pupil of the canonist Ivo of Chartres and Paschal see Monod, *Essai*, pp. 30-34 and Sprandel, *Ivo*, esp. p. 143.

Lambert of St. Bertin and the archdeacons William of Paris and Clarembald of Arras were the other signatories.⁴⁷

In a letter to the pontiff, Ivo apologized for his inability to come to Troyes,⁴⁸ and announced that he had sent instead three representatives for Chartres.⁴⁹ One of them was Ivo's chancellor Vulgrinus.⁵⁰ Another French see represented by a delegation was the church of Dol.⁵¹ But not only Italian, Spanish, and French participation is documented, that of delegates sent by King Henry I of England and Archbishop Anselm of Canterbury is also known. The attendance of William of Warelwast and the monk Baldwin had been requested by Paschal.⁵² The synod of Troyes was well attended indeed, and Suger's expression "universale concilium" seems appropriate.⁵³ This makes all the more noticeable, however, the absence of representatives from the empire.⁵⁴ Several German bishops had gathered for the meeting

---

⁴⁷ A letter of Bishop Lambert of Arras (ed. Bouquet no. 67), sent to Paschal in 1114, referred to the same decision: "de parochianis vero nostris circa capellam S. Mauritii commanentibus causa habita fuit in Trecensi concilio, praecepto vestro, coram cardinalibus et episcopis Morinensi, Ambianensi, Parisiensi, aliisque religiosis et synodalibus personis..." (*Recueil des historiens des Gaules et de la France* 15 [Paris 1878] 206-207).

⁴⁸ PL 162, ep. 175, col. 178: "... Parabam me pro viribus meis ad iter concilii a vestra paternitate indicti, sed, quia frequentia curiae vestrae ea tempestate, qua solitus eram, purgatorium accipere me non permisit, tota confluentia humorum repente in caput ascendit, ... ita ut nec breve iter aggredi valeam sine periculo corporis mei." Cf. the interpretation of the letter by N. H. Cantor, *Church, Kingship and Lay Investiture*, p. 211.

⁴⁹ PL 162, ep. 175, col. 178: "... Misi itaque tres ex archidiaconibus ecclesiae nobis commissae cum litteris nostris."

⁵⁰ Monod translated the name into French as Bougrin (*Essai*, p. 57).

⁵¹ A delegation from this church elected Ivo's chancellor Vulgrinus bishop of Dol at the council, evidently in the presence of Paschal and with his approval. Vulgrinus, however, refused to accept the honor, and was supported by Bishop Ivo, who wrote both to Paschal (PL 162, ep. 176 col. 178-179: "Reversus a concilio Trecensi filius noster Vulgrinus, ecclesiae nostrae cancellarius, anxie conquestus est quod Dolensis ecclesia, destinatis excellentiae vestrae quibusdam legatis suis, eum sibi in episcopum sub praesentia vestra elegerit ...") and to the clergy of Dol (ibid. ep. 178, col. 180). Dol at the time was involved in a bitter quarrel about the primacy of Tours. Dol claimed metropolitan rank at least since 845, and the pallium had been granted by Pope Gregory VII to Bishop Even who thus became archbishop. Pope Innocent III in 1199 finally decided against the claims of Dol whose clergy submitted to the decision in 1201. (See DHGE 14 [1960] 567-574, H. Waquet.)

⁵² Eadmer, *Historia novorum*, p. 185. On William see also Eadmer, *The Life of St. Anselm*, p. 97 n. 3 and particularly R. W. Southern, *Saint Anselm and His Biographer*, p. 172.

⁵³ Suger, *Vita Ludovici grossi*, p. 60. Cf. Tangl, *Teilnehmer*, pp. 186-187. In the early twelfth century the term was a synonym for "generale concilium." See H. Fuhrmann, "Das Ökumenische Konzil," especially part 4, pp. 680-686; in the notes in preparation for the Editio Romana of the ecumenical councils both Guastalla and Troyes are described as general synods (MS Barb. lat. 860, fol. 222r).

⁵⁴ This is frequently pointed out, e.g. Tangl, *Teilnehmer*, pp. 186-187; Knonau, *Jahrbücher* 6: 50; Giesbrecht, *Kaiserzeit*, 3: 781.

with Paschal at Châlons. The chief German source for these discussions, the *Annales Patherbrunnenses*, name in addition to lay nobility Otto of Bamberg, Erlung of Würzburg, and Bruno of Trier at the head of the delegation.[55] Suger, an eyewitness, named Duke Welf and the bishops of Halberstadt (Reinhard, 1106-1123) and Münster (Burchard, 1097-1118) in addition to Bruno.[56] They did not participate in the synod which immediately followed the interview, but other German bishops, who were not members of the embassy of Châlons, were also absent as evidenced by the suspensions and excommunications pronounced at the conclusion of the synod.

## The Canons

### *Previously Known Texts*

Since Martène's discovery of one set of Troyes canons in the autograph manuscript of the Annalista Saxo in Paris,[57] several advances have been made, particularly by Weiland[58] but also by Mansi. An additional canon promulgated at the 1107 synod is known on the basis of Paschal's letter JL 6158. As Mansi noted, this decree cited in support of Archbishop Richard of Narbonne (1106-1121) is clearly identified and presents no problems.[59] It escaped his attention, though, that JL 6145 also reports a decree from Troyes.[60] Variants of this canon are found in two other letters sent from France: JL 6144 to Reinhard of Halberstadt and JL 6143 to Gebhard of Constance.[61] The canon, furthermore, is part of the series of decrees in the Parisian codex. As such it will be incorporated in the edition below, but since JL 6145 to Archbishop Rothard of Mainz is the most explicit evidence for Paschal's use of the *Collectio canonum* of Cardinal Deusdedit at the

---

[55] P. 117. For Otto of Bamberg see Juritsch, *Bischof Otto I.*, pp. 90-91.
[56] Suger, *Vita Ludovici grossi*, p. 56. The question of their participation is discussed by Bogumil, *Das Bistum Halberstadt*, Exkurs 1, pp. 256-257; for Reinhard see also ibid. p. 22.
[57] MS BN lat. 11851, for a description see below p. 89.
[58] MGH Const. 1: 566-567, no. 396.
[59] Mansi 20: 1224. For the complete text of the letter see ibid., col. 1026-1027. It was originally published by Labbe-Cossart, 10: 670. Their source is not indicated, and could not be identified by me.
[60] Mansi nevertheless included JL 6145 together with the remainder of Martène's material from MS BN lat. 11851; in particular the canons and JL 6144. See Mansi 20: 1220-1224 and Martène-Durand, *Veterum scriptorum collectio* 1: 616ff. and 7: 68.
[61] JL 6144 is preserved in MS BN lat. 11851 and in the Codex Udalrici (Jaffé, *Monumenta Bambergensia* pp. 256-257, no. 139; Mansi 20: 1221-1222). For JL 6143 see Jaffé, *Monumenta Moguntina*, p. 384, no. 37.

French synod, or possibly an intermediate collection that was presumably used by both Deusdedit and Anselm of Lucca,[62] a closer look at JL 6145 is called for. The text is given as edited by Jaffé, *Monumenta Moguntina*, p. 385, no. 38.

> ... Ne igitur in impositione manuum ulterius locum excusandi per ignorantiam habere possis, et illud apostoli dicentis: *Nemini cito manus imposueris, ne communices peccatis alienis,*[63] et ex multis sanctorum patrum constitutionibus quaedam tibi scribere necessarium duximus. Ex canonibus apostolorum: *Si quis episcopus, secularibus potestatibus usus, ecclesiam per ipsas obtineat, deponatur et segregetur, omnes*que *qui illi communicant.*[64] Item ex concilio Antiocheno: *Si quis presbyter vel diaconus per secularem dignitatem ecclesiam Domini obtinuerit, et ipse et ordinator eius a communione modis omnibus segregentur et sub anathemate sint, sicut Simon Magus de Petro* apostolo.[65] Item *Stephanus martyr pontifex: Laicis quamvis religiosis nulla de ecclesiasticis facultatibus* aliquid *disponendi legitur usquam attributa facultas.*[66] *Item Symmachus: Provida sententia enervari convenit et in irritum deduci, ne in exemplum remaneat presumendi: ne quibuslibet laicis quamvis religiosis vel potentibus in quacumque civitate quolibet modo liceat aliquid decernere de ecclesiasticis facultatibus,* quas *solis sacerdotibus disponendi a Deo cura commissa docetur.*[67]
> 
> Nos quoque sanctorum canonum constitutiones sequentes cum fratribus nostris in Trecensi concilio statuimus: ut quicumque clericorum de hac hora investituram ecclesie vel ecclesiastice dignitatis de manu laici acceperit, et qui ei manum imposuerit, gradus sui periculo subiaceat et communione privetur.[68]

---

[62] See Fuhrmann, *Einfluss und Verbreitung*, 2: 517 and 526-527 with n. 268.

[63] 1 Tim. 5: 22. See also JL 6453.

[64] *Ex* Deusd. 4.19; Can Apostolorum 31 (H 29).

[65] *Ex* Deusd. 4.22; Can. Apostolorum 30 (H 29); Ans. 7.191 (MS Vat. lat. 1364, fol. 187v).

[66] *Ex* Deusd. 3.47, the only source for Martyr et pontifex; Ps.-Stephanus I, ep. 2.12 (H 186); cf. Deusd. 4.54; Ans. 5.10.

[67] *Ex* Deusd. 3.47, Conc. Roman. a. 502, cap. 3. Paschal reversed the sequence of the Stephanus and Symachus texts of Deusdedit and omitted the reference to Eulalius. For complete references see c. 4 of the Lateran council of 1110, below ch. 3, p. 119.

[68] This last paragraph only is found in JL 6144 and JL 6143. It reads as follows in JL 6143 (Jaffé, *Monumenta Moguntina*, p. 384): "... Neque illud concilii statutum te lateat: ut, quisquis clericus deinceps investituram alicuius ecclesie et dignitates de manu laici susceperit et ipse et qui ei manum imposuerit, gradus sui periculum subeat et communione privetur"; in JL 6144 (Jaffé, *Monumenta Bambergensia*, pp. 256-257): "... Statutum est enim in Trecensi concilio ut, si quis ex manu laica ecclesiae investituram acceperit, tam ipse quam ordinator eius deponatur et a communione ecclesiae removeatur." The *Annales Patherbrunnenses* also report the prohibition: "Apostolicus enim apud Trecas banno confirmavit, ut nemo investituram neque aecclesiasticam dignitatem a laicali manu susciperet, quoadusque quaestio haec inter eum et regem sinodaliter terminaretur" (ed. Scheffer-Boichorst, p. 118). The Correctores Romani in MS Vat. lat. 4891 and D'Aquino in MS Barb. lat. 860 identified the

## The Arsenal Tradition

A tenth-century manuscript fragment found in Paris at the Bibliothèque de l'Arsenal preserves as a twelfth-century addition the text of an address given at Troyes, it seems. It appears to be a speech in which the canons agreed upon by the council were promulgated at the conclusion of the meeting. There are no indications that we are dealing with an opening discourse delivered either by the pontiff or a speaker on his behalf.[69] Canons 1 and 13 of the text edited below show that the decrees are of papal origin although the text does not have the formality of the Guastalla decrees as they are known from Paschal's register, the Troyes *breviaria* published by Weiland, or Paschal's letter JL 6145. There is no reason to suspect the text as a forgery, however, for no apparent interest group stood to gain from the decrees. If anyone had wished to profit from the pronouncements, they would probably have added a plausible attribution. As it is the Arsenal decrees lack any inscription. Their informality might imply that they were taken down as personal notes from an address to the laity as c. 5 and the crusading decree in particular seem to indicate.

The codex, Bibliothèque de l'Arsenal 717, is described in the catalogue of the library adequately enough, although the twelfth-century addendum on fol. 8v is only incompletely identified as "Réglementation de la trêve des quatre jours. Commencement: 'Sanctorum Patrum vestigiis inherentes ...'."[70] Etienne Baluze[71] knew the manuscript. He transcribed its decrees in one of his notebooks[72] with the inscription "ex vetusta membrana Trecensi; Cod. 4067 bibliothecae regiae." Although the Arsenal codex contains no indication that the canons recorded were those of the council of Troyes in 1107, Baluze attributed them to this synod, enumerating his reasons:

---

decree as Guastalla legislation. The Troyes canon was repromulgated at the Lateran council of 1110. Its is incorporated in Gratian's *Decretum*, C.16 q.7 c.17. Friedberg's note accompanying c.17 (no. 179) — c.1 Conc. Trec. hab. ao. 1107 ap. Mansi XX.1221 — is a reference to JL 6145 which does not really indicate that the decree is c. 1.

[69] Cf. Blumenthal, "Ein neuer Text für das Reimser Konzil Papst Leos ix. (1049)?" DA 32 (1976) 23-48. Cf. also Somerville's reconstruction of the procedures at papal councils (*Decreta Claromontensia* p. 27ff. and pp. 33-35).

[70] *Catalogue des Manuscrits de la Bibliothèque de l'Arsenal*, ed. H. Martin, 2 (Paris 1886) 55 no. 717.

[71] G. Mollat, DHGE 6 (1932) 439-452, gives a succinct biography for Baluze.

[72] Paris, BN MS Baluze 7, fol. 164r-v. (L. Auvray and R. Poupardin, *Catalogue des manuscrits de la collection Baluze* [Paris 1921] 13-19.) The Arsenal shelf mark for royal MS 4067 is given by H. Omont, *Concordances des numéros anciens et des numéros actuels des manuscrits latins de la Bibliothèque Nationale* (Paris 1903).

Chronicon S. Petri Vivi Senon. narrat Paschalem II in Concilio Trecensi multum sollicitum fuisse de Hierosolymitano itinere et de treuia Dei quod respicit caput primum et septimum istorum decretorum.[73]

Richardus[74] et Boso cardinales[75] testantur in eodem Concilio Trecensi interdictam laicis possessionem rerum ecclesiasticarum, decimarum, et oblationum.[76] Quod pertinet ad tertium caput. Ac de capito investiturae mentionem etiam facit Urspergensis.[77]

In chronico Malleacensi scriptum est statutum in hoc Trecensi Concilio fuisse ut per nullam guerram incendia domorum fierent.[78] Quod respicit caput tertium.

Haec sunt quae me movent ut credam in hac membrana agi de Decretis Concilii quod apud Trecas habuit Paschalis Papa hujus nominis secundus; praesertim cum membrana illa ad nos pervenerit ex urbe Trecensi.[79] Necesse est autem ista contigisse post Concilium Claramontanum Urbani secundi in quo primum statuta est crux seu crucis assumptio pro expeditione in terram sanctam, et ante Concilium Lateranense Callisti secundi in quo finis impositus est controversiae de investituris. Nam in istis capitulis statuitur ut qui cruces et vota fecerunt, ea usque ad proximum Pasche persolvant. Tum extat etiam in

---

[73] *Chronicon Sancti-Petri-Vivi*, p. 515: "In quo [concilio] intentio eius [Paschalis II] maxima fuit de Hierosolymitano itinere et de tregwa Dei." See ibid. p. 527 = Mansi 21: 9-10 a letter of Richard, cardinal of Albano, legate, to the Deacon Peter of Mauriac from the council of Clermont in 1110: "Dominus papa Pascalis in concilio Trecensi omnes eos excommunicavit qui pacem violarent, et praecipue eos qui res ecclesiasticas usurparent, vel personas in aliquo injuste lederent ut nec in vita, nec morte ecclesiae communionem haberent, nisi digna satisfactione prius resipiscerent." See Hoffmann, *Gottesfriede*, pp. 225-226.

[74] Richard, cardinal bishop of Albano (1096-1113), former deacon of St. Stephen at Metz (Klewitz, "Kardinalskollegium," p. 210), accompanied Paschal on his French journey and continued to stay a further three years in France. See Schieffer, *Die päpstlichen Legaten*, p. 178.

[75] Cardinal priest of S. Anastasia (Klewitz, "Kardinalskollegium," p. 213 no. 10). Boso, cardinal of S. Anastasia, was Paschal's legate to Spain (1116-1117) and France when he wrote the letter to the bishop of Toulouse (see n. 76 below). G. Säbekow, *Die päpstlichen Legationen nach Spanien und Portugal bis zum Ausgang des $XII$. Jahrhunderts* (Berlin 1931) 36-37 no. 20.

[76] The letters of Richard and Boso to which Baluze referred were published by C. Douais, *Cartulaire de l'Abbaye de Saint-Sernin de Toulouse (844-1200)* (Paris and Toulouse 1887). Richard wrote to Bishop Amelius of Toulouse in favor of St. Sernin: "... Cum essemus Tolose apud vos in concilio quod ibidem celebravimus, instituta domini pape que in Trecensi concilio de decimis, et oblationibus et possessionibus ecclesiarum pertractaverat, nos ex precepto eius recensuimus, et recensentes excommunicatione nostra confirmavimus ..." (no. 282 ibid. pp. 196-197). Cardinal Boso wrote in very similar words backing up Richard's pronouncements and excommunications (ibid. p. 198 no. 283).

[77] Ekkehard, p. 294.

[78] *Chronicon of Maillezais*, ed. Marchegay-Mabille, p. 423: "Apud Trecas ... fuit concilium quod tenuit Paschalis papa; in quo decrevit ut per nullam guerram incendia domorum fierent, nec oves aut agni raperentur."

[79] See below pp. 88-89.

his capitulis decretum adversus investituras quod condi non potuit post Callistum secundum. Haec firmant, opinor, conjecturam de tempore istorum capitulorum.[80]

Baluze's arguments appear sound and can be further supported by a peace statute from the diocese of Thérouanne which Baluze himself had transcribed.[81] A twelfth- or thirteenth-century copy of the same text is found in MS Paris, BN lat. 152, fol. 44v-45r.[82] In 1891, M. Sdralek, and independently H. Wasserschleben,[83] published the decree from yet a different source: a manuscript preserved at the Herzog August Bibliothek Wolfenbüttel, Cod. Guelf. Gud. 212.[84] The section of the Pax Morinensis[85] reporting the Troyes legislation reads:[86]

> Postea quidem in Trecensi concilio a Paschali papa sancitum est ne incendium usquam aliquo tempore fiat et ut quelibet ecclesia rationabiles canonicasque consuetudines et iusticias conservande pacis inviolabiles retineret.[87]

---

[80] Paris, BN MS Baluze 7, fol. 165-165v. With the exception of the *Annales Hildesheimenses*, Baluze listed the same authorities as Labbe-Cossart.

[81] Paris BN MS Baluze 7, fol. 161r.

[82] P. Lauer, *Catalogue général des manuscrits latins* 1 (Paris 1939) 52: "Recueil de fragments de manuscrits réunis par Baluze." One section of this peace statute, recording the strengthening of the peace decrees by Pope Urban II at the council of Clermont is edited by Somerville, *Decreta Claromontensia* pp. 63-64 and 73-74.

[83] H. Wasserschleben, "Zur Geschichte der Gottesfrieden," ZRG Germ. Abt. 12 (1891) 112-117, pp. 115-116.

[84] M. Sdralek, *Wolfenbüttler Fragmente* (Münster 1891) 144-147; for a discussion of the text see ibid. pp. 79-85, and for a description of codex Guelf. Gud. 212, ibid. pp. 5-6. The peace legislation is part of section V of the codex as designated by Sdralek, and not of the *Collection in Nine Books* (subsequently cited as 9L), its main component. 9L is the work of Bishop John of Thérouanne, who participated in the council of Troyes. It is therefore interesting to note that the peace statute is contained in MS Paris, BN lat. 10743, fol. 7v-8r, one of the earliest copies of the *Collection in Ten Parts*, a revision of 9L carried out around 1123 by the Archdeacon Walter of Thérouanne. (Somerville. *Decreta Claromontensia*, p. 61ff. with further references.) On the dating of the decree see Hoffmann, *Gottesfriede*, p. 156 n. 75.

[85] For an analysis of the Pax Morinensis see Hoffmann, *Gottesfriede*, pp. 144-158.

[86] According to A. Luchaire, *La cour du roi et ses fonctions judiciaires sous le règne de Louis VI (1108-1137)*, Extrait des Ann. de la Fac. des Lettres de Bordeaux, no. 2 (1880) 8, a *pactum pacis* of Louis VI confirmed the peace statutes of the synod of Troyes. Hoffmann refers to the *pactum* as "Ausführungsbestimmungen" (*Gottesfriede*, p. 208), pointing out, however, that the only evidence in support of this hypothesis is a reference to it in two of Ivo's letters: "Decet enim regiam maiestatem vestram, ut pactum pacis quod Deo inspirante in regno vestro confirmari fecistis, nulla lenocinante amicitia vel fallente desidia violare permittatis" (Ep. 253, PL 162 col. 259; see also ep. 275, PL 162 col. 278).

[87] The text given here is from what is perhaps the earliest extant manuscript, BN lat. 10743 (10P), fol. 7v-8r. It is almost identical with Sdralek's text (*Wolfenbüttler Fragmente*, p. 145). I agree with Hoffmann, *Gottesfriede*, p. 226 n. 44, that the following phrase is very

The reference to c. 2 of Troyes as found in the Arsenal manuscript is unambiguous. The remark of the *Chronicon* of Maillezais that was noted by both Baluze and Sdralek[88] thus receives further support.

To sum up, the fortunate circumstances that contemporary chronicles and canonists include references to the synod of Troyes, and that the cartulary of St. Sernin at Toulouse incidentally preserved the remarks of an eyewitness, Richard cardinal of Albano, make it possible to identify the text in MS Arsenal 717 with near certainty as a group of canons which the assembly of Troyes had passed. It was evident in connection with the council of Guastalla how strongly Paschal relied on the example set by his predecessor at Piacenza; in France the decrees and proceedings of Clermont must have been taken into consideration. Apart from the reconciliation with the French kings,[89] the church faced the same problems in 1107 as in 1095. Manuscript tradition relating to Urban's synod indicates that he probably delivered two public addresses, one to the clergy at the opening of the synod and another, the crusade exhortation, to both clergy and laity at the conclusion of the assembly.[90] At Troyes as at Clermont a decree on crusaders, probably in support of Bohemond's efforts to raise an army,[91] is combined with the proclamation of pax decrees,[92] and a similar way to publicize the Troyes canons may well have been chosen.

The new text for the synod is edited below. In order to illustrate differences and similarities, as well as to allow a comprehensive picture of Paschal's French legislation, the *breviaria* of Weiland, divided in accordance with his edition into recension a and recension b, are presented in columns parallel with the Arsenal text after a description of the manuscripts. Relevant letters and chronicles are included as well to facilitate comparisons, but their variants are of course not incorporated into any one of the three known textual traditions.

---

probably an addition by the scribe indicating his reasoning: "Sicut enim nemo iura dicionum suarum propter has institutiones amittit, sic ecclesia iustitias et consuetudines suas, quas ad tuitionem bonorum ac correctionem pravorum diutino tempore tenuit, indissolubiles servabit."

[88] For Baluze see above n. 80; Sdralek, *Wolfenbüttler Fragmente*, p. 145 n. 1.
[89] See above p. 75.
[90] Somerville, *Decreta Claromontensia*, p. 101; D. Munro, "A Crusader," *Speculum* 7 (1932) 321-335.
[91] Cf. above, ch. 1, p. 28.
[92] For the Peace and Truce of God at the council of Clermont see Somerville, *Decreta Claromontensia*, p. 143 nos. 1 and 2 with references and H. Hoffmann, *Gottesfriede*, pp. 221-224. The papal pax tradition for France extends back to the council of Reims of 1049.

## The Manuscripts

Pa: Paris, Bibliothèque de l'Arsenal 717

This small codex of 8 folios written in a tenth-century hand contains two letters from archbishops of Lyons, an epistle sent by Bishop Amo[u]lo (841-852) to Bishop Teutbald (Teodbold, Thiebaud) of Langres (849-859), fol. 1r-5r and that sent by Bishop Agobard (814-840) to Bishop Bartholomew of Narbonne (828-844), fol. 5r-8r. The canons from Troyes are a twelfth-century addition on fol. 8v. At the bottom of fol. 1r a note is found: "Dono D. Camusat Trecensis 1640."[93] "Dans la bibliothèque des frères Dupuy,[94] où il passa ensuite, ce petit volume était côté 183. Entré à la Bibliothèque du Roi, il reçut le no. 4067 sur l'inventaire des manuscrits du Roi que Clément dressa en 1682.[95] Il était en déficit lors de l'impression du catalogue des manuscrits latins du dix-huitième siècle."[96] But fortunately the codex was not lost. It found its way into the library of the Marquis de Paulmy.[97]

Baluze had worked with Pa at the Bibliothèque Royale and transcribed the decrees from Troyes.[98] Some relatively recent annotations, possibly from the eighteenth century, in the margins of the first fly-leaf verso, connect the manuscript to one of Baluze's publications: "vide Baluze 1655 Tome II p. 135 et Tome I p. 197." In 1665 Baluze reedited a publication by Papire Masson.[99] The modern page references in Pa are indeed to these volumes: 1: 197-207 contains the letter of Agobard of Lyons, and 2: 135-147 the letter of Amolo.

---

[93] Nicolas Camusat (1575-1655), canon of the cathedral chapter of Troyes, "se livra aux études historiques, cherchant des documents dans toutes les bibliothèques et sauvant occasionnellement de la destruction des pièces intéressantes" (*Dict. de Biographie Française* 7 [1956] 1019-1020). Camusat was apparently very generous in donating manuscripts from Troyes (see L. Delisle, *Cabinet des Manuscrits* 2: 45), but it is not known to whom he presented this particular MS.

[94] The brothers Dupuy, Pierre (1582-1651 [?]) and Jacques (1591-1656) "furent nommés gardes de la bibliothèque du roi en 1645" (*Dict. de Biographie Française* 12 [1968] 596-597).

[95] Montfaucon, *Bibliotheca bibliothecarum manuscriptorum nova* 2 (Paris 1739) 747.

[96] H. Martin, *Catalogue des manuscrits de la Bibliothèque de l'Arsenal* 8 (1899) 291.

[97] Antoine-René de Voyer d'Argenson marquis de Paulmy, vicomte de Mouzé (1722-1787), chancellor of Queen Marie-Antoinette from May 1774. He is the founder of the Bibliothèque de l'Arsenal, located in the palace where he lived after 1770. His life has been described in detail by Martin, *Catalogue* 1, especially pp. 17-36. It is possible that Paulmy obtained the manuscript by way of exchange with the royal library. According to Delisle, J. N. Moreau (1717-1804), librarian of the queen, exchanged several manuscripts with de Paulmy in 1780, for example (Delisle, *Cabinet des manuscrits* 1: 571-572).

[98] Above p. 84.

[99] Cf. DHGE s.v. Baluze (cf. above n. 71): "*Sancti Agobardi archiepiscopi Lugdunensis opera. Item epistolae et opuscula Leidradi et Amulonis archiepiscoporum Lugdunensium necnon Flori diaconi liber de electionibus episcoporum.* 2 vol. petit in-8°, Paris, chez F. Muguet, 1666" (vol. 6, col. 445, no. 16). Reproduced in *Maxima bibliotheca veterum patrum*, Lyons 1677, 14: 234-329.

However, in 1665 Baluze did not yet know Pa. He stated explicitly in the introduction that his edition was based exclusively on the Masson manuscript: "damus igitur tibi novam Agobardi editionem, emendatam ad fidem codicis quo Massonus est usus, quem nobis ex Bibliotheca Regia subministravit Vir Illustrissimus Nicolaus Colbertus Episcopus Lucionensis. Ac ne quis dubitet quin is sit siremps (sic) Massoni liber, haec in fronte codicis scripta sunt manu Illustr. V. Iac. Augusti Thuani[100] EX LIBRIS PAPIRII MASSONI."[101]

Bibliography: H. Martin, *Catalogue des Manuscrits de la Bibliothèque de l'Arsenal* 2 (1886) 55-56 and 8 (1899) 291. The letters of Agobard and Amolo are edited from the codex in MGH *Epistolae Karolini aevi* 3 (1899) 206-210 and 363-368.

Pn: Paris, BN lat. 11851

The manuscript, the autograph of the chronicle of the Annalista Saxo, was edited by Georg Waitz under its old shelfmark St. Germain-des-Prés 440.[102] Until the French Revolution it remained at this Benedictine monastery where it was consulted by E. Martène, who published several of the marginal addenda of the codex, including the canons.[103] The addenda appear to have been written in the same early twelfth-century hand as the main body of the text. The numbered set of four canons from the council of Troyes is found in the margin of fol. 212v. As Pertz has shown, the manuscript belonged in the fourteenth century to Andreas Cirkenbach of Würzburg. He concluded that Pn originated in Germany. The codex was used by Weiland.

Bibliography: Pertz, *Archiv* 7 (1839) 547-550; Waitz, MGH SS 6: 548-552; L. Delisle, "Inventaire des manuscrits latins de Saint-Germain-des-Prés," BEC 26 (1864-65) 208.

G: Göttweig, Stiftsbibliothek 53 (56)[104]

The manuscript is fully described by M. Sdralek. The canons from Troyes are the most recent material forming an integral part of the canonical collection covering fol. 1r-129r of G which used to be bound separately. They are found on fol. 86r-86v. The canonical collection was analyzed by Schulte.[105] Sdralek concluded that G originated probably in Passau. The codex was used by Weiland.

Bibliography: M. Sdralek, *Die Streitschriften Altmanns von Passau und*

---

[100] Jacques-Auguste de Thou (d. 1617) was president of the Parlement of Paris. *Nouvelle Biographie Générale*, vols. 45-46 (1866) 255-262.

[101] Jean-Papire Masson (1544-1611); see ibid. vols. 33-34 (1861) 207.

[102] MGH SS 6: 542-777.

[103] Above p. 78.

[104] The handwritten catalogue of the abbey library was not accessible; and I could see the relevant folios only in microfilm.

[105] Schulte concluded that the collection was closely related to the Collectio Tripartita ("Rechtshandschriften," p. 569), but his arguments were criticized by Fournier ("Yves de Chartres," BEC 58: 411-412) and Sdralek (*Streitschriften*, pp. 65-66).

*Wezilos von Mainz* (Paderborn 1890) especially p. 64; idem, *De S. Nicolai Papae I epistolarum codicibus* (Breslau 1882) 17, n. 1; Schulte, "Die Rechtshandschriften der Stiftsbibliotheken," especially pp. 560-569; P. Fournier, "Les collections canoniques attribuées à Yves de Chartres," BEC 58 (1897) especially p. 411; M. B. Bennett, *Historical Libraries of Austria* (Palm Springs 1964) pp. 9-10.

M: Munich, Bayerische Staatsbibliothek, Clm. 3739 (August. eccl. 39)
This ninth-century manuscript from the cathedral of Augsburg contains very valuable marginal additions from the eleventh and twelfth century. The canon from Guastalla is found in the lower margin of fol. 7v,[106] and the canons from Troyes were added on the same folio in the left hand margin where they are separated from the ninth-century text by a vertical line. The codex was used by Weiland.

Bibliography: *Catalogus codicum latinorum Bibliothecae Regiae Monacensis* 1/2 (Munich 1871) 129-130.

The Text

Summary of the sigla.

Pa  Paris, Bibliothèque de l'Arsenal 717; Pa is the only codex for the Arsenal tradition.
Pn  Paris, BN lat. 11851; used by Weiland; it is the second manuscript for recension a.
G   Göttweig, Stiftsbibliothek 53 (56); it is the basic manuscript for recension a in accordance with Weiland's edition.
M   Munich, Bayerische Staatsbibliothek, Clm. 3739; M is the only codex for recension b.

The canons are enumerated in accordance with the sequence found in Pa. The sequence of the canons of recensions a and b is broken up in order to facilitate comparisons, but arabic numerals in parenthesis indicate the original place of the decree within the pertinent recension.

| *Arsenal Tradition* | *Recension a* | *Recension b* |
|---|---|---|
| **1** Sanctorum patrum uestigiis inherentes, quae a romanae sedis auctoritate decreta suscepimus caritati vestrae ad honorem dei et | Decreta Paschalis pape Trecis data[a] | Decreta Paschalis pape apud Trecas |

---

[106] See above p. 55.

| *Arsenal Tradition* | *Recension a* | *Recension b* |

sanctae ecclesiae inconcusso tenenda uigore committimus.

ᵃ Decretum Paschalis papae Trecis datum *Pn*

**2** De pace igitur quod ad communem spectat utilitatem premitentes, personis et rebus ecclesiasticis, mercatoribus, peregrinis plenarie pacis gratiam omnibus diebus conseruari uolumus. Milites uero et seruientes uel quicumque ad inuicem inimicantes quattuor diebus, uidelicet a quarta feria sole occidente usque ad secundam feriam ante solis ortum, pacis securitatem obtineant. Omnes etiam domus et molendina ab incendio erunt omni die quieta.[1]

[1] Cf. Somerville, *Decreta Claromontensia*, esp. p. 73 c. 1 and p. 94 cc. 16 and 18; Sdralek, *Wolfenbüttler Fragmente*, pp. 144-145; Hoffmann, *Gottesfriede*, pp. 156-157, p. 208, pp. 225-226 with references.

**3**[1] Sacerdotibus et leuitis tam sub anathemate quam sub periculo ordinis sui omnimodam iniungimus continentiam.

De coniugatisᵃ presbiteris nisi cessauerint ut officioᵇ careant simul et a choro moueantur, praecipiendo mandamus. Etᶜ si nec sicᵈ cessauerint, procul a liminibus aecclesiae pellanturᵉ etᶠ nec laicaᵍ communione fruantur.

De uxoratis et concubinatis presbiteris id statuimus, ut penitus ab altaris ministerio sequestrentur et aecclesiasticis rebus depriuentur. (c. 2)

| Arsenal Tradition | Recension a | Recension b |
|---|---|---|
| | Idem[h] de diaconibus statuimus. (c. 4) | |

[a] coniugatis—presbiteris] uxoratis sacerdotibus siue concubinariis *Pn*   [b] officio—moueantur] ab altari moueantur simul et de choro segregentur *Pn*   [c] Quod *Pn*   [d] sic] tunc *Pn*   [e] arceantur *Pn*   [f] et *om. Pn*   [g] laica] ipsa laicali *Pn*   [h] quoque *add. Pn*

[1] Cf. Nic. II, synodica generalis c. 3 (MGH Const. 1: 547, no. 384)   Greg. VII, conc. Roman. a. 1075 (Caspar, *Das Register Gregors VII*, book 2.62 = 1: 217): "Decreuimus enim, quod si quis eorum ordinum qui sacris altaribus administrant, presbyter scilicet diaconus et subdiaconus, uxorem uel concubinam habet nisi illis omnino dimissis dignam poenitentiam agant, sacris altaribus penitus administrare desistant nec aliquo ecclesiae beneficio ulterius potiantur sive potitis fruantur"; Urb. II, conc. Carom. a. 1095 no. 10 (Somerville, *Decreta Claromontensia*, p. 144); Conc. Pictav. a. 1100 c. 15 (Sdralek, *Wolfenbüttler Fragmente*, p. 137 and Mansi 20: 1124 c. 16).

**4** Ne presbiteri duas habeant matrices ecclesias interdicimus.

Cf. Nic. II, synodica generalis c. 8: "Nec aliquis presbyter duas aecclesias simul obtineat" (MGH Const. 1: 548, no. 384)   Urb. II, conc. Clarom. a. 1095, no. 13 (Somerville, *Decreta Claromontensia*, p. 145); conc. Pictau. a. 1100 as above c. 3   Burch. 2.96   Ivo Decr. 6.173

| | | |
|---|---|---|
| **5** Laicos ab inuestituris rerum aecclesiasticarum faciendis[1] et a minutis decimis uel oblationibus recipiendis omnino prohibemus.[2] | | |
| | Item quicumque[a] ab hac hora et[b] deinceps inuestituram episcopatus[c] uel[d] aliquam aecclesiasticam[e] dignitatem a laicali manu acceperit[f], si ordinatus fuerit, deponatur simul et ordinator eius.[3] (c. 2) | Si quis aecclesiae aut aecclesiasticae dignitatis ab aliqua laica persona inuestituram susceperit, et ipse et qui manum ei imposuerit deponantur et communione priuentur.[3] (c. 1) |

*Arsenal Tradition*        *Recension a*        *Recension b*

ᵃ Qui *Pn*    ᵇ et deinceps *om. Pn*    ᶜ episcopalem *Pn*    ᵈ seu *Pn*    ᵉ spiritualem *Pn*    ᶠ susceperit *Pn*

[1] Cf. Greg. vii, conc. Roman. a. 1080, c. 2 (Caspar, *Das Register Gregors vii.*, book 7 no. 14a = 2: 480)    Urb. ii, conc. Clarom. a. 1095 no. 18 (Somerville, *Decreta Claromontensia*, p. 145).

[2] Cf. Nic. ii, synodica generalis c. 5 (MGH Const. 1: 547, no. 384)    Greg. vii, conc. Roman. a. 1078, c. 7 (Caspar, *Das Register Gregors vii.*, book 6 no. 5b = 2: 404) = Ans. 5.45    Urb. ii, conc. Clarom. a. 1095 no. 21 (Somerville, *Decreta Claromontensia*, p. 146).

[3] Cf. Nic. ii synodica generalis c. 6 (MGH Const. 1: 547 no. 384)    Greg. vii, conc. Roman. a. 1078 c. 3 (Caspar, *Das Register Gregors vii.*, book 6 no. 5b = 2: 403)    Urb. ii, conc. Clarom. a. 1095 no. 17 (Somerville, *Decreta Claromontensia*, p. 145).

ᶠIllud etiam repetitum et confirmatum est quod in Trecensi concilio de inuestituris aecclesiasticis promulgatum est, quod ita se habet:] Constitutiones sanctorum canonum sequentes statuimus, ut quicumque clericorum ab hac hora inuestituram ecclesie uel ecclesiastice dignitatis de manu laici acceperit et qui ei manum imposuerit, gradus sui periculo subiaceat et communione priuetur. (Conc. Lateran. 1110, below p. 119.)

Nos quoque sanctorum canonum constitutiones sequentes cum fratribus nostris in Trecensi concilio statuimus, ut quicumque clericorum de hac hora inuestituram ecclesie, uel ecclesiastice dignitatis de manu laici acceperit, et qui ei manum imposuerit, gradus sui periculo subiaceat et communione priuetur. (JL 6145, above p. 83.)

**6** Iniungit etiam romana auctoritas illis omnibus qui cruces et uota fecerunt quod usque ad proximum pascha quod uouerunt et unde obligati tenentur persoluant.[1]

[1] Cf. Urb. ii, conc. Clarom. a. 1095 no. 3 (Somerville, *Decreta Claromontensia*, p. 143).

| Arsenal Tradition | Recension a | Recension b |

**7** Matrimonia contrahere uolentibus ratum et inuiolabile mandatum prefigimus ut non ante duodecim annos nec sine legitimis testibus illud presumant, nec iuncta coniugia nisi in episcopi dissoluantur presentia.[1]

[1] Cf. J. Freisen, *Geschichte des kanonischen Eherechts bis zum Verfall der Glossenliteratur* (Paderborn 1893, repr. Aalen 1963) 324-325; A. Esmein, *Le mariage en droit canonique*, 2nd ed. by R. Genéstal, 1 (Paris 1929) 236-242.

**8** Presbiteris et diaconibus longos capillos, rostratos sotulares, fixas uestes, laqueos in blialdis[a] uel camisiis habere uel aleis seruire prohibemus.[1]

[a] blialdis *scripsi* blialibus *Pa*

[1] Cf. G. Coolen, "Le costume écclésiastique," *Bulletin de la société des antiquaires de la Morinie* 20 (1964) 274-284.

**9** Laici nullum in atriis censum, nullas consuetudines uel iusticias deinceps accipiant.[1]

[1] Cf. Leo ix conc. Remen. a. 1049 c. 4 (Blumenthal, "Reims," DA 32 [1976] 30)   Nic. ii synodica generalis c. 5 (MGH Const. 1: 547, no. 384)   Urb. ii, conc. Clarom. a. 1095 no. 22 (Somerville, *Decreta Claromontensia*, p. 146).

**10** Si preda aecclesiastica ad quodcumque receptum[1] ducta, proclamatori requirenti

| Arsenal Tradition | Recension a | Recension b |

fuerit denegata, receptum illud a diuinis <officiis> praeter baptisma cessare uolumus.[2]

[1] Probably used in the sense of castle; Georges: "Zuflucht, Rückzug"; Niermeyer: "1) compulsory housing and entertainment, 2) le droit de disposer d'un château."

[2] Cf. Leo IX con. Remen. a. 1049 cc. 12 and 13 (Blumenthal, "Reims," DA 32 [1976] 32) Calixt. II, conc. Remen. a. 1119 (Mansi 21: 236-237 and Hoffmann, *Gottesfriede*, pp. 226-228).

**11** Arcas in aecclesiis poni nisi tempore guerre et pro positis precium exigi prohibemus.

**12** Ecclesias et sacerdotalia beneficia uendi uel emi penitus interdicimus.[1]

Si quis munus exigerit pro oblationibus fidelium uel pro prebendis canonicorum uel monachorum uel alicuius aecclesiastici ordinis, ab ecclesia eiciatur et communione priuetur (c. 4)

[1] Cf. Urb. II, conc. Clarom. a. 1095 no. 7 (Somerville, *Decreta Claromontensia*, p. 143).

⌜Apostolicaᵃ auctoritate commoniti precipimus ut quicumque aliquam aecclesiasticam dignitatem symoniacae accepit, dignitatem amittat aut communione fidelium careat.⌝ (c. 1)

ᵃ Apostolica—careat *om. Pn*

| Arsenal Tradition | Recension a | Recension b |
|---|---|---|
| | Decani quos[a] archipresbiteros uocamus[b], nisi adepto presbiteratus ordine, non sint, si[c] fuerint, dignitate[d] careant[e] donec[f] ordinentur[g], tunc[h] si digni sunt, restituantur. Archidiaconi, nisi adepto diaconatus ordine, non sint, si[i] fuerint, priorem sententiam subeant[j].[1] (c. 3) | Nullus sibi nomen alienum usurpet, ut plerique solent eos nominare archipresbiteros, qui non sunt presbiteri, archidiaconos, qui non sunt diaconi, decanos, qui non sunt presbiteri; id omnino interdicimus. (c. 3) |

[a] nos *add. Pn*   [b] uocamus archipresbiteris *tr. Pn*   [c] autem *add. Pn*   [d] beneficio et *praem. Pn*   [e] careant] priuentur *Pn*   [f] donec] quousque *Pn*   [g] ordinentur] ordinem adipiscantur *Pn*   [h] et *praem. Pn*   [i] autem *add. Pn*   [j] priorem—subeant] secundum sententiam de archipresbiteris datam iudicentur *Pn*

[1] Cf. Urb. II, conc. Clarom. a. 1095 no. 4 (Somerville, *Decreta Claromontensia*, p. 143)   Calixt. II, con. Lateran. a. 1123 c. 6 (Alberigo et al., *Conciliorum oecumenicorum decreta*, 2nd ed. 1962, p. 166).

**13** Quod si quis instigante, quod absit, diabolo temeritatis suae audatia sanctae romane sedis[a] uiolare decreta presumpserit sciat procul dubio a corpore Christi, quod est aecclesia, se penitus alienatum atque in mortem animae suae anathematis uinculo donec satisfaciat obligatum.

[a] *supra scriptum est*

---

Nos vero in concilio quod apud Trecas celebravimus, sanctorum patrum decreta sequentes tam episcopis, quam abbatibus et clericis ceteris interdiximus nec<sup>a</sup> ulterius excommunicatos vel interdictos ab alio in sua parochia reciperent. (JL 6158).

<sup>a</sup> *lege* ne

---

### OTHER NOTABLE DECISIONS OF THE COUNCIL

The significance of the synod of Troyes is primarily reflected in the list of participants and in the accounts of the meetings at St. Denis and Châlons-sur-Marne. The *Liber Pontificalis* refers to the assembly only in passing in general terms.[107] Yet the synod served to further clarify papal policies. A passage in the *Historia novorum* of Eadmer indicates the circumstances that surrounded the presence of William and Baldwin of England.[108] King Henry I and Anselm delayed the publication of the agreement which Paschal, the archbishop and Henry had reached between August 1105 and 23 March 1106,[109] until the ambassadors had returned from the synod. But Eadmer as well as other sources are completely silent on the nature of the connection between the French council and the English agreement. All that can be said is, therefore, that the renewed prohibition of investiture as well as the rejection of the demands of Henry V must have impressed upon the English that they could under no circumstance expect that Henry I would be allowed to continue the practice of investiture. The synod apparently supported Paschal's relaxation of the prohibition of homage at least tacitly, if it is permissible to assume that it is not a mere accident that no decree against lay homage has survived in any of the sets of decrees or letters coming from the council.

Papal decisions made at the synod are more evident in other instances. The pontiff showed his support of the French monarchy by dissolving the marriage of Louis, king designate, and Lucienne de Rochefort, a marriage

---

[107] Ed. Duchesne 2: 299: "Sic pertransivit usque Frantiam et Trecis concilium celebravit, in quo multa quae ordinanda erant ordinavit et quae destruenda erant bono fine destruxit."

[108] *Historia novorum*, pp. 184-185: "Adunatis autem ad curiam ejus [scilicet Henrici I] in Pascha terrae principibus, dilata est ecclesiarum ordinatio quam rex se facturum disposuerat, eo quod summus sedis apostolicae pontifex Paschalis Franciam venerat, et sibi ad concilium quod Trecis erat celebraturus a rege Henrico et ab Anselmo archiepiscopo saepe supra memoratos viros Willelmum et Balduinum mitti mandaverat."

[109] Henry retained homage but gave up investiture. An excellent account of the negotiations is given by Southern, *Saint Anselm*, pp. 170-179. See also Cantor, *Lay Investiture*, passim and esp. 268. The date 1106 is that of Paschal's letter of dispensation written to St. Anselm (JL 6073). See above pp. 15-18.

Luchaire found was considered at the time "peu conforme à la dignité royale."[110] At the same time, however, he rejected the candidacy of Gervais for the archbishopric of Reims: "Domnus papa Paschalis apud Trecas concilium celebravit in quo Gervasium indignum esse archiepiscopatu Remensi iudicavit."[111] Gervasius had been elected with royal support by one faction of the Reims clergy after the death of Manasses in September 1106,[112] and was invested by the king. Instead of Gervais, however, the council of Troyes elected Radulf le Vert, who had been provost of the cathedral of Reims, with the support of the 'papal' faction at the cathedral.[113] A letter of Paschal to the suffragan bishops of Reims, dated November 23, 1107, shows that Radulf was consecrated "iuxta apostolice sedis preceptum."[114] This telling phrase reflects the fact that Paschal's action at the synod created a difficult situation for France. For the next year a consecrated archbishop of Reims who was accepted by the papacy would be the opponent of a royal archbishop who actually was in possession of the see although unconsecrated. The inherent dangers became clear at the end of July 1108 at the death of Philip I when Louis VI could not be crowned at Reims. Becker delineates the solution of the conflict in 1108 in favor of Radulf that was arrived at with the aid of Ivo of Chartres.[115] It is here only necessary to show that the agreement at St. Denis had not included a renunciation of reform principles on the part of Paschal.

Paschal also intervened in the affairs of the diocese of Verdun, an imperial see, occupied by Richard of Grand-Pré to whom the pontiff had originally offered the archbishopric of Reims if the words of the *Gesta episcoporum Virdunensium* can be accepted.[116] Richard had rejected the offer,

---

[110] Luchaire, *Louis VI le Gros*, p. 27 no. 50.

[111] *Annales Cameracenses*, auctore Lamberto Waterlos, ed. G. H. Pertz, MGH SS 16: 509-554, p. 511: "Radulfus archiepiscopus Remensis consecratur. Domnus Odo primum Cameracum venit. Domnus papa Paschalis apud Trecas concilium celebravit in quo Gervasium indignum esse archiepiscopatu Remensi iudicavit." For the incident see particularly Becker, *Investiturproblem*, pp. 123-126 and Monod, *Essai*, p. 57 n. 4.

[112] *Gallia Christiana* 9 (1751) cols. 80-81.

[113] See *Gallia Christiana* 9, cols. 80-81 and the letter of the chanter and other clergy of Reims in support of the royal candidate Gervais addressed to Radulf in *Recueil des historiens des Gaules et de la France* 15: 199.

[114] Sdralek, *Wolfenbüttler Fragmente*, p. 114 no. 4 with further references.

[115] Becker, *Investiturproblem*, pp. 123-125.

[116] Laurentii de Leodio, *Gesta episcoporum Virdunensium*, MGH SS 10: 499-500, c. 15. E. Baluze gathered some notes concerning these events based on "Richardus Wasseburgicus, lib. iv, Antiquitatum Galliae Belgicae," which stress Paschal's motives (Paris, BN, MS Baluze 7, fol. 158r: "[Paschal] sedi Remensi praefecit Richardum Archidiaconum Virdunensem, quo eum abduceret Henrici Imperatoris partibus, et in suas transgredi beneficio insigni procuraret."). See R. Wassebourg, *Antiquitez de la Gaule Belgicque* (Verdun [?]

and was elected instead to the see of Verdun after the death of his predecessor, perhaps around Christmas 1106. He was invested with ring and staff by Henry v, apparently immediately after the synod of Troyes, and entered the city with Archbishop Bruno of Trier. He was never recognized by Paschal.[117] The *Gesta* report that Paschal condemned Richard at Troyes: "Richardum Virdunensem, qui se tradidit regiae curiae, et nos tradimus eum sathanae."[118] The dating of the events surrounding Richard is not very definite, but they clearly represent a direct challenge to Henry v which the latter was not slow to take up.

The exacerbation of the conflict between Henry v and the Apostolic See after the council of Guastalla is also reflected in a series of excommunications pronounced at Troyes, an indication of the cessation of the truce between the antagonists that Bruno of Trier and Paschal had apparently agreed upon at the council of Guastalla in 1106.[119] The most important evidence here is a passage in the *Annales Patherbrunnenses*:

> Ibi Ruothardus Magontiae archiepiscopus ab officio divino suspenditur, eo quod Uodonem Hildinesheimensem sine aecclesiae consensu restituit et quia Reinhardum contra iura canonum Halverstadensi aecclesiae ordinavit. Gebehardus Constantiensis similiter, quia his consensit, qui Godescalcum Mindensi aecclesiae loco episcopi intruserunt et quia Heinricum Magetheburgensi aecclesiae temerarie ordinavit, ab officio suspenditur. Coloniensis episcopus Frithericus cum suis suffraganeis ab officio divino suspenditur, quia huic sanctae sinodo se subtraxerat. Omnibus ibi aecclesiis apostolicus libertatem suam, ut ex praecepto canonum praelatos sibi eligant, quos dignos viderint, restituit.[120]

Additional information is found in JL 6143 to Gebhard of Constance,[121] JL 6144 to Reinhard of Halberstadt, and JL 6145 to Rothard of Mainz. According to the *Annales Patherbrunnenses* Rothard was suspended from office because he had reinstated Udo of Hildesheim in 1105[122] and con-

---

1549) 2 vols. in 1, 1: 246: "... trouvoit bon le dict Pape Pascal, Presenter ledict Arcevesche au dict Richard pour le retirer en l'obeyssance Romaine et luy faire laisser le party de l'Empereur Henry cinquième, auquel seurement et notoirement il adheroit."
[117] Guleke, *Kirchenpolitik*, p. 115 no. 9.
[118] *Gesta Virdunensium* c. 15, p. 500.
[119] Above p. 73. See also Henking, *Gebhard*, p. 94.
[120] Ed. Scheffer-Boichorst, pp. 117-118. The most recent discussion of the excommunications is found in Bogumil, *Das Bistum Halberstadt*, Exkurs 2, pp. 257-259.
[121] See Jaffé, *Monumenta Moguntina*, p. 384 no. 37; Brackmann GP 2/1: 135 no. 44; Knonau, *Jahrbücher* 6: 53-56 and n. 30. Cf. also Ladewig-Müller, *Regesta episcoporum Constantiensium* 1: 80-81, nos. 645-646.
[122] Cf. above p. 35. See also Heinemann, *Das Bistum Hildesheim*, pp. 49-57.

secrated Reinhard as bishop of Halberstadt at the end of March 1107 although he had been invested with ring and staff by Henry v.[123] An additional reason for papal displeasure with Rothard is given in JL 6145: Rothard had not come to Troyes. Nonetheless, because of the intercession of Bruno of Trier, Gebhard of Constance and the abbot of Hirsau[124] on behalf of Rothard, this very letter already lifted the suspension that had just been pronounced. The letter is undated,[125] but since it expressly reports the investiture decree from Troyes it seems to have been written not too long after the synod. As Scheffer-Boichorst points out, this pardon does not mean that the *Annales Patherbrunnenses* are unreliable.[126] Rothard's suspension is also reported in JL 6143 to Gebhard of Constance.[127] The letter shows that Gebhard, too, was suspended in accordance with the *Annales*, but that he had been pardoned out of consideration for his past support of the papacy and because of the intervention of bishops Otto of Bamberg and Wido of Chur, who alone among the suffragans of Mainz had been exempted from the suspension of Rothard and all his suffragans on the ground that they were present at Guastalla. Like Rothard, Gebhard was accused of absence from the synod as well as of involvement with the consecrations of Gottschalk of Minden and Henry of Magdeburg. Gottschalk was constituted bishop in place of the imperial bishop Widelo who was expelled by Henry v between Easter and Pentecost 1105;[128] Henry was installed by Gebhard in Magdeburg on 11 June.[129] In addition to Rothard and Gebhard, Archbishop Frederick of Cologne with his suffragans was suspended a second time.[130]

---

[123] On Reinhard's elevation to the bishopric of Halberstadt see Bogumil, *Das Bistum Halberstadt*, pp. 17-21 and 23-27.

[124] For Abbot Bruno (1105-1120) cf. H. Jakobs, *Die Hirsauer*, pp. 33-34. The incident is not mentioned.

[125] See Jaffé, *Monumenta Moguntina*, p. 384.

[126] *Annales Patherbrunnenses*, p. 118 n. 1. For JL 6145 see also Stimming, *Mainzer Urkundenbuch*, p. 338 no. 432.

[127] As in n. 121 above: "... Noveris praeterea fratrem nostrum Moguntinum cum omnibus suffraganeis suis praeter Babenbergensem et Curiensem qui synodo Longobardice interfuit, pro concilii absentia a suis officiis interdictos ... ." See also Stimming, *Mainzer Urkundenbuch*, pp. 339-340 no. 433.

[128] Knonau, *Jahrbücher* 5: 223. Guleke, *Kirchenpolitik*, p. 113. For Bishop Widelo see also the references given above, ch. 2 n. 160.

[129] Knonau, *Jahrbücher* 5: 228 and nn. 29 and 31. The report in the *Gesta archiepiscoporum Magdeburgensium* that Gebhard honored Henry with the pallium which had been sent by Paschal does not square with the accusation of unauthorized consecration. See Guleke, *Kirchenpolitik*, p. 115 no. 11 and now especially D. Claude, *Geschichte des Erzbistums Magdeburg*, pp. 380-390. Cf. Ladewig-Müller, *Regesta episcoporum Constantiensium*, 1: 77, nos. 620-622.

[130] *Annales Patherbrunnenses*, p. 118. For Archbishop Frederick I (1100-1131) see W. Neuss and F. W. Oediger, *Das Bistum Köln von den Anfängen bis zum Ende des 12. Jahrhunderts* 1 (Cologne 1964) 204-215.

As the discussion shows, however, Paschal's apparently sweeping suspension of German bishops, important as it is as an expression of principle, was quickly mitigated in most instances. It could not lie in Paschal's interest to break abruptly the ties to the German church that had so recently been reestablished at Guastalla.

# 4

# The Councils of 1108 and 1110

## THE COUNCIL OF BENEVENTO, OCTOBER 1108

### The Sources and Previous Scholarship

Ever since Baronius quoted a passage from the chronicle of Montecassino[1] scholars have known that Paschal's first council after his return from France late in August 1107[2] was held in the autumn of the following year at Benevento.[3] Two recensions of the *Annales Beneventani* also refer to the synod in connection with the consecration of Archbishop Landulf II of Benevento.[4]

### The Participants

Almost nothings is known about the participants. Paschal was ac-

---

[1] MGH SS 7: 777 (lib. IV c. 33); Baronius, *Annales Ecclesiastici*, 12: 65.

[2] Paschal's return to Rome was not effected without difficulties. See *Liber Pontificalis*, ed. Duchesne, 2: 299; *Liber Pontificalis Dertusensis*, ed. March, pp. 138-139 and the discussion by Knonau, *Jahrbücher* 6: 57-58 nn. 34 and 35 where further references to contrasting reports in several chronicles are given.

[3] Binius 3/2 (2nd ed.): 443; *Collectio regia* 26: 767; Labbe-Cossart 10: 757-758; Hardouin 6/2: 1889-1890; Coleti 12: 1139; Mansi 20: 1231-1232. Severinus Binius added in his second edition (1618) a passage from the chronicle of the monastery of St. Vincent near Volterra. Although the passage only records a visit of the pontiff to the monastery which is not related to the council of Benevento, it was repeated by all later scholars.

[4] Recensions A.1 and A.2, ed. Bertolini, p. 153 and the reference ibid. n. 3. A.1: "Paschalis papa venit Beneventum et facta synodo mense octobri consecravit Landulfum archiepiscopum .vi. idus novembris." Recension A.2 is very similar. Landulf was archbishop from 1108-1119.

companied by Bruno of Segni, at this time abbot of Montecassino.[5] The archbishop-elect of Benevento who was consecrated shortly after the synod probably also attended.

## The Canons

The chronicle of Montecassino is evidence that at least two canons were promulgated in 1108:

> In qua [synodo] videlicet vestigia praedecessorum suorum secutus constituit, ut quicumque investituram ecclesiae vel ecclesiasticam dignitatem de manu laici acceperit, et dans et accipiens communione privetur. Vestimenta vero saecularia et pretiosa clericis reprehendit, et talibus uti interdixit.[6]

Both canons repeat earlier legislation of the pontiff. The prohibition of investiture is recorded whenever any trace of the canons survived, and it was at Troyes that the pontiff is first known to have prohibited luxurious garments for the clergy.[7] M. Sdralek published from MS Wolfenbüttel, Herzog August Bibliothek Guelf. Gud. 212, a much fuller recension of the decree against investiture.[8] In the Gudianus the Benevento canon is found in Sdralek's section IV, and is, therefore, not part of the canonical *Collection in Nine Books* contained in the codex. The decree entered the canonical tradition through two other collections, the *Caesaraugustana*[9] and the

---

[5] "Mense itaque Octobrio adveniente, idem apostolicus ad hunc locum adveniens, sociato sibi nostro abbate synodum celebraturus Beneventum perrexit" (Chronicle of Montecassino, MGH SS 7: 777). Cf. Tangl, *Teilnehmer*, p. 187.

[6] MGH SS 7: 777.

[7] Above p. 94 c. 8.

[8] Sdralek, *Wolfenbüttler Fragmente*, p. 138, no. 19. For a description of the different parts of the manuscript see ibid. p. 6.

[9] This canonical collection from the early twelfth century originated either in northern Spain or southern France. It was named after the first manuscript of it which was discovered near Zaragoza. See van Hove, *Prolegomena*, pp. 328 and 421; Stickler, *Historia iuris canonici*, pp. 184-185; P. Fournier, "La collection canonique dite Caesaraugustana," *Nouvelle Revue d'Histoire de Droit Français et Etranger* 45 (1921) 52-79; Fournier-Le Bras, *Histoire* 2: 269-296; C. M. Batlle and P. M. Gassó, *Pelagii I papae epistulae quae supersunt*, Scripta et documenta 8 (Montserrat 1956) xxxv-xxxix; J. Tarré, "La Collection Caesaraugustana est attribuable à Renan, écolâtre de Barcelone, 1117-25," *Positions des thèses de l'Ecole de Chartes* (1927) part xx, pp. 133-134; M. Rodriguez, "Tres manuscritos del siglo XII con colecciones canónicas," *Analecta Sacra Tarraconensia* 32 (1959) 35-54. Tarré's thesis about the authorship of the collection is discussed by Batlle-Gassó; *Pelagii I papae epistulae*, p. xxxvii n. 31 where further references can be found. The modern sixteenth-century paper copy of the Salamanca codex of the *Caesaraugustana*, MS Universidad Civil 2644, in the Biblioteca Apostolica Vaticana is not MS Barb. lat. 535 as indicated by Fournier-Le Bras and van Hove, but MS Barb. lat. 897.

*Collection in Seven Books*¹⁰ from which it is edited below. It is also appended to the Naples codex of the *Collectio canonum* of Anselm of Lucca, Bibl. Naz. XII A.39, fol. 109v.

The 1108 text in the *Caesaraugustana* correspond closely to the text published by Sdralek. It is listed in Jaffé's *Regesta* as JL 6613 based on the publication of the canon by S. Loewenfeld from a Paris manuscript, BN Baluze 269, fol. 107r.¹¹ Baluze's manuscript (fol. 30v) indicates the source which had been used by him; it is his "codex Rivipullensis." Among the incipits from this manuscript from the Catalan monastery S. Maria de Ripoll which Baluze listed in MS 269 on fols. 30r and 30v is found: "fol. 55v *Ex divinae legis praeceptis Paschalis II*." The "codex Rivipullensis" can be identified with the help of this entry, for in one of the manuscripts of the *Collectio Caesaraugustana* (Paris, BN lat. 3875) the decree "Ex divinae legis praeceptis" is found on fol. 55v. The fact that MS BN lat. 3875 was indeed the codex used by Baluze is certain, for it is the former MS Baluze 91.¹²

While all manuscripts of the *Caesaraugustana* (with one exception) contain the canon from Benevento,¹³ this is only true for the oldest of the three manuscripts of the *Collection in Seven Books*, MS Vat. lat. 1346, where the decree is an addendum on fol. 183r. The text in Vat. lat. 1346 is longer than the versions known hitherto, and because of the Italian origin of the manuscript (it is also older than the earliest copy of the *Caesaraugustana*), probably superior in authority.

A canonical manuscript at the Biblioteca Nazionale in Naples, MS XII A

---

¹⁰ Van Hove, *Prolegomena*, pp. 328 and 421; Stickler, *Historia iuris canonici*, p. 187; Fournier-Le Bras, *Histoire*, 2: 185-192.

¹¹ S. Loewenfeld, "Papsturkunden in Paris," *Neues Archiv* 7 (1882) 144-167; Loewenfeld did not know that "Ex divinae legis praeceptis" was a canon from Benevento. For MS Paris, BN Baluze 269, see Auvray and Poupardin, *Catalogue Baluze*, p. 324. Fol. 107r is not described.

¹² For a description of the manuscript see Batlle-Gassó, *Pelagii I papae epistulae*, p. xxxvi.

¹³ Three recensions are known. (See the bibliography above n. 9.) The location of the canon in complete manuscripts of the *Caesaraugustana* as well as in manuscripts containing excerpts from the collection which were examined is as follows: Paris, BN lat. 3875 fol. 55v; Paris, BN lat. 3876 fol. 50v; Salamanca, Universidad Civil 2644 fol. 62r; Vatican City, Bibl. Apostolica Vat., Barb. lat. 897 fol. 156vb; Vatican City, Bibl. Apostolica Vat., Vat. lat. 5715 fol. 48r; Vatican City, Bibl. Apostolica Vat., Vat. lat. 4976 fols. 149v-150r. MS Barcelona, Archivio de la Corona de Aragón, San Cugat 63, according to Tarré a reorganized, abbreviated version of the *Collectio Caesaraugustana*, but described by Batlle and Gassó as *Collection in Six Books* (*Epistulae*, p. lxii, with the admission: "Quae quidem non esse videtur nisi *Coll. Caesaraugustana* in VI libros distributa"), no longer contains the Benevento canon.

27, *Corpus Decretalium*, dating from the late twelfth or early thirteenth century, preserves part of the canon on fol. 90r.[14]

The basic manuscript for the following edition is MS Vat. lat. 1346 (Va).[15] Variants will be given from Sdralek's edition of the text in MS Wolfenbüttel, Gud. 212 (Wg),[16] from the unpublished *Collectio Caesaraugustana* (Vba),[17] and from MSS Naples, Bibl. Naz. XII A.27 (Nb) and XII A.39 (N).[18] For the sake of completeness, the second canon will be given from the Monumenta edition of the *Chronica monasterii Casinensis* (MGH SS 7: 777, siglum Cr).

Ex concilio habito a domino Paschali papa secundo.[a]

1. Et[b] diuine legis preceptis instruimur[c] quod omnia tabernaculi utensilia a leuitis custodiantur[d] et tractentur. Et per Iezechielem prophetam[1] dominus precipit ut terra circa templum sanctificata sit et solis sacerdotibus concedatur.[e] Quamobrem laicis omnibus interdicimus ne[f] aecclesias cum possessionibus suis[g] teneant aut aliis tradant aut presbyteros seu clericos intrudant uel expellant.[h] Qui uero eas[i] tenere aut[j] in feudum aliis[k] dare aut presbyteros siue clericos intrudere seu expellere[l] aut quasi hereditaria predia[m] uendicare presumpserint, ab aecclesiarum liminibus[n] arceantur.[o] Si uero, quod absit, in hac obstinatia[p] mortui fuerint, et clericorum obsequiis[q] et aecclesiastica[r] careant sepultura. Aecclesiae[s] uero ipse[t] diuinis[u] destituantur officiis.

[a] a domino—secundo] *written over an erasure after 'habito' in the right hand margin. The former text is no longer legible. The new inscription appears to have been written by the same hand and with the same ink as the main text.* Ex secundo] Paschalis *II* Vba  Ex decretis Paschalis pape *II* apud Beneuentum *Wg*  Pascalis pape *Nb*  [b] Et] ex *Vba*  ut *Wg*  [c] instruimus *Vba*  [d] custodirentur *Vba Wg N*  [e] Et diuine—concedatur *om. Nb*  [f] Quamobrem—ne] Laici qui *Nb*  [g] cum possessionibus suis] cum suis possessionibus *tr. Vba Nb*  [h] aut—expellant *om. Vba Wg N*  [i] teneant—eas *om. Nb*  [j] aut] uel *Nb*  [k] in feudum aliis] aliis in feudum *Vba*  in foedum *Nb*  [l] aut presbyteros—expellere *om. Vba Wg Nb N*  [m] predia *om. Nb*  [n] limi-

---

[14] Cf. Fournier-Le Bras, *Histoire*, 2: 204 n. 1. The footnote may contain a misprint regarding MS Naples, Bibl. Naz. XII A 27. The Naples manuscript of the *Coll. Canonum* of Anselm of Lucca is MS XII A 37-39. Conceivably, MS XII A 27 is related to the *Caesaraugustana*, but as yet I have been unable to examine the codex closely in order to confirm this impression.

[15] For a description see below p. 113 and the references given in n. 10 above.

[16] *Wolfenbüttler Fragmente*, p. 138 no. 19.

[17] See n. 9 above. The examined MSS (see above n. 13) have been collated. They show no significant variants. The siglum stands for MS Biblioteca Apostolica Vaticana, Barb. lat. 897, fol. 156v.

[18] The unnumbered parchment folios of the codex measure 249 × 161 mm, showing red inscriptions and initials.

nibus] et diuinis officiis add. *Vba Wg N*      ᵒ ab aecclesiarum—arceantur] excommunicentur *Nb*      ᵖ Si uero—obstinatia] et si in hoc *Nb*      ᑫ et—obsequiis] et domini corporis communione *Wg N*      et dominice corporis communione careant *Vba*      communione similiter *Nb*      ʳ aecclesiastica] ecclesie *Nb*      ˢ Aecclesiae] Eodem *N*      ᵗ ipse om. *Nb*      ᵘ diuinis] dominicis *Vba Nb*

[1] Ez. 45: 1-4. Cf. in general J. Funkenstein, *Das Alte Testament im Kampf von regnum und sacerdotium zur Zeit des Investiturstreits* (Dortmund 1938).

**2.** ⌜Uestimenta uero saecularia et pretiosa clericis reprehendit, et talibus uti interdixit.⌝ ᵃ

ᵃ om. *Va Vba Wg Nb N*, exstat apud *Cr* tantum

### Other Notable Decisions of the Council

Apart from the canons, no conciliar decisions are known. The significance of the 1108 prohibition of lay investiture is set in relief through a letter of Paschal to Anselm of Canterbury (JL 6206), perhaps sent from the synod for it is dated Benevento, 12 October 1108. Paschal writes: "Porro quod in eisdem litteris significasti scandalizari quosdam, quod regem Teutonicum dare investituras ecclesiarum toleramus, nec tolerasse nos aliquando nec toleraturos scias. Expectavimus quidem ut ferocia gentis illius edomaretur; rex vero si in paternae nequitiae tramite perseveraverit, Beati Petri gladium quem iam educere coepimus procul dubio experietur."[19] Knonau's and Peiser's perspicacious observation that the decree was specifically directed against Henry v is supported by the new version of the text in MS Vat. lat. 1346. In the light of canons from Guastalla and Troyes that already excommunicated not only the recipient but also the grantor of investiture it can, however, no longer be asserted that the council of Benevento marked a hardening of Paschal's attitude towards the Empire.[20]

## THE LATERAN COUNCIL, 7 MARCH 1110

### The Sources and Previous Scholarship

In spite of the importance[21] of the Lateran council of 1110 which is reflected in the relatively numerous manuscripts transmitting its legislation,

[19] Eadmer, *Historia novorum*, pp. 202-203; see also Peiser, *Investiturstreit*, pp. 47-49.
[20] Ibid. and Knonau, *Jahrbücher* 6: 90.
[21] Henry v had sent an embassy to Rome in 1109. For details about their negotiations see Knonau, *Jahrbücher* 6: 105 and n. 22; ibid. p. 115 and nn. 5 and 6. The aims of the

the synod is mentioned neither by Baronius, nor by Binius or the *Collectio Regia*.[22] It is indicative of the general state of documentation preserved for this assembly that the first item discovered by Gabriel Cossart is a set of canons. Cossart added a reference to the *Chronicon Hildesheimense*.[23] His text remained unchanged until Mansi supplemented it with a description of the canons in the work of the "Annalista Saxo Eccardi."[24] More recently, Pflugk-Harttung edited a series of decrees which he believed were promulgated by Paschal in 1110,[25] and Weiland's text incorporates the results of further researches.[26]

## The Participants

As in the case of the Beneventan council of 1108 almost nothing is known about attendance. Nevertheless, the synod was convoked as "generale concilium" and one letter of invitation has come down to us (JL 6503). Paschal wrote to Bishop Wido of Chur (1096-1122):

> Pro quibusdam ecclesiae casibus, propter quos eam potentes occupant et affligunt et sibi quasi saecularia vendicare contendunt, generale concilium in urbe IIII. nonas proximi Marcii per dei gratiam celebrare disposuimus.

Ewald, who published the text, argued that although the letter of invitation might have been for the Lenten synod of 1116, it should be dated 1110.[27] Wido of Chur, however, is not known to have gone to Italy in 1110.

---

Germans are expressed in the *Tractatus de investitura episcoporum* MGH Lib. de lite, 2: 495-504. The legislation of 1110 may well be Paschal's final reply to Henry's military preparation and requests.

[22] Nevertheless, it was apparently known that Paschal held a council in 1110. See the reference in Pierre de Marca, *Histoire de Béarn*, 2nd ed. 2: 159, to the "Concile de Latran (qui est à mon advis celuy qui fut tenu l'an 1110)." The first edition of the *Histoire* appeared in 1640, thirty years before Labbe-Cossart's *Sacrosancta Concilia*.

[23] Labbe-Cossart 10: 764-765: "Chronicon Hildesheimense ad hunc ipsum annum meminit Lateranensis synodi, quam vocat gloriosam." See *Annales Hildesheimenses*, p. 61: "1110, ind. 2 Non. Mart. synodus gloriosa in Lateranensi aecclesia presidente domino papa Paschali celebratur." The text is derived from the *Annales Patherbrunnenses*.

[24] See Hardouin, 6/2: 1895-1898; Coleti 12: 1149-1152, and Mansi 21: 10; for the Annalista Saxo see Rep. Font. 2 (1967) 353. The annalist is probably dependent on the *Annales Patherbrunnenses*.

[25] *Acta inedita* 2: 197, no. 238.

[26] MGH Const. 1: 567-569.

[27] See P. Ewald, "Reise nach Italien im Winter von 1876 auf 1877," *Neues Archiv* 3 (1878) 169, no. 2 and Brackmann, GP 2/2: 88 n. 6; S. Löwenfeld has "litteras ad a. 1116 posuit ... sed P. Ewald et in editione sua et in N. Archiv VII, 205 recte eas ad a. 1110 referendas esse monuit, *quia ad statuta concilii a. 1110 non. martii celebrati spectare verisimilius est*" (italics are mine).

It is possible that JL 6258, a privilege for the monastery of Fruttuaria in the diocese of Turin, dated 13 March 1110, indicates that Bishop Mainard of Turin (1099-1116) had come to Rome for the 1110 synod.[28] Nevertheless, his presence is not quite certain.

A passage in the *Histoire de Béarn* by Peter de Marca is confusing.[29] De Marca gathered from the cartulary of the abbey of Lescar that Gui, bishop of Lescar, suffragan of Auch, pursued before Pascal II the fight for the restoration of the monastery Saint-Pé-de-Générez to the bishopric of Lescar that had already involved his predecessor Sance in a quarrel with the bishop of Tarbes:

> Gui adjouste qu'il avoit succédé à Sance et renouvelé cette plainte en présence de l'évesque de Bigorre Grégoire, par devant le pape Paschal second, au Concile de Latran (qui est à mon advis celuy qui fut tenu l'an 1110) et ensuite par devant les papes Gelase second et Calliste second au Consile de Tolose, tenu l'an 1124.[30]

Sance was bishop of Lescar from 1095-1115, his successor, Vitus or Guido de Loth,[31] from 1115 to 1141. The only Lateran council of Paschal II which he could have attended is therefore the council of 1116 and not 1110 as de Marca thought, but even this is uncertain since his opponent from Tarbes[32] cannot have been Grégoire.[33] On the whole, the passage in the *Histoire de Béarn* seems rather unreliable. It is certain, however, that the bishops of Lescar and Tarbes were not in Rome in 1110.

---

[28] Paschal wrote: "... Proinde nos illius [Countess Agnes] et vestris [abbot of Fruttuaria] per confratrem nostrum Mainardum Taurinensem episcopum precibus annuentes praesenti decreto sancimus ut eadem villae novae medietate semper in monasterii vestri possessione permaneat ...."

[29] I wish to thank Professor R. Somerville for this reference. P. de Marca, *Histoire de Béarn*, 2nd ed. 2: 157-161 (book 5, ch. 31); see also *Gallia Christiana* 1 (Paris 1715) 1289-1291.

[30] Marca, *Histoire de Béarn*, 2nd ed. p. 159.

[31] The name Vitus de Loth is found in Gams, *Series episcoporum*, p. 563. Vitus was identical with Guido or Gui. See *Gallia Christiana* 1: 1291.

[32] The seat of the bishop of the county of Bigorre (independent from 819 to 1607 when it became part of France, and today coextensive with the Département des Hautes-Pyrénées) was at Tarbes, also known by the Latin names Tarba, Tarba Bigerriorum, and Castrum Bigorrae. (Gams, *Series episcoporum*, p. 634.)

[33] The bishops of Tarbes listed by Gams are Pontius (ad a. 1103), Heraclius? (*sic*) and Guilielmus, 1120-1141. But see G. Balencie, "Chronologie des évêques de Tarbes," *Mélanges Léonce Couture* (Toulouse 1902) 97-113, 106: "5 mars 1116 Concile de Latran: Grégoire, évêque de Bigorre, y soutint contre Gui de Lons, évêque de Lescar, la validité du rattachement de Saint-Pé au diocèse de Tarbes." Other entries for Gregory do not exist. See also Denis Labau, "Contribution à l'histoire de l'évêché de Lescar (suite)," *Revue régionaliste des Pyrénées* 52 (1970) 64-71.

## The Canons

Already contemporaries recognized the significance of the legislation of 1110 for it was widely disseminated. Although only two or three of the canons were included by Gratian in the *Decretum*,[34] they are found in several contemporary canonical collections[35] and were also copied by monastic chroniclers. The majority of these manuscripts, transmitting either the complete set of decrees or excerpts, were unknown to Weiland[36] and a new edition is called for.

### Edition

A full collation of both the manuscripts known to Weiland and of those newly discovered shows that they can basically be divided into two groups (A and B) which are distinguished by the inclusion or omission of c. *Constitutiones* as c. 1. A third group of codices, treated as a subgroup of class B, is the result of a conflation between manuscripts of class A and B. The apparatus criticus of the text below illustrates clearly the relationship between the classes and their subgroups and forms the basis for the introductory discussion accompanying the manuscript descriptions for both groups.

The manuscripts of class A contain the most extensive set of canons from Paschal's Lateran council of 1110, c. 1 *Constitutiones* to c. 7 *Quicumque* in this particular sequence. Not all of them, however, include the prologue found in two of them, MS Orléans, b.m. 315 and MS Wolfenbüttel, Guelf. Gud. 212. This is also true for the earliest manuscripts of class A: Vat. lat. 1346, Vat. lat. 4977 and Montecassino 522. The three codices just mentioned contain canonical collections and on the final folios as an addition the 1110 canons. The canons have not been altered and remain a unit, but in the manner of canonical collections the prologue has been reduced to an inscription. The Orléans (date, 1256) and Wolfenbüttel (s. 12 ex./s. 13 in.) manuscripts, the only ones that include the prologue in

---

[34] C.16 q.7 c.17 and C.1 q.1 c.125. C.16 q.7 c.24 and c.25 are either fragments of the 1110 decrees or are derived from the First Lateran Council of 1123 where Pope Calixtus II repeated the 1110 canons (Alberigo, *Conciliorum oecumenicorum decreta*, pp. 163-170).

[35] The *Collection in Seven Books*, the *Collection in Three Books*, the *Collection of Santa Maria Novella* as well as an unidentified collection in eight books at Wolfenbüttel, Herzog August Bibliothek, contain the text in full apart from a single canon. Parts of the decrees are found in the *Collection in Ten Parts* and the *Collection in Nine Books* of MS Archivio S. Pietro C. 118.

[36] MGH Const. 1: 567-569, no. 397.

class A, are the youngest members of the group. Nonetheless the Orléans codex was selected as the basic manuscript for the edition. The reasons are twofold: (1) Orléans 315 contains the prologue and (2) its readings agree generally with the text found in the early 'canonical' class A manuscripts. The assumption is made that the canons were originally preserved and distributed with the prologue. This conclusion is supported by the text in manuscripts of class B from the early twelfth century. They preserve a more complete prologue than is the case for class A codices.

For the purposes of this edition a subgroup of manuscripts will be considered part of class A. All of them are manuscripts of canonical collections which include the text of the 1110 canons, albeit incomplete, for both the prologue and c. 7 *Quicumque* are missing. The omission of the prologue in canonical manuscripts is not surprising. The omission of c. 7, while showing that the manuscripts of the subgroup are secondary to the codices of class A, is also easily explained and does not detract from the overall value of the manuscripts.

C. *Quicumque* provides a hint that the Lateran synod was not only concerned with strengthening the spiritual weapons at the disposal of the church to confront Henry v and his armies. Questions of general concern were debated in 1110 as well as at Guastalla and Troyes, for the content of the canon has nothing in common with the anti-investiture theme of the bulk of the material that was transmitted from the council, but instead prohibits the plunder of shipwreck victims. This divergence of content is probably the reason why the unit of 1110 material as preserved in the earliest and best manuscripts was rapidly broken up in the course of transmission. Two examples illustrate the process. There is in the first place MS Florence, Bibl. Naz., C.S., A 4.269, the *Collection of Santa Maria Novella.* The 1110 decisions are among the additions made some time after the completion of the collection. They are found at the end of the codex and are not included in the other copies of the collection, Florence, Bibl. Marucelliana MS C.386 and Florence, Bibl. Riccardiana MS 3006 (olim 3108) which were identified by Hubert Mordek.[37] The canons in MS C.S. A 4.269 are complete but c. *Quicumque* was provided with a new inscription, "Ex Paschali papa," although it follows directly upon c. 6 *Si quis.* Evidently the conscientious scribe wanted to make sure that the readers would know that this incongruous final canon was still part of Paschal's 1110 legis-

---

[37] "Handschriftenforschungen in Italien," p. 629 n. 7. It should be noted that these manuscripts also do not contain JL 6611, an important Paschal fragment, which is an integral part of the *Collection of Santa Maria Novella* in MS Bibl. Naz., C.S. A.4 269 (fol. 54v, col. a).

lation. Less conscientious scribes, or scribes who thought they knew better, omitted the canon. This procedure is demonstrated by the manuscripts of the *Collection in Seven Books*. The earliest manuscript, Vat. lat. 1346, contains the complete set of known 1110 canons. In both of the later copies of the collection, Cortona 43 and Vienna, ÖNB 2186, which otherwise transcribe the 1110 text exactly as found in Vat. lat. 1346, c. *Quicumque* is missing. It should be pointed out that the authoritative MS Vat. lat. 1346 provides also the desired evidence that *Quicumque* was not a later addition to the body of text.

It is ironic that nonetheless *Quicumque* became a well-known piece of Paschal legislation in northern France. Probably through the mediation of the *Collection in Ten Parts* that will be discussed below, the canon protecting shipwreck victims passed into canonical books that do not contain other elements of the 1110 legislation. The manuscripts are not included in the edition. They are:

1. MS Avranches, b.m. 146 (109) (s. 12), fol. 166v.
2. MS Paris, BN lat. 3871 (s. 12), fol. 176v.
3. MS Paris, BN lat. 3872 (s. 12), fol. cxli verso.
4. MS St. Omer, b.m. 364 (s. 12), fol. 154v.
5. MS Troyes, b.m. 480 (s. 12), fol. 126v.

In each case the decree is preceded by an extensive inscription that reflects the prologue: "Ex concilio Rome celebrato Paschali II presidente." What was copied depended evidently on the interests of the compiler.

Before the manuscripts of class A are briefly described and listed, a few words have to be said about MS Montecassino 522. The codex is the basic manuscript for John T. Gilchrist's edition of the *Diversorum patrum sententie sive Collectio in LXXIV titulos digesta*.[38] At issue here is a text found on pp. 385-386 (ink; pencil: 390 and 391). These pages are badly damaged and what remains of the faded script is often barely legible. A careful examination of the codex has now shown that the damaged passages, hitherto not accurately identified,[39] constitute a transcription of the canons of 1110. This identification is secure, but the necessary emendations are so numerous that the reconstituted text could not be used in the edition in spite of the great authority of the codex.

* * *

---

[38] Monumenta Iuris Canonici, Series B: Corpus Collectionum, vol. 1, Città del Vaticano 1973. See pp. xxxii-xxxiv for a description and bibliography of the codex.

[39] See ibid. and M. Inguanez, *Codicum Casinensium manuscriptorum catalogus*, vol. 3 (Montecassino 1940-41) 178-181.

## The manuscripts of class A

Fc: Florence, Bibl. Naz., Conventi Soppressi A 4.269 (Santa Maria Novella) Parchment, first half twelfth century, 227 folios in 2 columns, illuminated initials and rubrics. The manuscript contains the canonical collection of Santa Maria Novella.[40] As an addition on fol. 224rb to fol. 224vb the 1110 canons were transcribed, providing a separate inscription for c. 7 *Quicumque*. The origin of the manuscript cannot yet be determined precisely. It is Tuscan[41] and was acquired from Prato for the Dominicans of Santa Maria Novella in Florence by Frater Gerardus Naso, probably during the thirteenth century. A late thirteenth- or early fourteenth-century hand added a note on fol. iv: "Frater Gerardus Naso emit istum librum a quodam Pratenii pro conuentu fratrum predicatorum Sancte Marie Nouelle de Florentia .f. xiiii, et expendit pro ligatura et reparatura et aliis circa f. iii, tali intencione ut si aliquis ostenderet [quod] liber esset suus reddat supradictam pecuniam et recipiat librum. Qui legit hoc oret [ut] Christus dominus sibi donet regnum celorum saluator uitae bonorum." Conceivably, the codex was at the cathedral of Prato by the middle of the twelfth century, for letters, concerning the quarrel between the cathedral of Prato and St. Just from the pontificates of Innocent II (1130-1143), Celestine II (1143-1144), Lucius II (1144-1145), and Eugene III (1145-1153), are found in the codex as additions.[42] These additions are written in a hand later than that which transcribed the Paschal canons.

O: Orléans, Bibl. mun. 315 (267bis)
Parchment, s. 13, 211 pages, 251 × 183 mm, red and blue initials. The manuscript contains the *Chronicon S. Petri-Vivi Senonensis* by Clarius and supplementa.[43] An entry signed Hugo Mathoud in the lower margin of fol. 3r shows that the codex had been borrowed for thirty years by Jacques Sirmond who returned it to its owners at the monastery of Saint-Pierre-le-Vif at Sens in 1652. It was probably before this return that the manuscript had been examined by Gabriel Cossart who discovered among the supplementa the canons from the Lateran synod of 1110 on p. 183. Cossart published them

---

[40] Fournier-Le Bras, *Histoire* 2: 151-155; P. Fournier, "Les deux récensions de la collection canonique romaine dite le Polycarpus," *Mélanges d'Archéologie et d'Histoire* 37 (1918-19) 55-101, pp. 55-56 n. 2; Stickler, *Historia iuris canonici*, pp. 176-177; van Hove, *Prolegomena*, p. 326.

[41] Mordek, "Handschriftenforschungen," p. 629 n. 7.

[42] The were published from this manuscript by F. Carlesi, *Origini della città di Prato* (Prato 1904). See p. 73 with further references and the documentary appendix pp. 147-152, nos. 4-11; see also R. Davidsohn, *Geschichte von Florenz* 1 (Berlin 1896) 432 n. 6; Kehr IP 3: 120 nos. 7 and 10, and p. 136 nos. 2 and 4; Pflugk-Harttung, *Acta inedita* 2: 282 no. 321 and p. 320 no. 357.

[43] *Catalogue Général, Départements* 12 (1889) 161-164. Cf. the edition of the *Chronicon* by Duru, *Bibl. historique de l'Yonne*, 2: 449-597, esp. p. 582. Duru used for the edition MS Auxerre, b.m. 179. The chronicle was first partially edited by Luc d'Achery, *Spicilegium* 2 (Paris 1657) 463ff.

from this codex in volume 10 of the *Sacrosancta Concilia* (pp. 764-765). He had, however, not identified his exemplar beyond noting that he had taken the canons from a copy of Clarius' chronicle "eo quod editum est auctiore." Since none of the hitherto known manuscripts of the chronicle of Saint-Pierre-le-Vif contained the canons, Cossart's codex was feared lost until it was identified by R. Somerville in the library at Orléans.[44] Weiland used the text published by Cossart. O is the basic manuscript for the edition of the 1110 canons below.

Va: Città del Vaticano, Biblioteca Apostolica Vaticana, Vat. lat. 1346
Parchment, s. 12 in., 195 folios, red, green, brown, and yellow initials. The carefully written manuscript originated probably in Rome or in its vicinity[45] and contains the *Collection in Seven Books*. The 1110 canons are found on fol. 183r, directly following the canon from Paschal's Beneventan council of 1108. The canons are an addendum.

Vb: Città del Vaticano, Biblioteca Apostolica Vaticana, Vat. lat. 4977
Parchment, s. 12, 89 folios, 241 × 169 mm, red initials. The manuscript, once the property of Antonio Agustín, was most recently described by J. T. Gilchrist.[46] The 1110 decisions were added on the last folio (89r-v).

Rv: Rome, Biblioteca Vallicelliana, C.24
The manuscript was described and partially analyzed earlier.[47] The canons from the Lateran council of 1110, which were transcribed in the codex on fol. 46r-47v by Francisco Torres and subsequently copied on fol. 26r-27r, were published by Pflugk-Harttung. Pflugk-Harttung's edition was used by Weiland. Canons 1-14 of Urban's council of 1095 at Piacenza follow in the manuscript Paschal's Lateran canons as canons x-xv.[48] Pflugk-Harttung assumed that this pontiff repromulgated the legislation of his predecessor; Weiland admitted this as a possibility, but did not include the Piacenza text under 1110.[49] There is scarcely any evidence to support Pflugk-Harttung's contention since the "codex antiquus" of Francisco Torres is unknown. It should be noted, however, that I found the c. *Statuimus quoque ut ieiunia* (c. 14 in Weiland's edition of Piacenza) with Paschal inscriptions in two canonical collections: the *Collection in Seven Books* and the *Collection in Ten Parts* (10P). It is also known that Paschal intended that the canons of

---

[44] I wish to thank Professor R. Somerville for this information.

[45] Batlle and Gassó, *Pelagii epistulae*, p. lviii: "ante a. 1118 Romae vel in locis circumiacentibus, probabilius exscriptus."

[46] *Diversorum patrum sententie*, p. lxi with bibliography. For the codex see also F. Gossman, *Pope Urban II and Canon Law*, The Catholic University of American Canon Law Studies 403 (Washington 1960), especially pp. 16-18 and 109.

[47] Above ch. 2 n. 98.

[48] Weiland numbered these Piacenza canons 1-14 (MGH Const. 1: 560-563). The text published by Pflugk-Harttung under 1110 is very similar, but the different division between the canons resulted in a different number of canons.

[49] MGH Const. 1: 568 sub 5.

Piacenza should be used as guidelines during the attempt to establish peace with the German empire.[50] Nevertheless, since Rv, a sixteenth-century manuscript, is not of outstanding authority by itself, the Piacenza canons will in this edition not be considered part of the legislation of 1110.

Wg: Wolfenbüttel, Herzog August Bibliothek, Cod. Guelf. Gud. 212 (Heinemann 4517)

The codex, formerly at the monastery of Saint-Germain-des-Prés, is described by Sdralek. Part 4, a collection of canonical excerpts on fol. 51v-59v includes on fol. 56v-57r the canons from the 1110 synod. The material was compiled by John, bishop of Thérouanne.[51]

\* \* \*

The manuscripts of the subgroup of A

1. The *Collection in Three Books.*[52]

Pi: Pistoia, Archivio capitolare 135 (109)[53]

Parchment, s. 12 in., 290 fols., written in 2 columns. The codex was most recently described by Mr. John Erickson,[54] who dated the manuscript and the collection it contains anywhere from late 1111 to ca. 1123[55] in agreement with Fournier but in contrast to van Hove who proposed a date 1104-1110. The 1110 decrees are found on fol. 58vb-59ra.

Vc: Città del Vaticano, Biblioteca Apostolica Vaticana, Vat. lat. 3831

Parchment, s. 12 in., 151 fols., written in 2 columns. The same bibliography as for Pi is applicable. The 1110 canons are found on fol. 34rb = 2.8.19-2.8.21.

2. The *Collection in Seven Books.*[56]

Co: Cortona, Pubblica Biblioteca Comunale e dell'Accademia Etrusca 43

---

[50] See JL 6050.

[51] Sdralek, *Wolfenbüttler Fragmente*, pp. 6 and 50 with n. 4, and Somerville, *Decreta Claromontensia*, pp. 56-57.

[52] Stickler, *Historia iuris canonici*, p. 179; van Hove, *Prolegomena*, p. 328; Fournier-Le Bras, *Histoire* 2: 198-203. The collection will be edited by Dom Picasso, Milan.

[53] The codex was consulted on microfilm kindly lent by the Institute of Medieval Canon Law, Berkeley.

[54] John H. Erickson, "The Collection in Three Books and Gratian's Decretum," *Bulletin of Medieval Canon Law*, n.s. 2 (1972) 67-75. See also, in addition to the references given by Erickson, R. Somerville, "The Council of Pisa, 1135," p. 102 and n. 27 as well as H. Mordek, "Proprie auctoritates apostolice sedis. Ein zweiter Dictatus papae Gregors VII.?" DA 28 (1972) 105-132. Somerville has shown that Mansi used the manuscript. Fournier, "Une collection canonique italienne du commencement du XIIe siècle," *Annales de l'Université de Grenoble* 6 (1894) 343-409, p. 343, was also aware of this fact; but Mansi can have made only occasional use of the codex. He overlooked the 1110 canons.

[55] Erickson, "Three Books," p. 69.

[56] See the bibliography given above ch. 4 n. 10.

The codex is best described by G. Mancini.[57] Many of its folios are unnumbered. The canons promulgated in 1110, with the exception of c. *Quicumque*, are found on an unnumbered folio (following fol. 41v) at the beginning of book 1. Again on an unnumbered folio (following fol. 215r) c. 14 of the council of Piacenza held by Pope Urban II in 1095[58] is transcribed as part of book 6 with an inscription attributing the decree to Pope Paschal II.

Vy: Vienna, Österreichische Nationalbibliothek, MS 2186 (jur. can. 80)
The 1110 text is part of book 1 of the collection and is found on fol. 48v-49r. The same bibliography applies as indicated above, ch. 4 n. 10.

3. The *Collection in Eight Books*.

Wh: Wolfenbüttel, Herzog August Bibliothek, cod. Guelf. Helmst. 308 (Heinemann 342)
Parchment, s. 12 ex./13 in., 137 fols., 295 × 193 mm, red, blue or green initials, rubrics, written in 2 columns. The manuscript contains a canonical collection in eight books. On fol. 129ra-129rb the 1110 legislation is found (8.11.3).

A second group of manuscripts for the 1110 decrees is class B. Class B is distinguished from class A through the omission of c. 1 *Constitutiones*. No other important variations separate the classes. MS Brussels, B.R. 11 196-11 197 and MS Rome, Vall. F.54 exemplify class B. They contain the prologue followed by c. 2 *Apostolorum* and conclude with c. 7 *Quicumque*. It is useless to speculate as to the possible author of this 1110 transmission.

A subgroup within class B is formed apparently through the conflation of a manuscript of type A with this class. The exemplar of this mixed redaction must have been MS Metz 221 (E 14) or its archetype. The author of the Metz entry which provided the basic text for Weiland's edition[59] seems to have copied a text of class B while having also access to a codex of class A. In addition, he must have known Paschal's Troyes legislation, for after the final canons of class B (*Quicumque*) he added the lemma: "Illud etiam repetitum et confirmatum est quod in Trecensi concilio de inuestituris aecclesiasticis promulgatum est, quod ita se habet," following up this remark with a copy of c. 1 *Constitutiones*, changing the reading "sanctorum canonum" to "patrum." Scheffer-Boichorst pointed out that the lemma could not be considered part of the text, and furthermore that the legislation

---

[57] *I Manoscritti della Libreria del Comune e dell'Accademia Etrusca di Cortona* (Cortona 1884) 28-29. See also G. Mazzatinti, *Inventari dei Manoscritti delle Biblioteche d'Italia*, vol. 18 (Florence 1912) 26-27 and P. Fournier, "Les deux récensions," p. 56 and the references given for the *Collection in Seven Books* in general.
[58] MGH Const. 1: 563.
[59] MGH Const. 1: 567-569.

referred to was not, as might be thought, the Troyes canon,[60] but indeed c. *Constitutiones* from 1110 in Cossart's manuscript of the *Chronicon Senonense*.[61] These observations remain valid even though the lemma can no longer be claimed as a contribution of the author of the *Annales Patherbrunnenses* as Scheffer-Boichorst thought.

Weiland's Metz codex is the only manuscript that exhibits both the lemma and the complete text of c. *Constitutiones*. The lemma with an abbreviation of the decree is found in a manuscript at Wolfenbüttel, cod. Guelf. 9.4 Aug. 4º, and in the *Annales Patherbrunnenses*.

\* \* \*

The manuscripts of class B

B: Brussels, Bibl. royale, 11 196-11 197
A copy of the Register of Pope Gregory I, this early twelfth-century manuscript, v.d. Gheyn Cat. no. 1235, contains on the first 10 folios the *Gesta Romanae aecclesiae contra Hildebrandum* by Cardinal Beno.[62] Between items 10 and 11 of this anti-Gregorian treatise, Paschal's canons from 1110 were inserted followed by the famous letter of Pope Gregory VII to Bishop Hermann of Metz (JL 5201).[63] The insertions occur on fol. 9ra.[64] An ex libris (fol. 1r, upper margin) yields the provenance of the codex: "Iste est liber hospitalis sancti Nicolai prope Cusam." The founder of the hospital, the humanist Nicholas Cusanus, cardinal of S. Pietro in Vincoli and bishop of Brixen,[65] had left it together with other volumes to his foundation.[66] The

---

[60] See C.16 q.7 c.17. On the basis of Mansi 20: 1221 Friedberg attributed *Constitutiones* to the council of Troyes. Paschal did indeed pronounce at Troyes the same prohibition as shown by JL 6145 to Archbishop Rothard of Mainz, but according to the manuscript evidence the canon was repeated in 1110.

[61] *Annales Patherbrunnenses*, p. 121 n. 4.

[62] Ed. K. Francke, MGH Libelli de lite 2 (1892) 369-422. Francke used B. Cf. Potthast, *Wegweiser*, 1: 146.

[63] Jaffé edited the letter from B (*Monumenta gregoriana*, Bibliotheca rerum germanicarum 2 [1865] pp. 465-467).

[64] In addition to J. van den Gheyn et al., *Catalogue des manuscrits de la Bibliothèque Royale de Belgique* 2 (1902) 237, see L. Bethmann, *Archiv* 7 (1839) 872-875. Bethmann indicated that a London manuscript, B.M. Cotton Tiberius B VIII, fols. 290-301, was related to the Brussels codex. I am indebted to Cynthia M. Pyle who kindly checked the London codex. It does not contain the Paschal canons.

[65] His dates are 1401-1464. A Cusanus bibliography for the years 1920-1961 was compiled by Hans Kleinen and Robert Danzer, *Mitteilungen und Forschungen der Cusanus Gesellschaft* 1 (1961) 95-126. See also P. O. Kristeller, "Nicolò Cusano agli inizi del mondo moderno," *Atti del Congresso internazionale in occasione del V centenario della morte di Nicolò Cusano*, pp. 175-193.

[66] G. Mantese, "Ein Notarielles Inventar von Büchern und Wertgegenständen aus dem Nachlass des Nikolaus von Kues," *Mitteilungen und Forschungen der Cusanus Gesellschaft* 2 (1962) 85-116.

codex was acquired from the hospital by the Museum Bollandianum in Antwerp as an old shelf-mark, " + 119," on the inside front cover shows, and from the Bollandists by the Bibliothèque royale. It was used by Weiland.

Rf: Rome, Biblioteca Vallicelliana, F.54
The late eleventh-, early twelfth-century manuscript consists of three parts which were bound together. The 1110 canons are part of the second section which was written in Beneventan script — with the sole exception of the canons themselves. They are found on fol. 169v.[67]

\* \* \*

The manuscripts of the subgroup of B

Mb: Metz, Bibl. mun. 221 (E 14)
The manuscript, with an ex libris from the church of St. Arnulph in Metz, was destroyed during the last war. In addition to the catalogue entry,[68] a brief description of the contents published by Waitz is useful.[69] The manuscript was used by Weiland, and his text is used in the present edition.

Wa: Wolfenbüttel, Herzog August Bibliothek, cod. Guelf. 9.4 Aug. 4° (Heinemann 2985)
The manuscript contains the *Diversorum patrum sententie* with various additions and was described most recently by Gilchrist.[70] The final addition on fol. 158vb-159ra are the canons of 1110.

*Annales Patherbrunnenses*, consisting of:
        Chronicon Coloniense (C)
        Annales Hildesheimenses (H)
        Annalista Saxo (An)

According to Scheffer-Boichorst, who reconstituted the lost *Annales Patherbrunnenses*,[71] the text of the Lateran council was inserted into the chronicle by its author,[72] a monk from the monastery of Abdinghof at Paderborn.[73] He

---

[67] A full bibliography is given by Gilchrist, *Diversorum patrum sententie*, pp. xlvii-xlix.

[68] *Catalogue Général, Départements* (Quarto series) 5: 96-97 and ibid. (Octavo series) 53: 12.

[69] *Archiv* 8 (1843) 453: "Liber S. Arnulphi. Orationes; am Schluss Cyceln 1064-1196 ohne Noten; dann allerlei chronologische Notizen. Auf dem vorletzten Blatte: Anno dominicae incarn. 1110 facta est in Lateranensi aecclesia synodus praesidente domino Paschale II papa indict. 3 Nonas Marcii, ubi haec capitula edita sunt. 'Apostolorum canonibus statutum est ...' etc. abgeschrieben. Noch einige Auszüge aus Canonen über das Verhältnis der geistlichen und weltlichen Gewalt ...."

[70] Pp. l-li.

[71] For a recent evaluation of the reconstruction of the lost *Annales Patherbrunnenses* see F.-J. Schmale, "'Paderborner' oder 'Korveyer' Annalen?" DA 30 (1974) 505-526, esp. p. 508. The relationship between the annals of Paderborn and its constituent parts is analyzed by Scheffer-Boichorst and will not be repeated here.

[72] *Annales Patherbrunnenses*, p. 87.

[73] Ibid. pp. 29 and 84-85. Cf., however, Schmale as above n. 71.

consequently edited the text. His edition was used by Weiland and also below although the variants in the apparatus criticus of Scheffer-Boichorst seem to indicate that it is unlikely that the text in C and An was derived from the same source. The *Annales Hildesheimenses* contain only the prologue.

* * *

The text

Summary of the sigla employed.

Class A:
    Fc   Florence, Bibl. Naz., C.S. A 4.269
    O    Orléans, Bibl. mun. 315
    Va   Vat. lat. 1346
    Rv   Rome, Vall. C.24
    Wg   Wolfenbüttel cod. Guelf. Gud. 212

Class A subgroup:
    Pi   Pistoia, Archivio cap. 135
    Vc   Vat. lat. 3831
    Co   Cortona, Pub. Bibl. 43
    Vy   Vienna ÖNB 2186
    Wh   Wolfenbüttel, cod. Guelf. Helmst. 308

Class B:
    B    Brussels, B.R. 11 196-11 197
    Rf   Rome, Vall. F.54

Class B subgroup:
    Mb   Metz, Bibl. mun. 221
    Wa   Cod. Guelf. 9.4 Aug. 4°
    C    Chronicon Coloniense
    H    Annales Hildesheimenses
    An   Annalista Saxo

consensus codicum B sine CHAn = Λ

Basic MS: O

Anno[a] dominice incarnationis .mcx.[b] in lateranensi ecclesia[c] presidente domno Paschali[d] .ii.[e] indictione .iii. nonas martii.[f]

    [a] Anno—martii *om. Va Vb Rv*    Ex decretis Paschalis pp. ii. *Va*    Paschalis pp. *Vb*    Ex dictis Paschalis pp. *Fc*    Paschalis pp. ii. *Rv Co Vy*    Pascalis .ii. *Pi Vc*    Anno] Item. Decreta ex concilio Paschalis quod habuit Rome *praem. B*    Anno—martii] Sinodus gloriosa non. mart. (non. mart. synodus *tr. H*) in lateranensi aecclesia praesidente domno papa Paschali celebratur, praesentibus plurimis episcopis et abbatibus (abbatibus, episcopis *An*), ubi omnium consensu haec capitula edita sunt *substit.* HCAn (praesentibus—sunt *om. H*)    [b] facta est *add.* Λ    [c] synodus *add.* Λ    [d] P. *tantum Wg*    [e] papa *add.* Λ    [f] martii] ubi haec capitula edita sunt *add.* Λ

**1.** ⌈Constitutiones[a] sanctorum canonum sequentes statuimus ut quicumque clericorum ab hac hora[b] inuestituram ecclesie[c] uel[d] ecclesiastice dignitatis de manu laici[e] acceperit et qui ei manum[f] imposuerit gradus sui periculo subiaceat et communione priuetur.⌉ [1]

[a] Constitutiones—priuetur *om.* Λ *cum CHAn*   [b] in antea *add. Rv*   [c] ecclesie] uel *praem. VaCoVy Wh*   [d] ecclesie uel *om. Vc*   [e] laica *Rv*   [f] manus *Vb*

[1] Cf. Canones Apostolorum c. 30 vers. Isidor. (H 29) as well as c. 29 vers. Dion. 1 and C. 30 vers. Dion. 2 (3) (Turner 1/1, 20)   Deusd. 4.22   Conc. Claromon. a. 1095 (Somerville, *Decreta Claromontensia,* p. 90 c. 2)   See above p. 71, c. 7 of Guastalla and above p. 93 c. 5 of Troyes   Grat. C. 16 q.7 c.17

**2.** Apostolorum canonibus statutum[a] est ut *omnium negotiorum ecclesiasticorum curam[b] episcopus habeat et ea uelut Deo[c] contemplante dispenset.*[1]

[a] instatutum *Pi*   institutum *Vc*   [b] curas *Vb*   [c] domino *B*

[1] Canones Apostol. vers. Dion. 1, 2 (3), c. 38 (Turner 1/1: 26)   Burch. 1.210

**3.** Item in[a] Antiocheno concilio statutum est ut *que sunt ecclesie sub omni sollicitudine et conscientia bona et fide[b] que in Deum est conseruentur; que etiam[c] dispensanda sunt iudicio[d] et potestate pontificis dispensentur, cui commissus est populus et anime que* intra[e] *ecclesiam[f] congregantur.*[1]

[a] et *praem. Rv*   [b] fide] non facta *add.* C   [c] et *Vc*   enim *VaCoVy Wh*   [d] et *praem. Rv*   [e] infra *An Wa*   [f] sunt *add. An*

[1] Conc. Antioch 1 vers. Dion. 1 and 2, c. 24 (Turner 2/2: 301-303)   Cf. Ans. 6.156

**4.** Item Stephanus[a] martyr[b] scribit[c]: *Laicis[d] quamuis religiosi sint nulli[e] tamen de ecclesiasticis facultatibus[f] aliquid disponendi legitur unquam attributa facultas neque deinceps fieri permittimus sed[g] omnino interdicentes prohibemus.*[1]

[a] papa *add. Vb*   papa et *add. Mb*   beatus *praem.* C   [b] martyri *Vb*   [c] scripsit *O*   [d] Laici *Vb Vy Wh C An*   [e] nulli] nullatenus *Rv*   [f] de aecclesiasticis facultatibus nulli tamen *tr. B*   [g] sed—prohibemus *scrip. cum cett., om. O Wg*

[1] Ps.-Stephanus I, ep. 2.12 (H 186.9-10; JK †131; F 3.806 no. 43) 74T c. 260 (inscr. Stephanus episcopus omnibus orthodoxis)   Cf. Ans. 5.10   Deusd. 3.47 and 4.54
H. Fuhrmann, *Pseudoisidorische Fälschungen* 2: 526 n. 268 (see also ibid. p. 584 nn. 431 and 432) suggests that Anselm of Lucca and Deusdedit who combined the Pseudo-Isidorian decretal of Pope Stephen with a reference to the Symachan synod of 502, may have used an intermediate collection. This is probably also true for Pope Paschal II because his inscription uses the insert "martyr," only present in the collection of Deusdedit, while the final subordinate clause "neque deinceps—prohibemus" is only found in 74T c. 260. Cf. above p. 69 c. 3 of the Anselm tradition for the council of Guastalla.

5. Si quis ergo<sup>a</sup> principum uel aliorum laicorum dispositionem seu<sup>b</sup> donationem<sup>c</sup> rerum siue<sup>d</sup> possessionum ecclesiasticarum<sup>e</sup> sibi uendicauerit<sup>f</sup> ut sacrilegus iudicetur. Clerici<sup>g</sup> uero seu<sup>h</sup> monachi qui eas per illorum<sup>i</sup> potestatem<sup>k</sup> susceperint<sup>l</sup> excommunicationi subiciantur.<sup>m</sup>

    <sup>a</sup> uero *Wg*    <sup>b</sup> seu] sua *VaCoVy Wh*    uel *An*    seu donationem *om. Wg*    <sup>c</sup> donationem] dominationum *Vc Rv*    <sup>d</sup> siue] seu *Rv*    <sup>e</sup> dispositionem—ecclesiasticarum] dispositionem aecclesiasticarum *tantum Vb*    ecclesiasticarum] aecclesiarum *Wa C*    <sup>f</sup> uendicauerit] aliquid *praem. Vb Rv*    <sup>g</sup> *lect. incerta Vb*    <sup>h</sup> seu] siue *An*    <sup>i</sup> eorum *Wg*    <sup>k</sup> potestatem illorum *tr. C*    <sup>l</sup> acceperint *Rv*    <sup>m</sup> *lect. incerta Vb*

6. Sunt praeterea quidam qui<sup>a</sup> uel uiolentia uel<sup>b</sup> fauore<sup>c</sup> non permittunt ecclesias<sup>d</sup> regulariter ordinari, hos etiam decernimus ut sacrilegos iudicandos. Qui uero ecclesias eorum uiolentia uel potestatiuo fauore susceperint, excommunicationi subiciantur.[1]

    <sup>a</sup> qui *om. O*    <sup>b</sup> potestatiuo *add. Mb*    <sup>c</sup> susceperint excommunicationi subiciantur *male add. Mb*    <sup>d</sup> ecclesiam *Vb*

    [1] Cf. Grat. C.1 q.1 c. 125 (Sunt quidam—iudicandos)

7. Quicumque<sup>a</sup> res naufragorum diripiunt ut raptores et fratrum necatores ab<sup>b</sup> ecclesie liminibus<sup>c</sup> excludantur.[1]

    <sup>a</sup> Quicumque—excludantur *om. CoVy*    *PiVc Wh*    Quicumque] *inscr.* Ex Paschali papa *praem. Fa*    <sup>b</sup> ab] *om. B*    <sup>c</sup> liminibus *om. Wa CAn*

    [1] Cf. Greg. *VII*, Reg. 5, 14a, Conc. Rom. a. 1078 c. 13

⌐Illud<sup>a</sup> etiam repetitum et confirmatum est quod in Trecensi concilio de inuestituris aecclesiasticis promulgatum<sup>b</sup> est, quod ita se habet: Constituciones<sup>c</sup> sanctorum<sup>d</sup> canonum sequentes statuimus ut quicumque clericorum ab hac hora inuestituram aecclesiae uel aecclesiastice dignitatis de manu laici acceperit et qui ei manum inposuerit, gradus sui periculo subiaceat et communione priuetur.⌐[1]

    <sup>a</sup> Illud—priuetur *om. A cum B Rf*    <sup>b</sup> confirmatum *An*    <sup>c</sup> Constituciones] *cf. supra c. 1*    patrum sequentes *add. Wa*    patrum *add. C*    patrum etc. *add. An*    <sup>d</sup> sanctorum—priuetur *om. Wa CAn*

    [1] See above p. 71 and 93.    Cf. Grat. C.16 q.7 c.17

## Fragments of the 1110 Decrees in Canonical Collections

A chief means of distribution of the 1110 decisions were canonical collections. Manuscripts preserving the complete or almost complete body of text were included in the edition, but several canons were incorporated into additional canonical collections in fragmentary manner.[74] Manuscripts containing only c. 7 *Quicumque* were discussed earlier.[75] C. 1 *Constitutiones* is found on fol. 282r of the *Chronological Decretal Collection* in MS Vat. lat. 3829[76] under the rubric: "Ex decretis Paschalis .ii. pp." and the inscription: "Ut per laicum nullus clericus aliquo honore inuestiatur. Paschalis .ii. pp. dixit." The single canon from 1110 is followed immediately by the *acta* of the Lateran council of 1112. The *Collection in Nine Books* in the Vatican manuscript, Archivio S. Pietro C. 118[77] preserved in addition to c. 1 *Constitutiones* (fol. 33r = 3.5.24) also an abbreviation of c.6 (fol. 25v = 3.1.24) which corresponds to Grat. C.1 q.1 c.25.

A yet more substantial part of the 1110 canons has been incorporated into the *Collection in Ten Parts* (10P).[78] Three of Paschal's decrees can be found in part 4 of the collection: c. 7 *Quicumque*[79] and c. 5 *Si quis* with c. 6 *Sunt preterea*. Canons 5 and 6 were entered as a unit.[80] 10P preserved the canons with inscriptions that clearly show that they were originally excerpted from a copy of the 1110 decrees with the prologue.[81] One of the variants of cc. 5 and 6 seems related to the text preserved in MS Guelf. Gud.

---

[74] Not included in this discussion are stray Paschal canons found occasionally in canonical manuscripts which do not add to available information. Also omitted are the 1110 canons cited in ep. 29 of Hildebert of Lavardin (PL 71, cols. 248-253).

[75] See above p. 110.

[76] Fournier-Le Bras, *Histoire* 2: 210-218; Batlle and Gassó, *Pelagii epistulae*, pp. xl-xli (*lege* fol. 287); H. Fuhrmann, "Ein Papst Ideo," in *Etudes d'histoire du droit canonique dédiées à Gabriel Le Bras* (Paris 1965) 89-98; Kuttner, "Some Roman Manuscripts," pp. 21-22 (a misprint altered the shelf-mark to Vat. lat. 3529).

[77] Fournier-Le Bras, *Histoire* 2: 203-208; van Hove, *Prolegomena*, p. 240 and p. 328; Stickler, *Historia iuris canonici*, p. 179.

[78] A bibliography for 10P is given above ch. 1 n. 82. For the connection between 10P and MS Gud. 212 see Somerville, *Decreta Claromontensia*, p. 60.

[79] Berlin, DS, Phillipps 1746 (Rose 95) 4.20.9 (fol. 71ra); Cambridge, Corpus Christi College 94, 4.21.9 (fol. 70r); Florence, B.Naz., C.S. D 2 1476, 4.21.7 (fol. 99v); Paris, BN lat. 10743, 4.21.9 (p. 224); Vienna ÖNB 2178 (jur. can. 91), 4.21.9 (fol. 86ra).

[80] Berlin, DS, Phillipps 1746, 4.28.3 (fol. 73vb); Cambridge, CCC 94, 4.29.3 (fol. 72v); Florence, B.Naz., C.S. D 2 1476, 4.29.3 (fol. 102v); Paris, BN lat. 10743, 4.29.3 (p. 231); Vienna, ÖNB 2178, 4.29.3 (fol. 89rb).

[81] The inscription to c. 7 reads: "Ex concilio Rome Paschali II presidente celebrato"; the inscription to cc. 5 and 6: "Ex concilio Romano Paschali .II. presidente habito."

212 (Wg),[82] but because of the fragmentary nature of the text in 10P it is not possible to consider the text preserved in this collection from northern France as either part of class A or class B. Altogether, Paschal is well represented in 10P, for in addition to these 1110 canons several other significant texts were preserved for Paschal's pontificate by the compiler, Walter, archdeacon of Thérouanne. Paschal's correspondence with Anselm of Canterbury in 1102 was already mentioned,[83] and Paschal's correspondence from 1111 and 1112 with Archbishop Guy of Vienne, later Pope Calixtus II, was also incorporated in the form of excerpts. The letters are highly critical of the prelate and must have been included in 10P in order to support the papal position after the 'pravilege' of April 1111.

OTHER NOTABLE DECISIONS OF THE COUNCIL

Apart from the canons, no synodal judgments have been transmitted.

---

[82] *Seu donationem* of c. 5 is omitted. The second variant is the omission of *ergo* also in c. 5. No variants are found in c. 7. C. 6, *Sunt praeterea quidam* is also transmitted in the margins of one of the manuscripts of Gerhoch of Reichersberg's *De edificio Dei*, ed. Ernst Sackur, MGH Libelli de lite 3 (1897) 131-202, p. 178.

[83] Above pp. 18-19.

# Conclusion

The pontificate of Paschal II was a very successful one seen in the light of the councils he celebrated between his accession and his capture by King Henry V in February 1111. Relative to other periods of papal history the evidence that can be assembled is still scanty; authenticity and precise attributions for conciliar canons are often difficult to establish and sometimes cannot be shown at all. Nevertheless, it has been possible to remove many uncertainties and to increase sources. Thus the main features of Paschalian policies begin to emerge. It may well be asked whether it is justified to place so much emphasis on decisions and discussions surrounding Paschal's Italian and French synods. Not all councils are of equal significance, but the terminology used to describe the meetings of Guastalla, Troyes and at the Lateran in 1110 clearly brings out their great importance to contemporaries. The term "general concilium," "generalis synodus," is used in 1106 and 1110, and several expressions of equal standing refer to 1107: "generalis tractatus," "universale concilium," "synodalis conventus," as well as "concilium generale." Under the reform papacy general synods took the place of the old and venerated ecumenical councils,[1] and ecumenical, in fact, were the import and validity of these synods celebrated by Paschal. The evidence shows that negotiations carried out at the curia in the interim between councils would later be discussed at the assemblies if warranted by their intrinsic importance. St. Anselm of Canterbury was not certain whether in addition to Paschal's letters rejecting the royal request for investiture of the English clergy, the pontiff had not indeed entrusted the royal emissaries with verbal assurances to the king, and therefore he dispatched a new delegation, just to make sure. But whatever the case may have been, verbal message or no, according to the *Liber Pontificalis* Paschal's dispensation to permit King Henry I of England in effect to require homage for the time being[2] was discussed by the assembly at

---

[1] Fuhrmann, "Das ökumenische Konzil," pp. 680-686.
[2] JL 6073: "... Tu autem ... ab illa prohibitione sive ut tu credis excommunicatione absolvimus quam ab antecessore nostro sancte memorie Urbano papa adversus investituras aut hominia factam intelligis .... Si qui vero deinceps preter investituras ecclesiarum prelationes

Guastalla and very likely also at Troyes in the presence of an English delegation that had specifically been requested to attend. It deserves notice that Henry I waited until after the French meeting before publicizing the compromise. The eminent position of the synods seems clear.

The letters, chronicles, canonical collections, Cardinal Boso's dossier excerpted from Paschal's register, and manuscript annotations where traces of conciliar legislation survived, reflect some well-marked characteristics. Most striking although not at all unexpected is the sense of continuity with previous papal policy which they convey. The *vestigia praedecessorum* are evident everywhere as this edition shows, and just as Pope Urban II considered himself the 'pedisequus' of Gregory VII,[3] Paschal can be justly described as the political heir of Urban. The German schism was the most serious problem facing Urban as well as Paschal. Paschal's German policy is completely inspired by the decrees of Piacenza and related considerations, from parallelism in intent to parallelism in location.[4] Although circumstances had temporarily shifted in favor of the papacy, Paschal faced at Guastalla the same task of reconciling schismatic German clergy which had earlier been confronted by his predecessor. As long as the legitimacy of the papacy was accepted, and the concerned cleric was not directly involved in simony or criminal behavior, Paschal as well as Urban unconditionally readmitted the offenders to communion with Rome and allowed them to retain their offices. Both popes relied on ancient precedents that permitted the rigor of the laws to be tempered "pro necessitate temporis et utilitate ecclesie."[5] Paschal, the former Rainer, cardinal priest of S. Clemente who had served as Urban's legate to Spain, participated in Urban's council of Bari held in 1098 (JL 5929) and probably also accompanied the pontiff to Clermont (cf. JL 5812, 5818, 5820, 5835 and 5855), provided continuity with

---

assumpserint, etiamsi regi hominia fecerint, nequaquam ob hoc a benedictionis munere arceantur donec per omnipotentis Dei gratiam ad hoc omittendum cor regium tue predicationis imbribus molliatur ...."

[3] See for instance JL 5348.

[4] For the canons of Piacenza see MGH Const. 1: 560-563, no. 393; on Urban's German policy in general see the recent contribution by Becker, "Urban II.," pp. 252-257. Cf. Klaus Ganzer, *Die Entwicklung des auswärtigen Kardinalats*, p. 48 n. 22 on the possibility that Paschal during his cardinalate accompanied Urban II to France.

[5] JL 6152. See in this connection in particular S. Kuttner, "Urban II and the Doctrine of Interpretation: A Turning Point?" *Post Scripta, Essays on Medieval Law and the Emergence of the European State in Honor of Gaines Post*, Studia Gratiana 15 (1972) 53-85, and the bibliography given there. The theory of dispensation goes back to late antiquity, and in particular to Popes Leo the Great, Nicholas I and Innocent I. For Urban II see also Becker, "Urban II.," p. 258 and for Paschal see, for example, the edition of the pertinent canons of Guastalla, and JL 6073 as well as JL 6152.

Urban's pontificate, a continuity which is equally evident in respects other than the councils, most notably in the monastic policies pursued and the further development of the cardinalate.

The *vestigia praedecessorum*, however, encompass more than the legislation of Paschal's immediate predecessor. "Ea vero que sacri apostolorum canones, et Antiochenum, ac universa concilia, et predecessores nostri, et precipue felicis memorie domnus Gregorius et Urbanus de his [investituris] prohibuerunt ... ego prohibeo ...," (JL 6325) wrote Paschal in a letter to Guy of Vienne after the debacle of Ponte Mammolo. The phraseology of the letter recalls Paschal's declaration at the Lateran council of 1112,[6] but as the texts of his early councils show, it does not represent a departure in policy. By preference Paschal relies in his legislation on precedents to which secular lawmakers would attribute usage from time immemorial. The "decreta patrum nostrorum," the "sanctorum patrum instituta," "constitutiones sanctorum canonum,"[7] in Paschal's terminology are canonical collections[8] in which he finds precedents for his own decisions. The ancient *Ordo de concilio celebrando* required the use of at least one canonical collection at every synod,[9] and with Pope Leo ix, the first of the reform popes, the use of canon law received new emphasis. Haphazard and occasional attempts to cite canon law were replaced by systematic use of the "decreta patrum," that is, ancient authorities whether they be patristic excerpts, papal "decretals," or conciliar canons. The use of canon law by Pope Gregory vii is still debated,[10] but the extensive and close reliance on canonical precedents in most of the examined legislation of Paschal ii cannot be doubted. The third canon of the Boso tradition for the council of Guastalla illuminates conciliar procedure during his pontificate. It refers in one breath to "capitula" from St. Augustine, a papal letter and a canon from an African council. These canons were evidently recited and pre-

---

[6] MGH Const. 1: 570-574, nos. 399 and 400.

[7] See the Index.

[8] Cf. W. Hartmann, "Beziehungen des Normannischen Anonymus zu frühscholastischen Bildungszentren," DA 31 (1975) 108-143, p. 114 n. 24 for the terminology used by Bernold of Constance.

[9] The pertinent bibliography and a summing up of the discussion surrounding the Ordo were recently given by H. Fuhrmann, "Rechtswissenschaft," p. 184 n. 21.

[10] From the extensive literature see in particular J. Gilchrist, "Gregory vii and the Juristic Sources of his Ideology," *Studia Gratiana* 12 (1967), Collectanea S. Kuttner 2, pp. 1-37 and E. Caspar, "Gregor vii. in seinen Briefen," *Historische Zeitschrift* 130 (1924) 1-30 as well as Fuhrmann, "Rechtswissenschaft," pp. 189-192. Cf. also G. Ladner, "Two Gregorian Letters: On the Sources and Nature of Gregory vii's Reform Ideology," *Studi Gregoriani* 5 (1956) 221-242 and H. Mordek, "Proprie auctoritates apostolice sedis," DA 28 (1972) 105-132. See also Karl F. Morrison, *Tradition and Authority in the Western Church 300-1140* (Princeton 1969), pp. 273-274.

sumably discussed at the synod in order to reach a "new" decision concerning contemporary schismatics, that is, the imperial clergy. The following canon 4, *Per multos*, embodies this decision. The decree expresses basic principles. The influence of Urban's council at Piacenza can be clearly perceived, but even greater reliance was placed on the laws of the ancient church as c. 3 shows. Under Paschal II the aspect of the Gregorian reform best described as "restoration"[11] is strongly emphasized. The *libertas ecclesiae* in Paschal's opinion is guaranteed by the ancient "praecepta canonum."

In the case of the synod of Guastalla it is impossible to determine which canonical collection or collections were used. The canons from the synod of Troyes as well as Paschal's letter dispatched from this council to Archbishop Rothard (JL 6145) are firm evidence for the use of the *Collectio canonum* of Cardinal Deusdedit on this latter occasion. Deusdedit (d. 1098/99) had dedicated his collection to Pope Victor III. He was a close collaborator of the papacy, so close indeed that Ernst Sackur dubbed him "court canonist."[12] He belonged to the inner circle of reformers and while it is difficult, not to say impossible, to equate the mentality of a particular pope with the attitude displayed in a canonical collection, it is clear that Paschal II did indeed rely greatly on the compilation of Deusdedit.[13] The *collectio canonum* of Deusdedit is in some ways less sophisticated than the compilation of his contemporary Anselm of Lucca, but it served well to buttress papal claims to primacy, both spiritually as well as with regard to temporal possessions of the Roman church. That the latter claim was not disregarded by Paschal is shown in the context of the early synods through the declaration of war against Benevento at the council of Melfi.

It would be an error, however, to conclude that Paschal and his advisers were one-sided and narrow-minded in their reliance on canonical collections. At the councils several compilations seem to have been used side by side with each other. At the Lateran synod of 1110 Paschal quoted from the *Diversorum patrum sententie* (*Collection in 74 Titles*). On another occasion he seems to have cited the *Decretum* of Burchard of Worms, a collection whose continued importance for Italy in the twelfth century is now

---

[11] See Ladner, "Two Gregorian Letters," and idem, *The Idea of Reform, its Impact on Christian Thought and Action in the Age of the Fathers* (Cambridge, Mass. 1959) Index, s.v. "Restoration."

[12] Ernst Sackur, "Der Dictatus papae und die Canonsammlung des Deusdedit," *Neues Archiv* 18 (1893) 137-153, esp. pp. 140-141. For Deusdedit in general see now Fuhrmann, *Einfluss und Verbreitung*, 2: 522-533 with further references.

[13] Cf. Blumenthal, "Patrimonia and Regalia in February 1111: Some Notes," *Law, Church and Society: Essays in Honor of Stephan Kuttner* (Philadelphia, 1977).

recognized.¹⁴ Familiarity with the work of Ivo (whom he met at Chartres in 1107) is a distinct possibility.¹⁵ Speaking generally, Paschal's canons frequently allude to Pseudo-Isidorian material, but the quotations are usually too imprecise to be traced back to a particular collection from which they might have been taken. Pseudo-Isidore and the *Collection in 74 Titles* are often still interpreted as uncompromising documents created, it is thought, to support the supremacy of the papacy. These generalizations are inaccurate.¹⁶ The decades from the 1070's to the 1120's are a period of luxuriant growth of canon law, brought eventually under control by Gratian's *Concordia discordantium canonum*, but interest in canon law does not imply rigidity in outlook nor exclusive reliance on law. In the case of the synods of Paschal II this is best shown by the remarkable canon from the Beneventan council of 1108 where the customary reference to the *canones apostolorum* as basis for the prohibition of lay investiture is replaced by a reference to Ezechiel to justify lay exclusion from ecclesiastical promotions. The pontiff's stress on antiquity and canonical precedent which he shares with all of the reformers but emphasizes particularly, served in part as a rebuttal of voices in the imperial camp accusing the papacy of unheard of innovations.¹⁷ It is notable that Paschal never claimed the right to create new legislation as Gregory VII had done.¹⁸

The reference to the Old Testament at Benevento vividly brings to mind the exalted position of the priesthood. Noblesse oblige, however, and like Urban II Paschal felt it incumbent upon him to reaffirm the status of the

---

¹⁴ As introduction to this collection see Stickler, *Historia iuris canonici*, pp. 154-159; van Hove, *Prolegomena*, pp. 320-321; Fournier-Le Bras, *Histoire* 1 (1931) 363-421; P. Fournier, "Etudes critiques sur le Décret de Burchard de Worms," *Nouvelle Revue historique de droit français et étranger* 34 (1910) 41-112, 213-222, 289-351, 564-584; G. Fransen, "La tradition manuscrite du Décret de Burchard de Worms," *Ius Sacrum: Klaus Mörsdorf zum 60. Geburtstag* (1969) 111-118; idem, "Burchard de Worms: quête des manuscrits," *Traditio* 26 (1970) 446-447; E. Van Balberghe, "Les éditions du Décret de Burchard de Worms," *Recherches de Théologie ancienne et médiévale* 37 (1970) 5-22; Fuhrmann, *Einfluss und Verbreitung*, 2: 442-485, esp. pp. 454-455; Mordek, "Handschriftenforschungen," esp. pp. 630-650.
¹⁵ See R. Somerville, "Two Notes on Scotland."
¹⁶ In addition to the three volumes of Fuhrmann, *Einfluss und Verbreitung* see idem, "Über den Reformgeist der 74-Titel-Sammlung (Diversorum patrum sententiae)," *Festschrift für Hermann Heimpel zum 70. Geburtstag* (Göttingen 1972) 2: 1101-1120 and the edition by Gilchrist, *Diversorum patrum sententiae*, pp. xvii-xxxi.
¹⁷ Cf. Placidus of Nonantola, *Liber de honore ecclesiae*, ed. L. von Heinemann and E. Sackur, MGH Libelli de lite 2 (1892) 566-639, c. 53 p. 589.
¹⁸ On the meaning of new law see Ladner, "Two Gregorian Letters," esp. pp. 236-242 and n. 49; Kuttner, "Urban II," esp. pp. 67-69. Fuhrmann, "Rechtswissenschaft," esp. pp. 185-187, 190-191 with up-to-date bibliographies for *Dictatus papae* c. 7.

episcopal ordo.[19] The set of canons appended to some manuscripts of the *Collectio canonum* of Anselm of Lucca focuses on the standards of life prescribed for a bishop and strongly confirms the subordination of monks and clergy to the diocesan bishop. The numbers of exempt or papally protected monasteries and communities of canons increased rapidly during Paschal's pontificate, and a reconfirmation of hierarchical principles must have been welcomed by the episcopate.

It is difficult to accuse Paschal II of unneccessary rigidity, or of an attempt to overthrow Lanfranc's system in England.[20] The successes of the first half of his pontificate would be inconceivable if he had not been a skilful negotiator. The international assemblies of Guastalla and Troyes presupposed accommodations with the French, English, and German governments respectively, even if the last was merely a temporary truce and the clash of 1111 could not be prevented. Serious negotiations always involve a give and take on both sides, and rigidity would preclude any papal "give." The fourth decree of Guastalla and Paschal's negotiations with King Henry I of England and St. Anselm of Canterbury are examples of papal dispensations discussed and confirmed by Paschal's councils. It does not matter in the present context who initiated the compromise in the case of England: king, archbishop or pope.[21] The only significant factor is Paschal's support of conciliatory policies and his withdrawal from the position he had taken at the Lateran council of 1102 when he repeated Urban's prohibition of homage. Urban had prohibited liege homage at the council of Clermont[22] and probably also at Bari, as well as in 1099.[23] Paschal had juridically ceded very little, he merely permitted consecration of ecclesiastics who had done homage to the king, but he obtained the English king's renunciation of investiture with ring and staff, the symbols for the mystical marriage between a priest and his church and for the *cura*

---

[19] For Urban see Becker, "Urban II.," p. 251.

[20] Cantor, *Church, Kingship and Lay Investiture*, p. vii: "Paschal II made the most vigorous attempt at the complete overthrow of Lanfranc's system, he is representative of the most radical group among the Gregorian reformers."

[21] See H. Hoffmann, "Ivo von Chartres," pp. 419-420; H. Böhmer, *Kirche und Staat in England und der Normandie* (Leipzig 1899) 157-162; Cantor, *Church, Kingship and Lay Investiture*, ch. 5, esp. pp. 253-273; P. Classen, "Das Wormser Konkordat in der deutschen Verfassungsgeschichte," *Investiturstreit und Reichsverfassung*, Konstanzer Arbeitskreis für mittelalterliche Geschichte, Vorträge und Forschungen 17 (1973) 411-460, pp. 417-420; cf. Fried, "Der Regalienbegriff im 11. und 12. Jahrhundert," DA 29 (1973) 450-528 and Benson, *Bishop-Elect*, pp. 203-250 who do not specifically discuss English events.

[22] Somerville, *Decreta Claromontensia* p. 78 (recension of Lambert of Arras): "Ne episcopus vel sacerdos regi vel alicui laico in manibus ligiam fidelitatem faciat."

[23] Classen, "Wormser Konkordat," pp. 417-418.

*animarum.* This victory was well worth extended negotiations. In spite of Paschal's general flexibility lay investiture was the point at which no compromise was possible. The prohibition of investiture was pronounced at each of the councils in turn and the abolition of this custom was of paramount importance for Paschal. In a letter to Anselm of Canterbury the pontiff exclaimed: "Si ergo virgam pastoralitatis signum, si anulum signaculum fidei tradit laica manus, quid in ecclesia pontifices agunt? Ecclesiae honor atteritur, solvitur disciplinae vigor, et omnis religio Christiana conculcatur, si quod novimus sacerdotibus solis deberi laica patiamur temeritate praesumi. Non est laicorum ecclesiam tradere, nec filiorum matrem adulterio maculare."[24] The unsanctified hands of laymen could not be permitted to transmit or even to touch symbols which were central to the church and her mysteries.

---

[24] JL 5928; Schmitt, *Opera*, ep. 281 (4: 196-198). Cf. in general Benson, *Bishop-Elect*, pp. 121-124.

# Appendix 1

# A Council of Dubious Authenticity: Benevento, Autumn 1102

On the basis of several documents which were issued at Benevento between 13 September and 12 December 1102, Jaffé postulated that Paschal spent August to December 1102 in this southern city.[1] The second redaction (A.2) of the *Annales Beneventani monasterii Sanctae Sophiae* records that during this period the pontiff held a council:

> [A.D.] mcii. [indictione] x. an. iiii domni secundi Pascalis pape idem papa Beneventi sinodum celebravit.[2]

This annotation is the only evidence for a council at Benevento in the winter of 1102.[3] It was not mentioned in the great conciliar works for a simple reason. The editors, including Mansi, knew only the first redaction of the *Annales Beneventani* (A.1) which had been edited by Nicola Aloisia in Muratori's *Antiquitates italicae medii aevi*[4] and this redaction reports for 1102 only a great famine.[5]

---

[1] See Jaffé, *Regesta* 1: 713. JL 5875 is dated 1101 and was issued at Capua (see Jaffé, *Regesta* 1: 709).

[2] *Annales Beneventani*, p. 152 and n. 2; for the *Annales* in general see above ch. 1 n. 4.

[3] Runciman, *History of the Crusades*, 2: 35 n. 1, thought that the meeting between a certain Bishop Manasses (Runciman could not identify his see) and Pope Paschal that was reported by Albert d'Aix occurred at the synod reported in the *Annales Beneventani*. Albert, however, does not refer to a synod: "... in amaritudine animi Romam tendens, ipsum imperatorem criminatus est in ecclesia Beneventana ..." (RCHOc 4: 584-5). Furthermore, the authenticity of this particular passage in Albert's narrative has now been convincingly rejected by J. G. Rowe, "Paschal II, Bohemund of Antioch and the Byzantine Empire," pp. 173-176.

[4] See the references given above ch. 1 n. 4.

[5] *Annales Beneventani*, p. 152 and n. 1: "Fuit fames valida, ita ut modius frumenti venderetur .c. denariis, et mortalitas hominum." Redaction A.2 recorded a famine for 1103 and 1104 (ibid.).

Hefele-Leclercq, following Jaffé, incorporated a mention of a council held at Benevento in 1102 into the *Histoire des Conciles*,[6] accepting the statement of the *Annales Beneventani* without hesitation. They are a very reliable source, but it is curious that only the second redaction, MS Vat. lat. 4939 mentions the synod. Redactions A.1 and A.3, both older than A.2 which was written in 1119,[7] pass it over in silence. Furthermore, the statement of A.2 is not supported by even a single additional piece of evidence. The letters which were sent from Benevento, JL 5921-5932, indicate only the following facts:

1) Paschal was accompanied temporarily by the chancellor, John of Gaeta,[8] who was occasionally represented by Equitius,[9] or by the cardinal deacon Galterius.[10]
2) Paschal received English messengers at Benevento.[11]

On the whole it appears doubtful that a synod took place at Benevento in the winter of 1102. The entry in redaction A.2 of the *Annales Beneventani* might refer to a special meeting of the pope and high dignitaries of the curia.[12]

---

[6] *Histoire* 5/1: 778: "Vers cette même époque [December 1102], le pape Pascal tint à Bénévent un concile dont nous ne connaissons que l'existence."

[7] *Annales Beneventani*, p. 31.

[8] JL 5921. Cf. for John of Gaeta in general D. Lohrmann, "Die Jugendwerke des Johannes von Gaeta," QFIAB 47 (1967) 355-445 and the bibliography indicated there.

[9] JL 5923: "Datum Beneventi per manum Equitii agentis vicem cancelları, .xi. kal. Decembr. ind. xi. Inc. Dominicae anno 1102, pontificatus autem domni Paschalis II papae .iv." See also JL 5925.

[10] For Galterius see Klewitz, "Kardinalskollegium," p. 221 n. 24.

[11] JL 5928-5930.

[12] Cf. R. Somerville's remarks on the pseudo-council of Limoges attributed to Pope Urban II, "The French Councils of Pope Urban II: Some basic Considerations," *Annuarium Historiae Conciliorum* 2 (1970) 56-65, esp. pp. 58-60.

# Appendix 2

# The Guastalla Canons and Gratian's *Decretum*

The little group of canons appended to several manuscripts of the *Collectio Canonum* of Anselm of Lucca could be identified as legislation promulgated by Pope Paschal II at Guastalla in 1106. With the exception of the decree *Nullus episcopus* all of them are found in the *Decretum* of Gratian, but none is correctly identified. It is the purpose of this appendix to examine Friedberg's attributions with regard to them. They are distributed as follows:

|  | Guastalla |  | *Decretum* |
|---|---|---|---|
| c. 1 | *Episcopi lectioni* | | C.2 q.7 c.60 |
| c. 2 | *Nullus episcopus* | | ... |
| c. 3 | *Nullus laicorum* | | C.16 q.7 c.18[1] |
| c. 4 | *Sicut domini* | | C.16 q.7 c.19 |
| c. 5 | *Abbatibus qui* | | C.18 q.2 c.18 |
| c. 6 | *Si quis clericus* | | C.16 q.7 c.16 |
| c. 7 | *Constitutiones* | | C.16 q.7 c.17[2] |

Friedberg's identification of C.2 q.7 c.60 as "caput incertum," of Pascalis

---

[1] The text in Gratian's *Decretum* ("Nullus laicorum ecclesias vel ecclesiarum bona occupet vel disponat. Qui vero secus egerit, iuxta B. Alexandri capitulum ab ecclesiae liminibus arceatur") is an abbreviation of the longer decree in the Anselm manuscripts ("Nullus laicorum ecclesias vel ecclesiarum bona occupet vel disponat. Sicut enim beatus Stephanus papa martyr scribit, laici quamvis religiosi sint, nulli tamen de ecclesiasticis facultatibus aliquid disponendi legitur umquam attributa facultas. Qui vero secus egerit iuxta beati Alexandri primi capitulum ab ecclesie liminibus arceatur"). Nevertheless, their identity seems certain because the connection between the prohibition of lay investiture and the reference to a capitulum of Pope Hadrian I (see the note of the Correctores accompanying C.16 q.7 c.18) occurs only at Guastalla.

[2] This canon is not found in the manuscripts of Anselm of Lucca, but in the Segni fragment and MS Barb. lat. 860; see above pp. 59-61.

or Pascasius is accompanied by a reference to Berardi.[3] Berardi was not sure whether the text ought to be attributed to Paschal I (817-824) or Paschal II, but concluded: "Ego potius eundem Canonem referrem ad constitutiones Synodi Regiaticinae temporibus Leonis IV Pontificis celebratae anno 850." As reason for his contention he quoted a decree from the Pavia council. It is indeed like C.2 q.7 c.60 concerned with episcopal morals, but is worded completely differently.[4] For this reason it seems possible to dismiss Berardi's argument.

C.18 q.2 c.18 also presents no problem. It is identified by Jaffé as a fragment from the pontificate of Paschal II (JL 6608). Friedberg followed Jaffé, only changing the word "fragment" to "fragment of a letter." This can now be replaced by the precise attribution of the canon to the council of Guastalla.

The block of Guastalla canons in C.16 q.7 is similarly identified as Paschal II material, but Friedberg's notes to canons 16-19 are contradictory and more difficult to evaluate. In n. 175 to Grat. C.16 q.7 c.16, *Si quis clericus*, Friedberg quoted Baluze and Berardi as authorities who attributed canons 16-19 to the council of Troyes in 1107,[5] and added a reference to Mansi's treatment of the synod.[6] In notes 185 and 186 to canons 18 and 19 of Grat. q.7 C.16, however, Friedberg also referred to them as fragments of Paschal letters, numbered JL 6609 and JL 6610 respectively.[7]

Manuscript evidence has made it possible to identify c.16 *Si quis clericus* to c.18 *Nullus laicorum* inclusively as canons promulgated at Guastalla. The Correctores manuscript Vat. lat. 4891, however, does not contain notes for c. 19 *Sicut domini*. In the *Decretum* c. 19 as well as the preceding

---

[3] C. S. Berardi, *Gratiani canones genuini ab apocryphis discreti*, 2 vols. (Venice 1777).

[4] Ibid. 2: 209: "... in Canone 1. illius Concilii ita legimus: Decrevit sancta Synodus domesticam, et interiorem Episcopi conversationem totius reprehensionis, atque suspicionis impenetrabilem fieri debere, ut juxta Apostolum provideamus bona, non solum coram Deo, sed etiam coram omnibus hominibus. Oportet igitur, cubiculo Episcopi, et secretioribus quibuslibet obsequiis sincerae opinionis Sacerdotes, et Clerici assistant, qui vigilantem, orantem, sacra eloquia scrutantem, Episcopum suum jugiter attendant, ejusque sancte conversationis testes, imitatores, et ad Dei gloriam praedicatores existant."

[5] "Hoc caput pariter ac tria sequentia ad Conc. Trecense hab. ao. 1107 pertinere, chronicorum auctoritate nisi suspicantur Baluzius et Berardus."

[6] It should also be noted that in his prolegomena (Gratian, *Decretum*, p. xxiii no. 28) Friedberg listed C.16 q.7 c.17 and c.16 as derived from the council of Troyes, held in 1107. No reasons are given.

[7] Friedberg noted that c.18 (or JL 6609) was not part of the canonical collection *Polycarpus* (2.4) as maintained by the Correctores. This is true in the case of the *Polycarpus* manuscripts I examined. Mr. Uwe Horst, Tübingen, is preparing an edition of the collection and should confirm Friedberg.

canons 16-18 are attributed to *Pascalis Papa*. The name is given in the inscription to c. 16; the reference in c. 17 is "idem," in canons 18 and 19 likewise "idem." In short, they give the appearance of a sequence,[8] a hypothesis that is supported by manuscript evidence as seen earlier.[9]

---

[8] It should be noted, however, that Gratian usually distributed his sources among the topics to which they belonged.

[9] Above, pp. 63-64.

# Appendix 3

# Fragmenta

A sixteenth-century manuscript of the Correctores Romani in the Biblioteca Vallicelliana in Rome, C.24, contains two sets of canons attributed to Pope Paschal II following an unnumbered paper folio after fol. 45 with the announcement *Duo concilia Paschalis II*. Fols. 46r-47v contain a first group of decrees, and fol. 48r a second one. The latter were copied again on fol. 36r.[1] Both groups were published together by Pflugk-Harttung with the inscription, "Kanones einer Lateransynode Paschals II: 1110, März 7. Lateran."[2] Weiland essentially incorporated Pflugk-Harttung's material in his edition of the Lateran council,[3] but he obliterated most indications given by Pflugk-Harttung about the manuscript distribution of the canons in MS Vall. C.24.

The canons on fols. 46r-47v, "Constitutiones sanctorum canonum ... more solito fiant," that are entered with the marginal note, "Haec fragmenta habuit Mich. Thomasius a Franc. Turriano, qui ea sua manu ex cod. antiquo transcripserat," can be distinguished as consisting of the class A recension of the 1110 decrees and canons 1-14 of Urban's council of Piacenza, written as unbroken sequence. The 1110 material was included in the edition of the canons of this synod in chapter 4.[4]

The concern of this appendix is a discussion of the second group of decrees on fol. 48r. It is here that confusion has arisen. Five canons are involved, *Paschalis Papae II in concilio. Cap. 2. Laicis quamuis ... destituantur officiis.* Pflugk-Harttung recognized the similarity of the two initial canons with parts of the 1110 decrees and therefore did not reproduce them together with the remaining three at the end of the 1110 and Piacenza

---

[1] See L. Gasparri, "Osservazioni," p. 481.
[2] J. von Pflugk-Harttung, *Acta pontificum Romanorum inedita*, 3 vols., Tübingen and Stuttgart 1881-86; 2: 197-198, no. 238.
[3] MGH Const. 1: 567-569, no. 397.
[4] Above pp. 113-114, no. 5. Siglum Rv.

series. The final three decrees from fol. 48r were numbered in his edition VI A, VII A, VIII A, and a note indicated a bit vaguely their special position.[5] Weiland reproduced all five canons as a note to c. 2 of the 1110 legislation, reducing Pflugk-Harttung's five decrees to two which he identified as a different recension of cc. 1 and 2 of the Lateran synod.[6] But as will be seen from the following edition the new capitula have little similarity with the text of these decrees. Marginal notes in the hand of Antonio Agustín[7] accompany cc. 1-3. They read:

> Callist. c. 4
> Callist. c. 4
> vide c. 6 alibi

and show that Agustín noted the relationship between the canons in the Vallicellianus and the Lateran council held by Pope Calixtus II in 1123.[8] One of the canons so marked by Agustín corresponds to Gratian, C.16 q.7 c.25 that already carries a Calixtus inscription: *Item Calixtus Papa. Si quis principum* .... The annotation of the *Correctores* in the *Editio Romana* is instructive: "Inter decreta Calixti, ex quo citatur, non est inventum. Habetur in decretis Paschalis II. manuscriptis cap. 5., set non est mutatum nomen Calixti, quia Pontifices isti, qui iisdem fere temporibus fuerunt, frequenter eadem decreta suorum antecessorum repetebant." Their caution was justified. The text as transmitted in MS Vall. C.24 and in Gratian C.16 q.7 c.25 represents c. 2 of Paschal's Lateran council of 1110, but Pope Calixtus II repromulgated the decree as part of c. 8 of the First Lateran Council.[9] It was probably a version of this c. 8 that Agustín had before him when he wrote his remarks into the margins of the Vallicellianus, for another section of c. 8 of Calixtus is similar to the first decree in the set of Paschal canons on fol. 48r although the canonical sources for the pontiffs differ. Where Paschal relied on the *Collection in 74 Titles*,[10] Calixtus quoted Pseudo-Stephanus I, ep. 2.12 in the Isidorian version without the addition "et martyr."[11] Nonetheless, it is this part of c. 8 of the Lateran synod that

---

[5] Pflugk-Harttung, *Acta inedita* 2: 198.

[6] MGH Const. 1: 568, no. 397: "Diversam prorsus recensionem capitum 1 et 2 ordine inverso servavit V [Vall. C.24] ...." The text is given in small print pp. 568-569. Pflugk-Harttung, who was followed by Weiland, did not give the inscription of the second set: *Paschalis II in concilio*.

[7] This information was kindly provided by S. Kuttner who added that the whole quire of fol. 41 to 48 belongs to the papers which Agustín received from Michael Thomasius.

[8] *Conciliorum Oecumenicorum Decreta*, ed. J. Alberigo et al. (Basel 1962), pp. 163-170.

[9] Ibid. p. 167.

[10] Above ch. 4, p. 119, c. 4.

[11] See F.3 p. 806 no. 43 for various possibilities.

seems to have induced Agustín to identify the canon as "Callist. c. 4." The reference to c. 5 in the remarks of the Correctores suggests that the group may have been working on the basis of Vall. C.24. In the following presentation the text from the codex is given in col. a. Col. b indicates parallels to Paschal's legislation as documented in this study. As a result it is noted that two of the decrees find their closest parallel in the canons of 1110, and the remaining three in those of the council of Guastalla held in 1106. Michael Thomasius perhaps compiled canons with an attribution to Paschal II that may have been scattered through his "codex antiquus." But this hypothesis is only a guess, for Thomasius' manuscript is unfortunately lost. It might be equally correct to assume that the inscription "in concilio" has to be taken literally and that the decrees which are here identified belong to a single one of Paschal's synods. The earliest synod conceivable would be the meeting in the Lateran in 1110 where Guastalla canons might have been repeated. These conjectures, however, do not solve the question. The decrees are therefore reproduced as Paschalian conciliar fragments of undetermined date in this appendix.

| Col. a | Col. b |
|---|---|
| Rome, Biblioteca Vallicelliana MS C.24, fol. 48r (copy fol. 36r) Paschalis II in concilio. | |
| 1. Cap. 2. Laicis quamuis religiosis nulla de ecclesiasticis dignitatibus aliquid disponendi legitur attributa facultas, neque deinceps fieri permittimus, sed omnino interdicentes prohibemus. | 1110 Lateran synod, c. 4 (above ch. 4, p. 119) without inscription. Cf. Gratian, C.16 q.7 c.24 and Alberigo, *Decreta*, p. 167 c. 8 |
| 2. Cap. 5. Si quis principum uel aliorum laicorum dispositionem seu dominationem rerum seu possessionum ecclesiasticarum sibi aliquid uendicauerit ut sacrilegus iudicetur. | 1110 Lateran synod, c. 5 (above ch. 4, p. 120) but briefer. Cf. Gratian, C.16 q.7 c.25 and Alberigo, *Decreta*, p. 167 c. 8. |
| 3. Si quis clericus, abbas uel monachus per laicos ecclesias obtinuerit, secundum sanctorum apostolorum canones et Antiocheni concilii capitulum excommunicationi subiaceat. | 1106 council at Guastalla c. 6 (above ch. 2, p. 70). Gratian, C.16 q.7 c.16. |

**4.** Nullus laicorum ecclesias uel ecclesiarum bona occupet uel disponat. Qui uero secus egerit, iuxta beati Alexandri capitulum ab ecclesiae liminibus arceatur.

1106 council at Guastalla c. 3 (above ch. 2, p. 69) but briefer. Gratian, C.16 q.7 c.18.

**5.** Sicut Domini uestimentum scissum non est sed de eo sortiti sunt, ita nec ecclesia scindi debet, quia in unitate tota consistit. In potestatem ergo proprii episcopi ecclesiae reducantur, et ab ipso sicut in sacris canonibus cautum est ordinentur, alioquin et ecclesiae ipsae et clerici earundem diuinis destituantur officiis.

1106 council at Guastalla c. 4 (above ch. 2, p. 69). Gratian, C.16 q.7 c.19.

# Bibliography

### Printed Works Cited*

Achery, Luc d'. *Spicilegium sive collectio veterum aliquot scriptorum qui in Galliae bibliothecis ... latuerant.* 2nd ed. Edited by E. Baluze et al. 3 vols. Paris 1723.

Alberigo, Joseph et al. edd. *Conciliorum oecumenicorum decreta.* 2nd ed. Basel etc. 1962.

Albert, E. *Note sur un passage à Privas attribué au pape Pascal II (1099-1118).* Paris 1893.

*Annales Beneventani.* Edited by Georg Heinrich Pertz. Monumenta Germaniae Historica. Scriptores, vol. 3 (1839), pp. 173-185.

———. "Gli Annales Beneventani." Edited by O. Bertolini. *Bullettino dell'Istituto Storico Italiano per il Medio Evo e Archivio Muratoriano* 42 (1923) 1-163.

*Annales Besuenses.* Edited by Georg Heinrich Pertz. Monumenta Germaniae Historica. Scriptores, vol. 2 (1829), pp. 247-250.

*Annales Cameracenses auctore Lamberto Waterlos.* Edited by Georg Heinrich Pertz. Monumenta Germaniae Historica. Scriptores, vol. 16 (1859), pp. 509-554.

*Annales Elnonenses maiores.* Edited by Georg Heinrich Pertz. Monumenta Germaniae Historica. Scriptores, vol. 5 (1854), pp. 11-17.

*Annales Hildesheimenses.* Edited by Georg Waitz. Scriptores rerum germanicarum in usum scholarum. Hanover 1878.

*Annales Patherbrunnenses: eine verlorene Quellenschrift.* Edited by Paul Scheffer-Boichorst. Innsbruck 1870.

*Annales S. Benigni Divionensis.* Edited by Georg Waitz. Monumenta Germaniae Historica. Scriptores, vol. 5 (1854), pp. 37-50.

*Annales S. Disibodi.* Edited by Georg Waitz. Monumenta Germaniae Historica. Scriptores, vol. 17 (1861), pp. 4-30.

*Annalista Saxo.* Edited by Georg Waitz. Monumenta Germaniae Historica. Scriptores, vol. 6 (1844), pp. 542-777.

Anselm, St., archbishop of Canterbury. See *Sancti Anselmi ... opera omnia.*

Anselm II, bishop of Lucca. *Collectio canonum.* See Thaner, Friedrich, ed.

Arnold, Klaus. *Johannes Trithemius (1462-1516).* Quellen und Forschungen zur Geschichte des Bistums und Hochstifts Würzburg, vol. 23. Würzburg 1971.

---

* A table of abbreviations is found above, pp. ix-xi. Manuscript catalogues are generally not included in the bibliography.

Balberghe, Emile Van. "Les éditions du Décret de Burchard de Worms." *Recherches de Théologie ancienne et médiévale* 37 (1970) 5-22.
Baldwin, Marshall Whithed. *The First Hundred Years.* A History of the Crusades, vol. 1; edited by Kenneth M. Setton. Philadelphia 1958.
Balencie, G. "Chronologie des évêques de Tarbes." In *Mélanges Léonce Couture*, pp. 97-113. Toulouse 1902.
Baronius, Caesar. *Annales Ecclesiastici.* Vol. 12. Rome 1607.
——. *Annales Ecclesiastici cum critica historico-chronologica.* Edited by Antonio Pagi. Vol. 18. Lucca 1746.
Batlle, Columba M. and P. M. Gassó. *Pelagii I papae epistulae quae supersunt.* Scripta et documenta, vol. 8. Montserrat 1956.
Becker, Alfons. *Papst Urban II. (1088-1099) part 1: Herkunft und kirchliche Laufbahn; der Papst und die lateinische Christenheit.* Monumenta Germaniae Historica. Schriften, vol. 19/1. Stuttgart 1964.
——. *Studien zum Investiturproblem in Frankreich.* Saarbrücken 1955.
——. "Urban II. und die deutsche Kirche." In *Investiturstreit und Reichsverfassung*, edited by J. Fleckenstein, pp. 241-275. Konstanzer Arbeitskreis für mittelalterliche Geschichte. Vorträge und Forschungen, vol. 17. Sigmaringen 1973.
Behrendt, Roland. "Abbot John Trithemius (1462-1516), Monk and Humanist." *Revue Bénédictine* 84 (1974) 212-229.
Bellini, A. "Il beato Landolfo da Vergiate." *Archivio Storico Lombardo* 49 (1922) 332-349.
*Benonis aliorumque cardinalium schismaticorum contra Gregorium VII. et Urbanum II. scripta.* Edited by Kuno Francke. Monumenta Germaniae Historica. Libelli de lite, vol. 2 (1893), pp. 369-422.
Benson, Robert L. *The Bishop-Elect: A Study in Medieval Ecclesiastical Office.* Princeton 1968.
Berardi, C. S. *Gratiani canones genuini ab apocryphis discreti.* Vol. 2. Venice 1777.
Bernold of Constance. *De Berengarii haeresiarchae damnatione multiplici.* Edited by Pierre Chifflet. Patrologia series latina, vol. 148, cols. 1449-1460.
——. *De excommunicatis vitandis.* Libellus X. Edited by Friedrich Thaner. Monumenta Germaniae Historica. Libelli de lite, vol. 2 (1892) pp. 112-142.
Bernheim, Ernst. *Das Wormser Konkordat und seine Vorurkunden.* Untersuchungen zur deutschen Staats- und Rechtsgeschichte, vol. 81. Breslau 1906. Reprint Aalen 1970.
Bertolini, O., ed. "Gli Annales Beneventani." See *Annales Beneventani.*
Bertram, Adolf. *Geschichte des Bisthums Hildesheim.* Vol. 1. Hildesheim 1899.
Bethell, Denis. "Two Letters of Pope Paschal II to Scotland." *Scottish Historical Review* 49 (1970) 33-45.
Binius, Severinus. *Concilia generalia et provincialia...* 4 vols. in 5. Cologne 1606. 2nd ed. Cologne 1618.
Blume, Fritz. *Iter Italicum.* 4 vols. in 2. Berlin and Stettin 1824-36.
Blumenthal, Uta-Renate. "Codex Guarnerius 203: A Manuscript of the Collection

in 74 Titles at San Daniele del Friuli." *Bulletin of Medieval Canon Law*, n.s. 5 (1975) 11-33.
———. "Ein neuer Text für das Reimser Konzil Papst Leos IX. (1049)?" *Deutsches Archiv* 32 (1976) 23-48.
Boehmer, Heinrich. *Die Fälschungen Erzbischof Lanfranks von Canterbury.* Studien zur Geschichte der Theologie und der Kirche 8. Leipzig 1902.
———. *Kirche und Staat in England und der Normandie im XI. und XII. Jahrhundert: Eine historische Studie.* Leipzig 1899.
Bogumil, Karlotto. *Das Bistum Halberstadt im 12. Jahrhundert: Studien zur Reichs- und Reformpolitik des Bischofs Reinhard und zum Wirken der Augustiner- Chorherren.* Mitteldeutsche Forschungen, vol. 69. Cologne 1972.
*Boso's Life of Alexander III.* Introduction by Peter Munz. Translated by G. M. Ellis. Totowa N.J. 1973.
Brackmann, Albert, ed. *Germania pontificia; sive, Repertorium privilegiorum et litterarum a Romanis pontificibus ante annum MCLXXXXVIII Germaniae ecclesiis, monasteriis, civitatibus singulisque personis concessorum* .... Vol. 1: *Provincia Salisburgensis et episcopatus Tridentinus*; Berlin 1910-11. Vol. 2: *Provincia Maguntinensis*, Part 1: *Dioeceses Eichstetensis, Augustensis, Constantiensis 1*; Berlin 1923. Vol. 3: *Provincia Maguntinensis*; Part 3: *Dioeceses Strassburgensis, Spirensis, Wormatiensis, Wirciburgensis, Bambergensis*; Berlin 1935.
———. *Studien und Vorarbeiten zur Germania Pontificia.* Vol. 3: Die Bistümer Würzburg und Bamberg in ihrer wirtschaftlichen Bedeutung für die Geschichte des deutschen Ostens; Part: 2: *Bamberg*, edited by Heinrich Büttner. Berlin 1937.
Bresslau, Harry. *Handbuch der Urkundenlehre.* 3rd ed. Vol. 1. Berlin 1958.
———. *Jahrbücher des deutschen Reichs unter Konrad II.* Jahrbücher der deutschen Geschichte, vol. 11, part 2. Leipzig 1884.
Brooke, Zachary N. *The English Church and the Papacy.* Cambridge 1952.
———. "Lay Investiture and its Relation to the Conflict of Empire and Papacy." The Raleigh Lecture on History. *Proceedings, British Academy* 25 (1939) 217-247.
Bruns, Hermann T. *Canones Apostolorum et conciliorum saeculorum IV. V. VI. VII.* Vol. 1 Berlin 1839.
Burchard of Worms. *Decretum.* Patrologia series latina, vol. 140, cols. 537-1090.
Büttner, Heinrich. "Das Erzstift Mainz und die Klosterreform im 11. Jahrhundert." *Archiv für Mittelrheinische Kirchengeschichte* 1 (1949) 30-64.
Cadderi, A. *Conone di Preneste.* Collana di studi storici religiosi letterari, vol. 6. Rome 1974.
Campi, Pietro M. *Dell'Historia ecclesiastica di Piacenza.* Vol. 2. Piacenza 1651.
Cantor, Norman F. *Church, Kingship, and Lay Investiture in England: 1089-1135.* Princeton 1958.
Carlesi, Ferdinando. *Origini della città e del comune di Prato.* Prato 1904.
Caspar, Erich. "Gregor VII. in seinen Briefen." *Historische Zeitschrift* 130 (1924) 1-30.

——, ed. *Das Register Gregors VII*. Monumenta Germaniae Historica. Epistolae selectae. Vol. 2, fasc. 1-2. Berlin 1920-23. Reprint Berlin 1967.
——. "Studien zum Register Gregors VII." *Neues Archiv* 38 (1973) 143-226.
Cauchie, Alfred. *La querelle des investitures dans les diocèses de Liège et de Cambrai*. Paris 1890.
Cazzani, Eugenio. *Vescovi e Arcivescovi di Milano*. Milan 1955.
Cheney, C. R. "Textual Problems of the English Provincial Canons." In *La Critica del Testo. Atti del 2° Congresso internazionale della Società Italiana di Storia del Diritto*. Vol. 1, pp. 165-188. Florence 1971. Reprinted in idem, *Medieval Texts and Studies*, pp. 111-137. Oxford 1973.
*Chronica monasterii Casinensis*. Edited by Wilhelm Wattenbach. Monumenta Germaniae Historica. Scriptores, vol. 7 (1846), pp. 551-844.
*Chronica Regia Coloniensis*. Edited by Georg Waitz. Scriptores rerum germanicarum in usum scholarum. Hanover 1880.
*Chronicon S. Andreae castri Cameracensii*. Edited by Ludwig Bethmann. Monumenta Germaniae Historica. Scriptores, vol. 7 (1846), pp. 526-550.
*Chronicon S. Maxentii Pictavense (vulgo dicitur Malleacense)*. Edited by Paul Marchegay and Emile Mabille. Chroniques des Eglises d'Anjou, pp. 349-433. Paris 1869.
Clarius of Sens. *Chronicon Sancti-Petri-Vivi Senonensis*. Edited by L. M. Duru. Bibliothèque historique de l'Yonne. Vol. 2: 451-597. Auxerre 1863.
Classen, Peter. "Heinrichs IV. Briefe im Codex Udalrici." *Deutsches Archiv* 20 (1964) 115-129.
——. "Das Wormser Konkordat in der deutschen Verfassungsgeschichte." In *Investiturstreit und Reichsverfassung*, ed. J. Fleckenstein. Konstanzer Arbeitskreis für mittelalterliche Geschichte. Vorträge und Forschungen, vol. 17, pp. 411-460. Sigmaringen 1973.
Claude, Dietrich. *Geschichte des Erzbistums Magdeburg bis in das 12. Jahrhundert*. Teil 1. Mitteldeutsche Forschungen 67/1. Cologne and Vienna 1972.
Coleti, Niccolò. *Sacrosancta concilia ad regiam editionem exacta ...*. 23 vols. Venice 1728-33.
*Collectio Canonum in V Libris*. Edited by Mario Fornasari. Corpus Christianorum, Continuatio Mediaevalis, vol. 6. Turnhout 1970.
*Conciliorum omnium generalium et provincialium collectio regia*. 37 vols. Paris 1644.
*Constitutiones et acta publica ...*. Edited by Ludwig Weiland. Monumenta Germaniae Historica. Legum Sectio 4, vol. 1. Hanover 1893.
Coolen, G. "Le costume ecclésiastique." *Bulletin de la Société des antiquaires de la Morinie* 20 (1964) 274-284.
*Corpus iuris canonici*. Edited by Emil Friedberg. 2 vols. Leipzig 1879-81.
Cyprian. *Liber de unitate ecclesiae*. Edited by E. Baluze. Patrologia series latina, vol. 4, cols. 493-520.
Davidsohn, R. *Geschichte von Florenz*. Vol. 1. Berlin 1896.
*Decretales Gregorii IX*. See *Corpus iuris canonici*.

Deér, Josef. "Der Anspruch der Herrscher des 12. Jahrhunderts auf die apostolische Legation." *Archivum Historiae Pontificiae* 2 (1964) 117-186.

———. *Papsttum und Normannen: Untersuchungen zu ihren lehnsrechtlichen und kirchenpolitischen Beziehungen.* Studien und Quellen zur Welt Kaiser Friedrichs II., vol. 1. Cologne 1972.

Delisle, Léopold. *Cabinet des Manuscrits.* 3 vols. Paris 1868-1881.

———. "Inventaire des manuscrits latins de Saint-Germain-des-Prés." *Bibliothèque de l'Ecole des Chartes* 26 (1864-65) 185-214.

———. "Notice sur des manuscrits du fonds Libri conservés à la Laurentienne." *Notices et Extraits des manuscrits de la Bibliothèque Nationale et autres bibliothèques* 32 (1886) 1-120.

Deusdedit. *Collectio Canonum.* See *Die Kanonessammlung des Kardinals Deusdedit.*

Donizo. *Vita Mathildis.* Edited by Ludwig Bethmann. Monumenta Germaniae Historica. Scriptores, vol. 12 (1856), pp. 348-409.

Douais, C. *Cartulaire de l'Abbaye de Saint-Sernin de Toulouse (844-1200).* Paris and Toulouse 1887.

*Eadmeri historia novorum in Anglia.* Edited by M. Rule. Rerum Britannicarum medii aevi scriptores (Rolls series), vol. 81. London 1884.

*Eadmeri monachi Cantuariensis historiae novorum sive sui saeculi libri VI.* Edited by John Selden. London 1623.

*Eadmer's History of Recent Events in England.* Translated by G. Bosanquet. London 1964.

Eadmer. *The Life of St. Anselm: Archbishop of Canterbury.* Edited and translated by R. W. Southern. Oxford 1962.

Ehrle, Fritz. "Zur Geschichte der Katalogisierung der Vatikana." *Historisches Jahrbuch* 11 (1890) 718-727.

Ekkehard of Aura. *Chronica.* Edited by Schmale and Schmale-Ott. See *Frutolfs und Ekkehards Chroniken.*

*Ekkehardi Uraugiensis Chronica.* Edited by Georg Waitz. Monumenta Germaniae Historica. Scriptores, vol. 6 (1844), pp. 1-267.

Elze, Reinhard. *Die Ordines für die Weihe und Krönung des Kaisers und der Kaiserin.* Fontes iuris germanici antiqui in usum scholarum ... editi, vol. 9. Hanover 1960.

Endlicher, Stephan Ladislaus. *Rerum hungaricarum monumenta Arpadiana.* St. Gall 1849.

*Epistolae Karolini aevi.* Monumenta Germaniae Historica. Vol. 3. Berlin 1899.

Erickson, John H. "The Collection in Three Books and Gratian's Decretum." *Bulletin of Medieval Canon Law*, n.s. 2 (1972) 67-75.

Esmein, Adhémar. *Le mariage en droit canonique.* 2nd rev. ed. by R. Génestal. 2 vols. Paris 1929-35.

Eubel, Conrad. *Hierarchia catholica medii aevi.* Vol. 1. 2nd rev. ed. Münster 1913. Vol. 3. 1st ed. Münster 1910.

Ewald, Paul. "Reise nach Italien im Winter von 1876 auf 1877." *Neues Archiv* 3 (1878) 139-181.

———. "Reise nach Spanien im Winter von 1878 auf 1879." *Neues Archiv* 6 (1881) 219-398.
Fabre, Paul. *Etude sur le Liber Censuum de l'Eglise Romaine.* Bibliothèque des Ecoles Françaises d'Athènes et de Rome. Fasc. 62. Paris 1892.
———. "Les vies de papes dans les manuscrits du Liber Censuum." *Extraits des Mélanges d'Archéologie et d'Histoire.* Ecole Française de Rome, vol. 6. Rome 1889.
Fasoli, Gina. "Rileggendo la 'Vita Matildis' di Donizone." In *Studi Matildici: Atti e Memorie del II Convegno di Studi Matildici, Modena-Reggio Emilia, 1-3 maggio 1970.* Deput. di Storia Patria per le Ant. Prov. Modenesi. Biblioteca n.s. vol. 16, pp. 15-39. Modena 1971.
Fejér, György. *Codex diplomaticus Hungariae ecclesiasticus ac civilis.* Vol. 2. Buda 1829.
Ficker, Julius. *Forschungen zur Reichs- und Rechtsgeschichte Italiens.* Vol. 4. Innsbruck 1874.
Fliche, Augustin and Victor Martin, edd. *Histoire de l'église depuis les origines jusqu'à nos jours.* Vol. 8: *La réforme grégorienne et la reconquête chrétienne (1057-1123).* Edited by A. Fliche. Paris 1950.
Fournier, Paul. "Les collections canoniques attribués à Yves de Chartres." *Bibliothèque de l'Ecole des Chartes* 57 (1896) 645-698; 58 (1897) 26-77, 293-326, 410-444, 624-676.
———. "Études critiques sur le Décret de Burchard de Worms." *Nouvelle Revue historique de Droit français et étranger* 34 (1910) 41-112, 213-222, 289-351, 564-584.
———. "Les deux récensions de la collection canonique romaine dite le Polycarpus." *Mélanges d'Archéologie et d'Histoire* 37 (1918-19) 55-101.
———. "Observations sur diverses récensions de la Collection Canonique d'Anselme de Lucques." *Annales de l'Université de Grenoble* 13 (1901) 427-458.
———. "Une collection canonique italienne du commencement du xiie siècle." *Annales de l'Université de Grenoble* 6 (1894) 343-409.
——— and Gabriel Le Bras. *Histoire des collections canoniques en occident: depuis les Fausses Décrétales jusqu'au Décret de Gratien.* Vol. 2. Paris 1932. Reprint Aalen 1972.
Fransen, Gérard. "Réflections sur l'étude des collections canoniques à l'occasion de l'édition d'une lettre de Bruno de Segni." *Studi Gregoriani* 9 (1972) 515-533.
———. "La tradition manuscrite du Décret de Burchard de Worms." In *Ius Sacrum: Klaus Mörsdorf zum 60. Geburtstag,* pp. 111-118. Munich 1969.
———. "Trois notes." *Traditio* 26 (1970) 444-447.
Freisen, J. *Geschichte des kanonischen Eherechts bis zum Verfall der Glossenliteratur.* Paderborn 1893. Reprint Aalen 1963.
Fried, Johannes. "Der Regalienbegriff im 11. und 12. Jahrhundert." *Deutsches Archiv* 29 (1973) 450-528.
*Frutolfs und Ekkehards Chroniken und die Anonyme Kaiserchronik.* Edited and translated by Franz-Josef Schmale and Irene Schmale-Ott. Ausgewählte

Quellen zur deutschen Geschichte des Mittelalters. Freiherr vom Stein-Gedächtnisausgabe, vol. 15. Darmstadt 1972.

Fuhrmann, Horst. *Einfluss und Verbreitung der pseudoisidorischen Fälschungen.* Monumenta Germaniae Historica. Schriften, vol. 24 in 3 parts. Stuttgart 1972, 1973, 1974.

——. "Ein Papst Ideo. (Zu Collectio Lipsensis, tit. 27.5)." *Études d'histoire du droit canonique dédiés à Gabriel Le Bras,* vol. 1, pp. 89-98. Paris 1965.

——. "Das Ökumenische Konzil und seine historischen Grundlagen." *Geschichte in Wissenschaft und Unterricht* 12 (1961) 672-695.

——. "Das Reformpapsttum und die Rechtswissenschaft." In *Investiturstreit und Reichsverfassung,* ed. J. Fleckenstein. Konstanzer Arbeitskreis für mittelalterliche Geschichte. Vorträge und Forschungen, vol. 17, pp. 175-203. Sigmaringen 1973.

——. "Über den Reformgeist der 74-Titel-Sammlung (Diversorum patrum sententiae)." In *Festschrift für Hermann Heimpel zum 70. Geburtstag,* vol. 2, pp. 1101-1120. Göttingen 1972.

——. "Zwei Papstbriefe aus der Überlieferung der Rechtssammlung 'Polycarpus'." In *Aus Reichsgeschichte und Nordischer Geschichte* (Festschrift Karl Jordan). Kieler Historische Studien, vol. 16, pp. 131-140. Stuttgart 1972.

*Fundatio monasterii Arroasiensis auctore Galtero abbate.* Edited by O. Holder-Egger. Monumenta Germaniae Historica. Scriptores, vol. 15/2 (1888), pp. 1117-1125.

Funkenstein, J. *Das Alte Testament im Kampf von regnum und sacerdotium zur Zeit des Investiturstreits.* Diss. Basel. Dortmund 1938.

*Gallia Christiana.* Vol. 1 (Paris 1715). Vol. 9 (Paris 1751).

Gams, Pius Bonifacius. *Series episcoporum ecclesiae catholicae.* Reprint Graz 1957.

Ganzer, Klaus. *Die Entwicklung des auswärtigen Kardinalats im hohen Mittelalter: Ein Beitrag zur Geschichte des Kardinalkollegiums vom 11. bis 13. Jahrhundert.* Bibliothek des Deutschen Historischen Instituts in Rom, 26. Tübingen 1963.

Gasparri, Laura. "Osservazioni sul codice Vallicelliano C.24." *Studi Gregoriani* 9 (1972) 467-513.

Geisthardt, Fritz. *Der Kämmerer Boso.* Historische Studien, vol. 293. Berlin 1936.

Gerhoch of Reichersberg. *De edificio Dei.* Excerpts. Edited by Ernst Sackur. Monumenta Germaniae Historica. Libelli de lite, vol. 3 (1897), pp. 131-202.

*Gesta archiepiscoporum Salisburgensium.* Edited by Wilhelm Wattenbach. Monumenta Germaniae Historica. Scriptores, vol. 11 (1854), pp. 1-103.

*Gesta episcoporum Cameracensium.* Edited by Ludwig Bethmann. Monumenta Germaniae Historica. Scriptores, vol. 7 (1846), pp. 393-525.

*Gesta Treverorum.* Edited by Georg Waitz. Monumenta Germaniae Historica. Scriptores, vol. 8 (1848), pp. 111-204.

Giesebrecht, Wilhelm von. *Geschichte der deutschen Kaiserzeit.* 4th ed. Vol. 3. Braunschweig 1876-77.

Gigalski, Bernhard. *Bruno, Bischof von Segni, Abt von Monte-Cassino (1049-1123), sein Leben und seine Schriften: Ein Beitrag zur Kirchengeschichte im Zeitalter des Investiturstreites und zur theologischen Litteraturgeschichte des Mittelalters.* Kirchengeschichtliche Studien, vol. 3/4. Münster 1898.

Gilchrist, John T., ed. *Diversorum patrum sententie sive Collectio in LXXIV titulos digesta.* Monumenta Iuris Canonici. Series B: Corpus Collectionum, vol. 1. Vatican City 1973.

———. "Gregory VII and the Juristic Sources of His Ideology." *Studia Gratiana* 12. Collectanea S. Kuttner 2 (1967) 1-37.

Giraud, M. *Essai historique sur l'abbaye de S. Barnard et sur la ville de Romans; première partie accompagnée de pièces justificatives inédites, entre autres du Cartulaire de Romans annoté.* Lyons 1856.

Girgensohn, Dieter. "Miscellanea Italiae pontificiae: Untersuchungen und Urkunden zur mittelalterlichen Kirchengeschichte Italiens I." *Nachrichten der Akademie der Wissenschaften in Göttingen I. Philologisch-Historische Klasse.* 1974, 4, pp. 129-196.

Gisbert, Erich. "Die Bischöfe von Minden bis zum Ende des Investiturstreits." *Mindener Jahrbuch* 5 (1930/31) 5-80.

Giulini, G. *Memorie spettanti alla storia, al governo, ed alla descrizione della città e della campagna di Milan.* Vols. 4 and 5. Milano s.d.

Gladel, Nikolaus. *Die trierischen Erzbischöfe in der Zeit des Investiturstreits.* Kaldenkirchen 1932.

*Goffridi abbatis Vindocinensis libelli.* Edited by Ernst Sackur. Monumenta Germaniae Historica. Libelli de lite, vol. 2 (1892), pp. 676-700.

Goiffon, E. *Bullaire de l'Abbaye de Saint-Gilles.* Nimes 1882.

Gossman, Francis J. *Urban II and Canon Law.* The Catholic University of America Canon Law Studies, vol. 403. Washington 1960.

Gottlob, Theodor. *Der kirchliche Amtseid der Bischöfe.* Kanonistische Studien und Texte, vol. 9. Bonn 1936.

Gratian. *Decretum.* See *Corpus iuris canonici.*

Grégoire, Réginald. *Bruno de Segni, exégète médiéval et théologien monastique.* Centro italiano di studi sull'alto medioevo, vol. 3. Spoleto 1965.

Grobecker, Max. *Studien zur Geschichtsschreibung des Albert Krantz.* Hamburg 1964.

Grundmann, Herbert. *Geschichtsschreibung im Mittelalter: Gattungen-Epochen-Eigenart.* Göttingen 1965.

Guerrini, Paolo. "Un cardinale Gregoriano a Brescia, il vescovo Arimanno." *Studi Gregoriani* 2 (1947) 361-385.

Guleke, Hermann. *Deutschlands innere Kirchenpolitik von 1105 bis 1111.* Dorpat 1882.

Güterbock, Ferdinand. "Possessi imperiali matildine tra Parma e Piacenza." *Archivio Storico Lombardo,* n.s. 1 (1936) 255-276.

Guttenberg, Erich Freiherr von. *Das Bistum Bamberg, Teil 1.* Germania Sacra, Zweite Abteilung, vol. 1, part 1. Berlin and Leipzig 1937.

Haller, Johannes. *Das Papsttum: Idee und Wirklichkeit.* 2nd ed. Vol. 2. Esslingen 1962.
*Handbook of Dates for Students of English History.* Edited by C. R. Cheney. Royal Historical Society Guides and Handbooks, vol. 4. London 1945.
Hardouin, Jean. *Acta conciliorum* .... 11 vols. Paris 1714-15.
Hartmann, Wilfried. "Beziehungen des Normannischen Anonymus zu frühscholastischen Bildungszentren." *Deutsches Archiv* 31 (1975) 108-143.
Hauck, Albert. *Kirchengeschichte Deutschlands.* Vol. 3. Leipzig 1896.
Hausmann, F. *Reichskanzlei und Hofkapelle unter Heinrich v. und Konrad III.* Monumenta Germaniae Historica. Schriften, vol. 14 (1956).
Hefele, Carl Joseph von and H. Leclercq, *Histoire des conciles.* Vol. 5/1. Paris 1912.
Heinemann, Wolfgang. *Das Bistum Hildesheim im Kräftespiel der Reichs- und Territorialpolitik vornehmlich des 12. Jahrhunderts.* Quellen und Darstellungen zur Geschichte Niedersachsens, vol. 72. Hildesheim 1968.
Henking, Carl. *Gebhard III., Bischof von Constanz: 1084-1110.* Stuttgart 1880.
Hiestand, Rudolf. "Legat, Kaiser und Basileus; Bischof Kuno von Praeneste und die Krise des Papsttums von 1111/1112." In *Aus Reichsgeschichte und Nordischer Geschichte.* Kieler Historische Studien, vol. 16, pp. 141-152. Stuttgart 1972.
Hils, Kurt. *Die Grafen von Nellenburg im 11. Jahrhundert.* Forschungen zur Oberrheinischen Landesgeschichte, vol. 19. Freiburg 1967.
Hinschius, Paul. *Das Kirchenrecht der Katholiken und Protestanten in Deutschland. System des Katholischen Kirchenrechts mit besonderer Rücksicht auf Deutschland.* Vol. 2, Berlin 1878. Vol. 3, Berlin 1883. Vol. 5, Berlin 1893. Reprint Graz 1959.
——, ed. *Decretales Pseudo-Isidorianae et Capitula Angilramni.* Leipzig 1863.
Hirschfeld, Theodor. "Das Gerichtswesen der Stadt Rom vom 8. bis 12. Jahrhundert wesentlich nach stadtrömischen Urkunden." *Archiv für Ukrundenforschung* 4 (1912) 419-562.
*Historia Compostellana.* Edited by Enrico Florez. España Sagrada, vol. 20. Madrid 1791. (Patrologia series latina, vol. 170, cols. 879-1236.)
Hlawitschka, Eduard. *Studien zur Äbtissinnenreihe von Remiremont.* Veröffentlichungen des Instituts für Landeskundes des Saarlandes. Vol. 9: Saarbrücken 1963.
Hoffmann, Hartmut. *Gottesfriede und Treuga Dei.* Monumenta Germaniae Historica. Schriften, vol. 20 (1964).
——. "Ivo von Chartres und die Lösung des Investiturproblems." *Deutsches Archiv* 15 (1959) 393-440.
——. "Petrus Diaconus, die Herren von Tusculum und der Sturz Oderisius II. von Montecassino," *Deutsches Archiv* 27 (1971) 1-109.
——. "Studien zur Chronik von Montecassino." *Deutsches Archiv* 29 (1973) 59-162.
Hofmeister, Adolf. "Das Wormser Konkordat: zum Streit um seine Bedeutung." In

*Festschrift Dietrich Schäfer,* pp. 64-148. Jena 1915. Reprinted separately with preface by R. Schmidt, Darmstadt 1962.

Holtzmann, Walter. *Papsturkunden in England.* Vol. 1: *Bibliotheken und Archive in London.* Abhandlungen der Gesellschaft der Wissenschaften zu Göttingen, philologisch-historische Klasse, n.s. vol. 25. Berlin 1930. Vol. 2: *Die kirchlichen Archive und Bibliotheken.* Abhandlungen der Gesellschaft der Wissenschaften zu Göttingen, philologisch-historische Klasse, 3rd ser., nos. 14 and 15. Berlin 1935 and 1936.

——. *Das Register Papst Innocenz' III. über den deutschen Thronstreit: Regestum domni Innocentii tertii pape super negotio Romani imperii.* 2 vols. in 1. Bonn 1947-48.

Hóman, B. *Geschichte des ungarischen Mittelalters.* 2nd ed. Vol. 1. Budapest 1935.

Hove, Alfons van. *Prolegomena ad codicem iuris canonici.* Commentarium Lovaniense in codicem iuris canonici. 2nd ed. Mechlin and Rome 1945.

Hüls, Rudolf. "Das Kardinalskollegium in seiner Entstehungszeit und die Regioneneinteilung Roms." Ph.D. dissertation. Göttingen 1975. [Not seen.]

Jaffé, Philip. *Monumenta gregoriana.* Bibliotheca rerum germanicarum, vol. 2. Berlin 1865. Reprint Aalen 1964.

——. *Monumenta Moguntina.* Bibliotheca rerum germanicarum, vol. 3. Berlin 1866. Reprint Aalen 1964.

——. *Monumenta Bambergensia.* Bibliotheca rerum germanicarum, vol. 5. Berlin 1869. Reprint Aalen 1964.

——. *Regesta pontificum romanorum.* 2nd rev. ed. Edited by S. Loewenfeld, F. Kaltenbrunner, and P. Ewald. 2 vols. Leipzig 1885 and 1888. Reprint Graz 1956.

Jakobs, Hermann. *Die Hirsauer. Ihre Ausbreitung und Rechtsstellung im Zeitalter des Investiturstreites.* Kölner historische Abhandlungen, vol. 4. Cologne 1961.

Jedin, Hubert and John Dolan, eds. *Handbook of Church History.* Vol. 3: *The Church in the Age of Feudalism.* Edited by Friedrich Kempf et al., translated by A. Biggs. New York 1969.

Jenal, Georg. *Erzbischof Anno II. von Köln (1056-75) und sein politisches Wirken: Ein Beitrag zur Geschichte der Reichs- und Territorialpolitik im 11. Jahrhundert.* Monographien zur Geschichte des Mittelalters, vol. 8 in 2 parts. Stuttgart 1974 and 1975.

Juritsch, Georg. *Geschichte des Bischofs Otto I. von Bamberg, des Pommern-Apostels (1102-1139).* Gotha 1889.

*Die Kanonessammlung des Kardinals Deusdedit.* Edited by Victor Wolf von Glanvell. Vol. 1 [unicum]. Paderborn 1905. Reprint Aalen 1967.

Kantorowicz, Ernst H. "Inalienability." *Speculum* 29 (1954) 488-502.

——. *The King's Two Bodies: A Study in Mediaeval Political Theology.* Princeton 1957.

Kastner, Jörg. *Historiae fundationum monasteriorum: Frühformen monastischer In-*

*stitutionsgeschichtsschreibung im Mittelalter.* Münchener Beiträge zur Mediävistik und Renaissance-Forschung, vol. 18. Munich 1974.

Kay, R. L. "Mansi and Rouen: A Critique of the Conciliar Collections." *Catholic Historical Review* 52 (1966) 155-185.

Kehr, Paul. "Die Belehnungen der süditalienischen Normannenfürsten durch die Päpste (1059-1192)." *Abhandlungen der Preussischen Akademie der Wissenschaften zur Berlin, philosophisch-historische Klasse,* 1934-35, pp. 1-52.

———. "Le Bolle Pontificie che si conservano negli Archivi Senesi." *Bullettino Senese di Storia Patria,* vol. 6 (1899).

———. "Papsturkunden in Campanien." *Nachrichten der Kgl. Gesellschaft der Wissenschaften zu Göttingen, philologisch-historische Klasse,* 1900, pp. 286-344.

———. "Papsturkunden in Sizilien." *Nachrichten der Kgl. Gesellschaft der Wissenschaften zu Göttingen, philologisch-historische Klasse,* 1899, pp. 283-337.

———, ed. *Italia pontificia; sive, Repertorium privilegiorum et litterarum a romanis pontificibus ante annum MCLXXXXVIII Italiae ecclesiis, monasteriis, civitatibus singulisque personis concessorum* .... Vol. 3: *Etruria;* Berlin 1908. Vol. 5: *Aemilia sive provincia Ravennas;* Berlin 1911. Vol. 6: *Liguria sive provincia Mediolanensis,* part 1: *Lombardia;* Berlin 1913; part 2: *Pedemontium, Liguria maritima;* Berlin 1914. Vol. 7: *Venetia et Histria,* part 1: *Provincia Aquilensis;* Berlin 1923. Vol. 8: *Regnum normannorum - Campania;* Berlin 1935. Vol. 9: *Samnium, Apulia, Lucania;* edited by Walther Holtzmann; Berlin 1962. Vol. 10: *Calabria - Insulae;* edited by Dieter Girgensohn; Berlin 1975.

Kempf, Friederich et al. *The Church in the Age of Feudalism.* See Jedin, Hubert and John Dolan, eds. *Handbook of Church History.*

Kleinen, Hans and Robert Danzer. "Eine Cusanus Bibliographie 1920-1961." *Mitteilungen und Forschungen der Cusanus Gesellschaft* 1 (1961) 95-126.

Klewitz, Hans-Walter. "Die Entstehung des Kardinalkollegiums." *Zeitschrift der Savigny Stiftung für Rechtsgeschichte, Kanonistische Abteilung* 25 (1936) 115-221. Reprint in idem, *Reformpapsttum und Kardinalkolleg,* pp. 10-134. Darmstadt 1957.

———. "Studien über die Wiederherstellung der römischen Kirche in Süditalien durch das Reformpapsttum." *Quellen und Forschungen aus italienischen Archiven und Bibliotheken* 25 (1934-35) 105-157.

Knonau, Gerold Meyer von. *Jahrbücher des Deutschen Reiches unter Heinrich IV. und Heinrich V.* Jahrbücher der Deutschen Geschichte, vol. 17. 7 vols. Leipzig 1890-1909.

Krantz, Albert. *Rerum germanicarum historici clarissimi ecclesiastica historia, sive metropolis* .... Edited by Johannes Wolf. Frankfurt am Main 1567.

Kristeller, Paul Oskar. "The Contribution of Religious Orders to Renaissance Thought and Learning." *American Benedictine Review* 21 (1970) 1-55. Reprinted in idem, *Medieval Aspects of Renaissance Learning,* edited by Edward P. Mahoney. Durham 1974.

———. "Nicolò Cusano agli inizi del mondo moderno." *Atti del Congresso inter-*

*nazionale in occasione del v centenario della morte di Nicolò Cusano, Bressanone 6-10 settembre 1964*. Facoltà di Magistero dell'Università di Padova, vol. 12 (s.d.), pp. 175-193.

——. *Latin Manuscript Books Before 1600: A List of the Printed Catalogues and Unpublished Inventories of Extant Collections*. 3rd rev. ed. New York 1960.

Kuttner, Stephan. "L'Édition Romaine des conciles généraux et les actes du premier concile de Lyon." In *Miscellanea historiae pontificiae*. Vol. 3/5, pp. 3-40. Rome 1940.

——. "Notes on the Presentation of Text and Apparatus in Editing Works of the Decretists and Decretalists." *Traditio* 15 (1959) 452-464.

——. "Some Methodological Considerations." *Traditio* 11 (1955) 435-439.

——. "Some Roman Manuscripts of Canonical Collections." *Bulletin of Medieval Canon Law*, n.s. 1 (1971) 7-29.

——. "Urban II and the Doctrine of Interpretation: A Turning Point?" In *Post Scripta. Essays on Medieval Law and the Emergence of the European State in Honor of Gaines Post*, edited by Joseph R. Strayer and Donald E. Queller. Studia Gratiana, vol. 15 (1972), pp. 53-85.

——. "Urban II and Gratian." *Traditio* 24 (1968) 504-505.

—— and Robert Somerville. "The So-Called Canons of Nîmes (1096)" *Tijdschrift voor Rechtsgeschiedenis* 38 (1970) 175-189.

Kurze, Wilhelm. "Der Adel und das Kloster S. Salvatore all'Isola im 11. und 12. Jahrhundert." *Quellen und Forschungen aus italienischen Archiven und Bibliotheken* 47 (1967) 446-573.

Labau, Denis. "Contribution à l'histoire de l'évêché de Lescar (suite)." *Revue régionaliste des Pyrénées* 52 (1970) 64-71.

Labbe, Philippe and Gabriel Cossart, eds. *Sacrosancta concilia ad regiam editionem exacta ....* 16 vols. Paris 1671-72.

Ladewig, Paul and Theodor Müller. *Regesta episcoporum Constantiensium: Regesten zur Geschichte der Bischöfe von Constanz*, vol. 1. Innsbruck 1895.

Ladner, Gerhart B. *The Idea of Reform, Its Impact on Christian Thought and Action in the Age of the Fathers.* Cambridge, Mass. 1959.

——. "Two Gregorian Letters: On the Sources and Nature of Gregory VII's Reform Ideology." *Studi Gregoriani* 5 (1956) 221-242.

*Landulphi Junioris sive de Sancto Paulo Historia Mediolanensis ab anno MXCV usque ad annum MCXXXVII*. Rerum Italicarum Scriptores. 2nd ed. Vol. 5/3, edited by C. Castiglioni. Bologna s.d.

*Laurentii de Leodio gesta episcoporum Virdunensium*. Edited by Georg Waitz. Monumenta Germaniae Historica. Scriptores, vol. 10 (1852), pp. 486-525.

Leonardi, Claudio. "Per una storia dell'edizione romana dei Concili ecumenici (1608-1612) da Antonio Agustín a Francesco Aduarte." *Studi e Testi*, vol. 236, Mélanges Eugène Tisserant, vol. 6 (1964), pp. 583-637.

*Le Liber Censuum*. Edited by Paul Fabre and Louis D. Duchesne. Bibliothèque des Écoles Françaises d'Athènes et de Rome. Vols. 1-2, Paris 1889-1910; vol. 3, edited by G. Mollat, Paris 1952.

*Le Liber Pontificalis.* Edited by Louis D. Duchesne. Bibliothèque des Écoles Françaises d'Athènes et de Rome. Vol. 2. Paris 1892, reprinted 1955. Vol. 3, edited by C. Vogel, Paris 1957.

*Liber Pontificalis prout exstat in codice manuscripto Dertusensi.* Edited by Josephus M. March. Barcelona 1925.

Loewenfeld, S. "Papsturkunden in Paris." *Neues Archiv* 7 (1882) 144-167.

Lohrmann, Dietrich. "Die Jugendwerke des Johannes von Gaeta." *Quellen und Forschungen aus italienischen Archiven und Bibliotheken* 47 (1967) 355-445.

Luchaire, Achilles. *La cour du roi et ses fonctions judiciaires sous le règne de Louis vi (1108-1137).* Extrait des Annales de la Faculté des Lettres de Bordeaux, no. 2 (1880).

———. *Louis vi le Gros: Annales de sa vie et de son règne (1081-1137).* Paris 1890.

Lühe, Wilhelm. *Hugo von Die und Lyon, Legat von Gallien.* Breslau 1898.

Mabillon, Jean. *Annales Ordinis Sancti Benedicti* .... Vol. 5. Lucca 1742.

Mann, Horace K. *The Lives of the Popes.* 2nd rev. ed. Vol. 8. London 1925.

Mansi, J. D. *Sacrorum conciliorum nova et amplissima collectio* .... Vol. 20. Venice 1775.

———. *Sanctorum conciliorum et decretorum collectio nova.* 6 vols. Lucca 1748-1752.

Mantese, Giovanni. "Ein notarielles Inventar von Büchern und Wertgegenständen aus dem Nachlass des Nikolaus von Kues." *Mitteilungen und Forschungen der Cusanus Gesellschaft* 2 (1962) 85-116.

Marca, Pierre de. *Histoire de Béarn.* Paris 1640. 2nd rev. ed., edited by V. Dubarat. 2 vols. Pau 1912.

Martène, Edmond und Ursin Durand; *Thesaurus novus anecdotorum.* Vol. 4. Paris 1717.

———. *Veterum Scriptorum et monumentorum historicorum ... amplissima collectio.* Vol. 1, Paris 1724. Vol. 7, Paris 1733.

Martinus Polonus. *Chronicon pontificum et imperatorum.* Edited by Ludwig Weiland. Monumenta Germaniae Historica. Scriptores, vol. 22 (1872), pp. 377-475.

Masnovo, O. "Pier Grosolano e il suo epitafio." *Archivio Storico Lombardo,* ser. 5, 49 (1922) 1-28.

Mayer, Hans Eberhard. *The Crusades.* Translated by John Gillingham. Oxford 1972.

Mezey, Ladislas. "Ungarn und Europa im 12. Jahrhundert, Kirche und Kultur zwischen Ost und West." In *Probleme des 12. Jahrhunderts*, edited by Theodor Mayer. Konstanzer Arbeitskreis für mittelalterliche Geschichte. Vorträge und Forschungen, vol. 12, pp. 255-272. Constance 1968.

Monod, Bernard. *Essai sur les rapports de Pascal II avec Philippe I$^{er}$ (1099-1108).* Paris 1907.

Montfaucon, Bernard. *Bibliotheca bibliothecarum manuscriptorum nova.* 2 vols. Paris 1739.

Moos, Peter von. *Hildebert von Lavardin, 1056-1133: Humanitas an der Schwelle*

*des Höfischen Zeitalters.* Pariser Historische Studien, vol. 3. Stuttgart 1965.
Mordek, Hubert. "Handschriftenforschungen in Italien." *Quellen und Forschungen in italienischen Archiven und Bibliotheken* 51 (1971) 626-651.
——. "Proprie auctoritates apostolice sedis: Ein zweiter Dictatus papae Gregors VII.?" *Deutsches Archiv* 28 (1972) 105-132.
Morrison, Karl F. *Tradition and Authority in the Western Church 300-1140.* Princeton 1969.
Munier, Charles, ed. *Concilia Africae A. 345 - A. 525.* Corpus Christianorum Series Latina 259. Turnhout 1974.
Munro, Dana C. "A Crusader." *Speculum* 7 (1932) 321-335.
Munz, Peter. *Boso's Life of Alexander III.* See Boso.
Neuss, Wilhelm and Friedrich Wilhelm Oediger. *Das Bistum Köln von den Anfängen bis zum Ende des 12. Jahrhunderts.* Vol. 1. Cologne 1964.
Ordericus Vitalis. *The Ecclesiastical History of Orderic Vitalis.* Edited by Marjorie Chibnall. Vol. 2. Oxford 1969.
——. *Historia ecclesiastica libri XIII.* Edited by Augustus Le Prevost. Vol. 4. Paris 1852.
Ortmanns, Kurt. *Das Bistum Minden in seinen Beziehungen zu König, Papst und Herzog bis zum Ende des 12. Jahrhunderts. Ein Beitrag zur Germania Pontificia.* Reihe der Forschungen im Schäuble Verlag 5. Bensberg 1972.
Overmann, A. *Die Besitzungen der Grossgräfin Mathilde von Tuscien nebst Regesten ihrer Urkunden.* Berlin 1893.
——. *Gräfin Mathilde von Tuscien, ihre Besitzungen. Geschichte ihres Gutes von 1115-1230 und ihre Regesten.* Innsbruck 1895.
Partner, Peter. *The Lands of St. Peter: The Papal State in the Middle Ages and the Early Renaissance.* Berkeley 1972.
Peiser, Gerson. *Der deutsche Investiturstreit unter König Heinrich V. bis zum päpstlichen Privileg vom 3. April 1111.* Berlin 1883.
Peitz, W. M. *Regestum domni Innocentii tertii pape super negotio Romani imperii (Reg. Vat. 6), riprodotto in fototipia a cura della Biblioteca Apostolica Vaticana.* Codices e Vaticanis selecti, vol. 16. Rome 1927.
Peri, Vittorio. "Due Protagonisti dell'editio romana dei concili ecumenici: Petro Marin ed Antonio d'Aquino." *Studi e Testi,* vol. 237. Mélanges Eugène Tisserant, vol. 7 (1964), pp. 131-239.
Petersmann, Johanna. "Die kanonistische Überlieferung des Constitutum Constantini bis zum Dekret Gratians." *Deutsches Archiv* 30 (1974) 356-449.
Pflugk-Harttung, J. von. *Acta pontificum romanorum inedita: Urkunden der Päpste vom Jahre 748-1198.* Vol. 1, Tübingen 1881. Vols. 2 and 3, Stuttgart 1884-86.
——. "Briefe aus den Jahren 1047-1146." *Neues Archiv* 6 (1881) 626-636.
——. *Iter Italicum.* 2 vols. Stuttgart 1883.
Pirrus, Rocco. *Sicilia sacra, disquisitionibus et notitiis illustrata ....* Leiden s.d.
Placidus de Nonantola. *Liber de honore ecclesiae.* Edited by Ludwig von Heinemann and Ernst Sackur. Monumenta Germaniae Historica. Libelli de lite, vol. 2 (1892), pp. 566-639.

Potthast, August. *Bibliotheca historica medii aevi. Wegweiser durch die Geschichtswerke des europäischen Mittelalters von 375-1500.* Berlin 1862.
Prawer, Joshua. *Histoire du Royaume Latin de Jérusalem.* Translated by G. Nahon. Vol. 1. Paris 1969.
Pray, G. *Annales Regum Hungariae.* Vol. 1. Vienna 1763.
Pullapilly, Cyriac K. *Caesar Baronius, Counter-Reformation Historian.* Notre Dame and London 1975.
Quentin, Henri. *Jean-Dominique Mansi et les grandes collections conciliaires. Etude d'histoire littéraire suivi d'une correspondance inédite de Baluze avec le Cardinal Casanate et de lettres de Pierre Morin, Hardouin, Lupus, Mabillon et Montfaucon.* Paris 1900.
Quétif, J. and J. Echard. *Scriptores ordinis praedicatorum recensiti.* 2 vols. in 4. Paris 1719-23.
*Quinque compilationes antiquae.* Edited by Emil Friedberg. Leipzig 1882.
Ramackers, Johannes. *Papsturkunden in Frankreich.* Neue Folge, vol. 3: *Artois.* Abhandlungen der Gesellschaft der Wissenschaften zu Göttingen, philologisch-historische Klasse. Dritte Folge, vol. 23. 1940.
——. *Papsturkunden in Frankreich.* Neue Folge, vol. 4: *Picardie.* Abhandlungen der Gesellschaft der Wissenschaften zu Göttingen, philologisch-historische Klasse. Dritte Folge, vol. 27. 1942.
——. *Papsturkunden in den Niederlanden.* Abhandlungen der Gesellschaft der Wissenschaften zu Göttingen, philologisch-historische Klasse. Dritte Folge, vol. 9. Berlin 1933-34.
Rassow, Peter. "Der Kampf Kaiser Heinrich iv. mit Heinrich v." *Zeitschrift für Kirchengeschichte* 47 (1928) 451-465.
—— "Über Erzbischof Ruthard von Mainz (1089-1109)." *Die Geschichtliche Einheit des Abendlandes.* Kölner Historische Abhandlungen, vol. 2. Cologne and Graz 1960.
*Recueil des historiens des Gaules et de la France.* Vol. 15. Edited by Léopold Delisle. Paris 1878.
Reincke, H. "Albert Krantz als Geschichtsschreiber und Geschichtsforscher." *Festschrift der Hamburgischen Universität für W. von Melle.* Hamburg 1933.
Rodriguez, Florencio Marcos. "Tres manuscritos del siglo *XII* con collecciones canónicas." *Analecta Sacra Tarraconensia* 32 (1959) 35-44.
Röhricht, R. *Geschichte der Kreuzzüge im Umriss.* Innsbruck 1898.
Rowe, J. G. "Paschal ii and the Relation between the Spiritual and Temporal Powers in the Kingdom of Jerusalem." *Speculum* 32 (1957) 470-501.
——. "Paschal ii, Bohemund of Antioch and the Byzantine Empire." *Bulletin of the John Rylands Library* 49 (1966) 165-202.
Rozière, Eugène de, ed. *Cartulaire de l'Église du Saint Sépulcre de Jérusalem.* Paris 1849.
Runciman, Steven. *A History of the Crusades.* Vols. 1 and 2. Cambridge, Engl. 1951 and 1952. Reprint New York 1964 and 1965.
Säbekow, Gerhard. *Die päpstlichen Legationen nach Spanien und Portugal bis zum Ausgang des xii. Jahrhunderts.* Berlin 1931.

Sackur, Ernst. "Der Dictatus papae und die Canonsammlung des Deusdedit." *Neues Archiv* 18 (1893) 137-153.
*Sancti Anselmi Cantuariensis archiepiscopi opera omnia.* Edited by F. S. Schmitt. 6 vols. Edinburgh 1945.
Santifaller, Leo. *Neuere Editionen mittelalterlicher Königs- und Papsturkunden; eine Übersicht unter Mitwirkung von Mitgliedern des Instituts für österreichische Geschichtsforschung.* Österreichische Akademie der Wissenschaften. Mitteilungen der Wiener Diplomata Abteilung der MGH. Vienna 1958.
Schellhass, Karl. "Deutsche und Kuriale Gelehrte im Dienste der Gegenreformation." *Quellen und Forschungen aus italienischen Archiven und Bibliotheken* 14 (1911) 287-314.
———. "Wissenschaftliche Forschungen unter Gregor XIII. für die Neuausgabe des Gratianischen Dekrets." In *Papsttum und Kaisertum, Forschungen zur politischen Geschichte und Geisteskultur des Mittelalters Paul Kehr zum 65. Geburtstag dargebracht*, ed. Albert Brackmann, pp. 674-690. Munich 1926. Reprinted Aalen 1973.
Schieffer, Theodor. *Die päpstlichen Legaten in Frankreich vom Vertrage von Meersen (870) bis zum Schisma von 1130.* Berlin 1935.
———. "Der Stand des Göttinger Papsturkunden-Werkes." In *Jahrbuch der Akademie der Wissenschaften in Göttingen 1971*, pp. 68-79. Göttingen 1971.
Schlechte, Horst. *Erzbischof Bruno von Trier.* Leipzig 1934.
Schmale, Franz-Josef. "Fiktionen im Codex Udalrici." *Zeitschrift für bayerische Landesgeschichte* 20 (1957) 437-474.
———. "'Paderborner' oder 'Korveyer' Annalen?" *Deutsches Archiv* 30 (1974) 505-526.
———. *Studien zum Schisma des Jahres 1130.* Forschungen zur kirchlichen Rechtsgeschichte und zum Kirchenrecht, vol. 3. Cologne and Graz 1961.
———. "Systematisches zu den Konzilien des Reformpapsttums im 12. Jahrhundert." *Annuarium Historiae Conciliorum* 6 (1974) 21-39.
———. "Überlieferungskritik und Editionsprinzipien der Chronik Ekkehards von Aura." *Deutsches Archiv* 27 (1971) 110-134.
Schmale-Ott, Irene. "Die Rezension C der Weltchronik Ekkehards." *Deutsches Archiv* 12 (1956) 363-387.
———. "Untersuchungen zu Ekkehard von Aura und zur Kaiserchronik." *Zeitschrift für bayerische Landesgeschichte* 34 (1971) 403-461.
Schmitt, F. S. "Zur Entstehungsgeschichte der handschriftlichen Sammlungen der Briefe des Hl. Anselm von Canterbury." *Revue Bénédictine* 48 (1936) 300-317.
———. "Zur Überlieferung der Korrespondenz Anselms von Canterbury: Neue Briefe." *Revue Bénédictine* 43 (1931) 224-238.
Schreiber, Georg. *Kurie und Kloster im 12. Jahrhundert.* Kirchenrechtliche Abhandlungen 65-68. 2 vols. Stuttgart 1910. Reprint Amsterdam 1965.
Schulte, Johann Friedrich von. "Die Rechtshandschriften der Stifsbibliotheken von Göttweig ... Ord. S. Bened." *Sitzungsberichte der Kaiserlichen Akademie der Wissenschaften Wien* 57 (1867) 559-616.

Schum, Wilhelm. "Kaiser Heinrich v. und Papst Paschalis II. im Jahre 1112." *Jahrbücher der Akademie zu Erfurt*, n.s. 8 (1877) 191-318.

Schumann, Otto. *Die päpstlichen Legaten in Deutschland zur Zeit Heinrichs IV. und Heinrichs V. (1056-1125)*. Diss. Marburg 1912.

Sdralek, Max. *De S. Nicolai Papae I epistolarum codicibus*. Breslau 1882.

——. *Die Streitschriften Altmanns von Passau und Wezilos von Mainz*. Paderborn 1890.

——. *Wolfenbüttler Fragmente: Analekten zur Kirchengeschichte des Mittelalters aus Wolfenbüttler Handschriften*. Kirchengeschichtliche Studien, vol. 1. Münster 1891.

Seherus. *Primordia Calmosiacensia*. Edited by Philipp Jaffé. Monumenta Germaniae Historica. Scriptores, vol. 12 (1856), pp. 324-347.

Simeoni, Luigi. "Il contributo della contessa Matilde al papato nella lotta per le investiture." *Studi Gregoriani* 1 (1947) 353-372.

Somerville, Robert. "The Council of Beauvais, 1114." *Traditio* 24 (1968) 493-503.

——. "The Council of Clermont (1095), and Latin Christian Society." *Archivum Historiae Pontificiae* 12 (1974) 55-90.

——. "The Council of Pisa, 1135." *Speculum* 45 (1970) 98-114.

——. *The Councils of Urban II, 1: Decreta Claromontensia*. Annuarium Historiae Conciliorum Supplementum, vol. 1. Amsterdam 1972.

——. "The French Councils of Pope Urban II; Some Basic Considerations." *Annuarium Historiae Conciliorum* 2 (1970) 56-65.

——. "Honorius II, Conrad and Lothar III." *Archivum Historiae Pontificiae* 10 (1972) 341-346.

——. "Miscellany: Two Notes on Scotland and the Medieval Papacy." *The Innes Review* 23 (1972) 149-151.

——. "An Unknown Letter of Pope Paschal II." *Speculum* 47 (1972) 737-741.

——. See also S. Kuttner and R. Somerville.

Southern, R. W. *Saint Anselm and His Biographer: A Study of Monastic Life and Thought 1059 - c. 1130*. Cambridge, Engl. 1963.

Sprandel, Rolf. *Ivo von Chartres und seine Stellung in der Kirchengeschichte*. Pariser Historische Studien, vol. 1. Stuttgart 1962.

Sproemberg, Heinrich. "Urban II und das kanonische Recht." *Zeitschrift der Savigny Stiftung für Rechtsgeschichte, Kanonistische Abteilung* 51 (1965) 254-263.

Steffen, C. "Untersuchungen zum 'Liber de scriptoribus ecclesiasticis' des Johannes Trithemius." *Archiv für Geschichte des Buchwesens* 10 (1970) cols. 1247-1354.

Stein, Henri. *Bibliographie générale des cartulaires français*. Manuels de bibliographie historique, vol. 4. Paris 1907.

Stevenson, E. "Osservazioni sulla Collectio Canonum di Deusdedit." *Archivio della R. Società Romana di Storia Patria* 8 (1885) 305-398.

Sthamer, Eduard. "Das Chartular von Sant'Angelo in Formis." *Quellen und For-*

*schungen aus italienischen Archiven und Bibliotheken* 22 (1930-31) 1-30.
Stickler, Alphonsus M. *Historia Iuris Canonici Latini.* Vol. 1: *Historia Fontium.* Turin 1950.
Stimming, Manfred, ed. *Mainzer Urkundenbuch.* Vol. 1: *Die Urkunden bis zum Tode Erzbischofs Adalberts ı. (1137).* Darmstadt 1932.
Suger. *Vie de Louis le Gros.* Edited and translated by Henri Waquet. Les classiques de l'histoire de France au moyen âge. Paris 1929.
Szentpétery, I. and I. Borsa. *Regesta regum stirpis Arpadianae critico-diplomatico.* Vol. 1. Budapest 1923.
Tangl, Georgine. *Die Teilnehmer an den allgemeinen Konzilien des Mittelalters.* Weimar 1932. Reprint Darmstadt 1969.
Tarré, J. "La Collection Caesaraugustana attribuable à Renan, écolâtre de Barcelona, 1117-25." *Positions des thèses de l'École des Chartes,* vol. 20 (1927).
Thaner, Friedrich, ed. *Anselmi Lucensis collectio canonum una cum collectione minore.* 2 fasc. in 1. Innsbruck 1906-15. Reprint Aalen 1965.
Theiner, Augustin. *Disquisitiones criticae in praecipuas canonum et decretalium collectiones.* Rome 1836.
Thomas, Heinz. "Studien zur Trierer Geschichtsschreibung des 11. Jahrhunderts, insbesondere zu den Gesta Treverorum." *Rheinisches Archiv* 68. Bonn 1968.
*Tractatus de investitura episcoporum.* Edited by Ernst Bernheim. Monumenta Germaniae Historica. Libelli de lite, vol. 2 (1892), pp. 495-504.
*Translatio S. Modoaldi.* Edited by Philipp Jaffé. Monumenta Germaniae Historica. Scriptores, vol. 12 (1856), pp. 284-310.
Turner, Cuthbert Hamilton, ed. *Ecclesiae occidentalis monumenta iuris antiquissima, canonum et conciliorum Graecorum interpretationes Latinae.* Vols. 1 and 2. Oxford 1899-1907.
Udalschalk. *De Eginone et Herimanno.* Edited by Philip Jaffé. Monumenta Germaniae Historica. Scriptores, vol. 12 (1856), pp. 429-448.
Ullman, B. L. and P. A. Stadter. *The Public Library of Renaissance Florence: Niccolò Niccoli, Cosimo de' Medici and the Library of San Marco.* Padua 1972.
Váczy, P. von. *Die erste Epoche des ungarischen Königtums.* Pécs 1936.
Vehse, Otto. "Benevent als Territorium des Kirchenstaates bis zum Beginn der avignonesischen Epoche. I. Teil." *Quellen und Forschungen aus italienischen Archiven und Bibliotheken* 22 (1930-31) 87-160.
*Vitae nonnullorum pontificum Romanorum a Nicolao Aragonii S.R.E. cardinali conscriptae.* Edited by N. Aloisia. Rerum Italicarum Scriptores. Vol. 3/1. Milan 1723.
Wassebourg, R. *Antiquitez de la Gaule Belgicque.* 2 vols. in 1. [Verdun?] 1549.
Wasserschleben, H. "Zur Geschichte der Gottesfrieden." *Zeitschrift der Savigny Stiftung für Rechtsgeschichte, Germanistische Abteilung* 12 (1891) 112-117.
Wattenbach, Wilhelm. "Aus Stuttgart und Schaffhausen." *Neues Archiv* 6 (1880) 447-451.
―― and Robert Holtzmann. *Deutschlands Geschichtsquellen im Mittelalter.* Rev. ed. by F.-J. Schmale. 3 vols. Darmstadt 1967-71.

Watterich, Wilhelm. *Pontificum romanorum ... vitae.* Vol. 1. Leipzig 1862.
Weiss, Ursula-Renate. *Die Konstanzer Bischöfe im 12. Jahrhundert. Ein Beitrag zur Untersuchung der reichsbischöflichen Stellung im Kräftefeld kaiserlicher, päpstlicher und regionaldiözesaner Politik.* Konstanzer Geschichts- und Rechtsquellen, vol. 20. Sigmaringen 1975.
William of Tyre. *Historia rerum in partibus transmarinis gestarum.* Recueil des historiens des croisades. Historiens occidentaux. Vol. 1/1. Paris 1844.
Williams, Schafer. *Codices Pseudo-Isidoriani: A Palaeographico-Historical Study.* Monumenta iuris canonici, series C: Subsidia. Vol. 3. New York 1971.
Wilmart André. "La tradition des lettres de S. Anselme." *Revue Bénédictine* 43 (1931) 38-54.
Yewdale, Ralph Bailey. *Bohemond I, Prince of Antioch.* Princeton 1924. Reprint Amsterdam 1970.
Zerbi, Piero. "Pasquale II e l'ideale della povertà della chiesa." *Annuario dell'Università cattolica del Sacro Cuore.* Milan 1964-65.

# INDEX OF INCIPITS OF PASCHALIAN CANONS

The numbers in italics indicate the pages on which the canon is discussed.

Abbatibus qui 70; *132*
Aliud quoque 51; *44, 49*
Anno postea 54
Apostolica auctoritate 95
Apostolorum canonibus 119; *115, 120n*
Arcas in 95

Circa solutionem 52
Constitutiones sanctorum 59, 60, 61, 65, 71, 93, 119, 120; *62, 64, 65, 109, 115-116, 121, 125, 132, 135*

De coniugatis 91
De pace igitur 91
De uxoratis 91
Decani quos 96

Ecclesias et 95
Episcopi lectioni 68; *132*
Et divine legis 105

Iamdiu a prauis 53, 64; *44, 65*
In hoc concilio 52
In Langobardia 43
In qua videlicet 103
Iniungit etiam 93
Item in Antiocheno 119
Item quicumque 92
Item Stephanus martyr 119; *in JL 6145* 83; *82*

Laici nullum 94
Laicis quamuis 137; *135*; *in JL 6145* 83
Laicos ab inuestituris 92

Matrimonia contrahere 94

Ne presbiteri duas 92
Nullus abbas 54, 57; *46*
Nullus episcopus 69; *132*
Nullus laicorum 59, 60, 64, 69, 132n, 138; *63, 65, 132, 133*
Nullus sibi 96
Nuper in 20n

Per multos 53, 55; *126*
Postea quidem 86
Presbiteris et 94

Qua de re 18; *15n*
Quia, inquit, tunicam 21
Quicumque res 120; *109-111, 112, 115, 121*
Quod si quis 96
Quoniam aecclesia 56

Sacerdotibus et 91
Sanctorum patrum vestigiis 90, 84
Si preda 94
Si quis aecclesiae 92
Si quis clericus 59, 60, 65, 70, 137; *59, 62, 65, 132, 133*
Si quis erfo 120; *110, 121*
Si quis munus 95
Si quis principum 137
Sicut domini 69, 138; *60, 132, 133*
Sunt preterea 120; *121, 122n*

Unde in concilio 30
Uestimenta vero 103, 106

# MANUSCRIPT INDEX

Avranches, Bibliothèque municipale, MS 146: 111

Bamberg, Staatsbibliothek, MS Lit. 140 (Ed. II. 16): 56
—, MS Patr. 30 (B. III. 25): 56
Barcelona, Archivio de la Corona de Aragón, MS San Cugat 63: 104 n
Berlin, Deutsche Staatsbibliothek, MS Phillipps 1746: 19n, 20n, 121n
Besançon, Bibliothèque municipale, MS 398: 49, 50
Brussels, Bibliothèque royale, MS 11196-11197: 115, 116

Cambridge, Corpus Christi College, MS 94: 19n, 20n, 121n
—, MS 269: 58n
Cortona, Pubblica Biblioteca Comunale e dell'Accademia Etrusca, MS 43: 111, 114

Florence, Biblioteca Marucelliana, MS C 386: 110
Florence, Biblioteca Mediceo-Laurenziana, MS Ashburnham 53: 58, 63, 65
—, MS San Marco 499: 58, 58n, 63, 66
Florence, Biblioteca nazionale, MS Conventi soppressi A. 4. 269: 110, 112
—, MS Conventi soppressi D. 2. 1476: 19n, 20n, 121n
Florence, Biblioteca Riccardiana, MS 228: 44, 44n, 46n, 47, 50, 51
—, MS 3006: 110
Frankfurt am Main, Stadt- und Universitätsbibliothek, MS Barth. 50: 55

Göttweig, Stiftsbibliothek, MS 53 (56): 78, 89, 96
—, MS 85 (8): 55
Graz, Universitätsbibliothek, MS 351: 58, 63, 66

Huesca, Biblioteca Provincial, MS 20: 58n

London, British Library, MS Cotton Claudius E.V: 17n
—, MS Cotton Tiberius B.VIII: 116n
—, MS Cotton Titus A.IX: 15n

Madrid, Biblioteca Nacional, MS 4207 (P.95): 51, 54
Metz, Bibliothèque municipale, MS 221 (E.14): 115, 117
Montecassino, Archivio della Badia, MS 522: 109, 111
Munich, Bayerische Staatsbibliothek, Clm 3739 (August., eccl. 39): 50, 55, 78, 90

Naples, Biblioteca nazionale, MS XII A 27: 104, 105, 105n
—, MS XII A 37-39: 58, 63, 67, 104, 105, 105n
—, MS VI E 43: 8n

Orléans, Bibliothèque municipale, MS 315 (267bis): 109-110, 112

Paris, Bibliothèque de l'Arsenal, MS 717: 84, 88, 96
Paris, Bibliothèque nationale, MS Baluze 7: 84n, 86n, 98n
—, MS Baluze 91: 104
—, MS Baluze 269: 104
—, MS, Collection Duchesne, vol. CXIV: 14n
—, MS lat. 152: 86
—, MS lat. 1275: 14n
—, MS lat. 3871: 111
—, MS lat. 3872: 111
—, MS lat. 3875: 104, 104n
—, MS lat. 3876: 104n
—, MS lat. 4284: 20, 20n, 70
—, MS lat. 10743: 19, 20n, 86n, 121n

# MANUSCRIPT INDEX

—, MS lat. 11851: 78, 82n, 89, 96
Parma, Biblioteca Palatina, Fondo Parmense 976: 58, 67
Pistoia, Archivio capitolare del Duomo, MS 135 (109): 114

Rome, Biblioteca Vallicelliana, MS C.16: 50, 54
—, MS C.24: 47, 48, 48n, 61n, 113, 135, 136, 137
—, MS C.25: 48
—, MS F.54: 115, 117

Saint Omer, Bibliothèque municipale, MS 364: 19, 20n, 111
Salamanca, Universidad Civil, MS 2644: 103n, 104n
San Daniele del Friuli, Biblioteca Civica Guarneriana, MS 203: 52
Schaffhausen, Ministerialbibliothek, MS 46: 46n, 57

Tarbes, Bibliothèque municipale, MS Glanage VI: 14n
Troyes, Bibliothèque municipale, MS 480: 111

Vatican City, Biblioteca Apostolica Vaticana, Archivio Segreto, MS Miscell Arm XV.1: 46n
—, MS Miscell. Arm. XXXV.18: 46n
Vatican City, Biblioteca Apostolica Vaticana, MS Archivio della Basilica di San Pietro C.118: 109n, 121n
—, MS Barb. lat. 535: 103n
—, MS Barb. lat. 538: 46n, 57
—, MS Barb. lat. 860: 60, 61, 61n, 62, 64, 81n, 83n, 132n
—, MS Barb. lat. 897: 103n, 104n, 105n
—, MS Ottob. lat. 3057: 2n
—, MS Palat. lat. 587: 50, 55
—, MS Reg. lat. 972: 20, 20n
—, MS Vat. lat. 1339: 61n, 62n
—, MS Vat. lat. 1346: 52, 104, 105, 106, 109, 111, 112
—, MS Vat. lat. 1361: 58, 62n, 68
—, MS Vat. lat. 1364: 53, 70, 83n
—, MS Vat. lat. 1984: 2n, 45
—, MS Vat. lat. 3829: 121n
—, MS Vat. lat. 3831: 114
—, MS Vat. lat. 3958: 48n
—, MS Vat. lat. 4891: 59, 59n, 60n, 61, 62, 83n, 133
—, MS Vat. lat. 4928: 8n
—, MS Vat. lat. 4939: 8n, 131
—, MS Vat. lat. 4976: 104n
—, MS Vat. lat. 4977: 109, 113
—, MS Vat. lat. 5717: 104n
—, MS Vat. lat. 6948: 61n
—, MS Vat. lat. 8486: 2n, 44n
Vienna, Österreichische Nationalbibliothek, MS 1705: 56
—, MS 2178: 19n, 20n
—, MS 2186: 111, 115

Wolfenbüttel, Herzog August Bibliothek, Cod. Guelf. 9.4 Aug. 4°: 116, 117
—, Cod. Guelf. Gud. 212: 86, 103, 105, 109, 114, 121n
—, Cod. Guelf. Helmst. 308: 115

# GENERAL INDEX

Abinghof, monastery of (Paderborn), 117
Acatius, patriarch of Constantinople (472-489) 57
Adelgot, archbp. of Magdeburg (1107-1119) 40
Agobard, archbp. of Lyons (814-840) 88
Agustín, Antonio (1517-1586), archbp. of Tarragona 48, 48n, 113, 136, 136n
Alberic, card. pr. of S. Pietro in Vincoli (ca. 1100): at Melfi 9
Albert, archbp. of Siponto: at Melfi 9
Aldo, bp. of Piacenza (1096-1118) 36n; at Châlons-sur-Marne 79n; at Guastalla 42n; at Troyes 79, 80
Alexander, monk of Christ Church, Canterbury 16n
Alexander I, pope (105-115?) 60, 65
Alexander III, pope (1159-1181) 48
Alfons VI, king of Castile and León (1072-1109): papal letter JL 5840 8
Amelius, bp. of Toulouse 85n
Amiens, diocese of, see Godfrey, bp. of
Amoulo, archbp. of Lyons (841-852) 88
Anaclete II, see Petrus, son of Petrus Leonis
Anastasius, card. pr. of S. Clemente (ca. 1102-1125): at Lateran council (1102) 17
anathema (anathemizare) 21, 71, 77; with declaration of obedience 13, 21, 72-73
*Annales Beneventani monasterii Sanctae Sophiae* 8, 8n, 10, 130
*Annales Hildesheimenses* 117, 118
*Annales Patherbrunnenses* 82, 83n, 116, 117; and Guastalla 42n, 71, 73; and Troyes (1107) 77-78, 79, 99-101
*Annales S. Disibodi* 22
Annalista Saxo 78, 82, 89, 107, 117
Anselm, archbp. of Canterbury (1093-1109) 122; compromise of 1107 19, 97; embassies to Paschal II 81, 123; excommunication of Henry I 30n; and homage 18; and investiture 20; papal letters JL 5908 14, 15, 16, 17-18, 19; JL 5928 27, 129; JL 6028 24, 30-31; JL 6073 19n, 97n; JL 6206 106; Paschal's dispensation for 18, 19n, 97n; second exile from England 16n, 30-31; supported by Paschal II 20, 31
Anselm, bp. of Lucca (d. 1086): *Collectio Canonum* of 83, 104, 105, 126, 128, 132n; **5.10** 69, 83n, 119; **5.45** 93; **6.113** 69; **6.156** 119; **7.191** 70, 83n; **8.34** 53; and Guastalla canons 58, 62-65; manuscripts with Guastalla canons 58, 63
Anso, governor of Benevento 10
Antioch, council of (341) 125; c.**24** 119; *see also Canones Apostolorum*, c. **30**
Antwerp, Museum Bollandianum 117
apostolicus 21, 22, 27, 33, 45, 52, 99
Apulia 11, 16, 28
Aquileia, *see* Udalric, patriarch of
Aquino, Antonio d': and Correctores Romani 60-61; and Gratian c.**16** q.7 c.**17** 64
Arras, diocese of: *see* Clarembald, archdeacon of; Lambert, bp. of; Ste. Marie, cathedral church of; St. Mauritius, church of; St. Vaast, abbey of
Ashburnham, Lord 66
Auch, *see* William II, archbp. of
Augsburg, city of: Paschal II expected at 41
—, diocese of: canons from, at Guastalla 41; papal letters JL 5971 36; JL 6103 36; JL 6119 36; *see also* Hermann, bp. of; SS. Ulrich and Afra, monastery of
Augustine, bp. of Hippo (354-430), 20; epistle **185** 52-53
Autenrieth, J. 63n
Azelin, chanter of St. Vannes, Verdun 41

Baldwin, king of Jerusalem (1100-1118) 26
Baldwin, monk of abbey of Bec, 16n, 81, 97
Baluze, E.: and Arsenal codex 84-87, 88-89; and codex Rivipullensis 104
Bari, council of (1099) 128

Baronius, C.: *Annales Ecclesiastici* 4, 11, 12-13, 14, 36, 38, 48, 49, 50, 76, 102, 107
Bartholomew, bp. of Narbonne (828-844) 88
Bec, abbey of: visit of Anselm, archbp. of Canterbury, to 31; *see also* Baldwin, monk of
Becker, A. 98
Benevento: Anso, governor of 10; Dacumarius, governor of 10; excommunication of 10-11; war of Paschal II against 10; *see also* S. Sophia, monastery of
Benevento, council of (1102): dubious 130-131
Benevento, council of (1108) 102-106, 107; investiture prohibited at 103-104, 105; Old Testament sources at 127
Beno, schismatic card. pr. of SS. Martino e Silvestro (d. after 1098): *Gesta Romanae aecclesiae contra Hildebrandum* 116
Berardi, C. S. 77, 133
Berardo, card. d. of S. Angelo (d. 1130): at Guastalla 42n; at Troyes 79
Bernardi degli Uberti, abbot of Vallombrosa, card. pr. of S. Crisogono, bp. of Parma (1106-1133): at Guastalla 41; at Lateran Council (1102) 18
Bernier, abbot of Bonneval: papal letter JL 6139 79
Bernold of Constance (d. 1100): author of *De Berengarii haeresiarchae damnatione multiplici* (?) 56; *De excommunicatis vitandis* ... 53
Berta, abbess of S. Maria Theodatae 42
Bertolini, O. 8n
Besançon, *see* St. Vincent, monastery at
Bible, Ezechiel **45.1-4** 105, 127; John **19.23f.** 69; 1 Tim. **3.7** 68; **5.22** 83
Binius, S. 4, 37, 76, 102n, 107
Biondo (Blondus), Flavio (1392-1463) 43
bishops 58, 68, 69, 70, 71, 128
Bohemond of Antioch 28
Bologna, diocese of 52, 54
Bonosius (d. ca. 400) 57
Boso, card. pr. of S. Anastasia (ca. 1113-ca. 1117) 85, 85n

Boso, card. pr. tituli Pastoris (1165-1178) 44n; and Guastalla canons 44-46, 50; and Roselli 47, 48-50; vita of Paschal II 44-47, 49, 124
Boutourlin, Count, library of 66
Bresslau, H. 46
*breviaria* (of canons): from Guastalla 65; from Lateran council (1112) 46, 51, 57; from Troyes 87
Bruges, cathedral chapter of 42
Bruno, bp. of Segni (1079-1123): at Benevento (1108) 103; at Guastalla (?) 42, 60n; and Guastalla canons 60n; held synod of Poitiers (1106) 28; at Lateran council (1105) (?) 28; at Melfi 9; and Montecassino 12
Bruno, archbp. of Trier (1102-1124) 72, 99; ambassador of Henry V 25-26, 36, 73, 75, 82, 99; at Guastalla 26, 39; invested by Henry IV 72; papal letter JL 6099 22, 72; and Rothard, archbp. of Mainz 100
Burchard, bp. of Münster (1097-1118) 82
Burchard, bp. of Worms (1000-1025): *Decretum*, 55, 126; **1.210** 119; **2.96** 92; **3.109** 70

Caecilian, bp. of Carthage (311-ca. 337) 52
Calixtus II, pope (1119-1124), *see* Guy, archbp. of Vienne; Reims, archdiocese of, council (1119); Rome, Lateran council (1123); Toulouse, council of (1119)
Cambrai, diocese of, *see* Odo, bp. of; Walcher, bp. of
Campagna 16
Camusat, Nicholas, canon of chapter of Troyes (1575-1655) 88
*Canones Apostolorum* 125; c.**29** 119; c.**30** 60, 65, 70, 83, 119; c.**31** 70, 83; c.**38** 119
canonical elections 77, 120
Canterbury: seizure of lands of church of 30n; *see also* Anselm, archbp. of
Canterbury, Christ Church, *see* Alexander, monk of; Eadmer, monk of
Cantor, N. H. 2, 128n
Capua 29; *see also* S. Maria, convent of; Sennes, archbp. of

Cardinals, *see* Alberic (S. Pietro in Vincoli); Anastasius (S. Clemente); Beno (schismatic; SS. Martino e Silvestro); Berardo (S. Angelo); Bernard degli Uberti (S. Crisogono); Boso (S. Anastasia); Boso (tituli Pastoris); Cono (Palestrina); Cusanus, Nicolas (S. Pietro in Vincoli); Deusdedit (S. Pietro in Vincoli); Diani, Pietro (S. Cecilia); Diviso (SS. Martino e Silvestro); Galo (SS. Martino e Silvestro); Galterius (ca. 1100); John (Tusculum); John of Gaeta (S. Maria in Cosmedin); Landulf (S. Lorenzo in Lucina); Milo (Palestrina); Oddo II (Ostia); Richard (Albano); Riso (S. Lorenzo in Damaso); Robert Parisiensis (S. Eusebio); Roselli, Nicholas (Aragon); Ugo (SS. Cosma e Damiano)

Carthage, council of (401): c.**68**, vers. Dion. 52, 53

*Cassatio* (of investiture privilege of 1111) 38, 49

Castiglioni, E. 24n, 29n

Celestine II, pope (1143-1144) 112

Châlons-sur-Marne: negotiations at 75-76, 82; *see also* St. Etienne, cathedral

Charles the Great (768-814) 75

Chartres, diocese of, *see* St. Peter's abbey

Chaumouzey, monastery of (Toul) 41

*Chronica monasterii Casinensis* 3, 12; and Benevento council (1108) 102, 103 105; and Lateran council (1105) 26; papal letter JL 6070 33

*Chronicon Coloniense* 117

*Chronicon Hildesheimense* 107

*Chronicon Malleacense/Chronicon Sancti Maxentii Pictavense/Chronicon of Maillezais* 77, 85

*Chronicon Sancti-Petri-Vivi Senonensis*, *see* Clarius of Sens

*Chronological Decretal Collection* of MS Vat. Lat. 3829 121

Ciavarella, A 67

Cirkenbach, Andreas, of Würzburg (14th cent.) 89

Clarembald, archdeacon of Arras: at Troyes 81

Clarius of Sens: *Chronicon Sancti-Petri-Vivi Senonensis* 77, 85, 112

clerical garments 72; and Benevento council (1108) 103, 106; and Troyes council 94, 101

Clermont, council of (1095) 4, 18, 18n, 70, 73, 86, 87; and canons and legislation of Paschal II 84, 87, 92, 93, 94, 95, 96, 119; lay homage prohibited at 128; and Paschal II 70

Cluny, monastery of: papal letter JL 6154 80; Paschal II at 74

*Codex*: at papal curial 10n

Codex Udalrici 50, 56

Colbert, N. 89

Coleti, N. 24, 37, 49, 50, 77

*Collectio Caesaraugustana* 103, 104, 105

*Collectio Regia* 76, 107

*Collection in Three Books* 109n

*Collection in Five Books* 61n

*Collection in Seven Books* 52, 104, 109n, 111, 113

*Collection in Nine Books* 86n, 103, 109n

*Collection in Ten Parts* 19, 20, 86n, 109n, 111, 113, 121-122

*Collection in Thirteen Books* 62, 62n, 63, 68

*Collection in Seventy-Four Titles*, *see Diversorum patrum sententie*

Collection of MS Archivio S. Pietro C. **118** 109n, 121

*Collection of Santa Maria Novella* 109n, 110, 112

Coloman, king of Hungary (1095-1116) 38, 49

"concilium generale" 35n, 107, 123

"concilium universale" 123

Concordat of Worms: and agreements of 1111 1

Cono, prior of canons of Arouaise, later card. bp. of Palestrina (ca. 1108-1122) 79n; papal letter JL 6136 79

Corbie, monastery of 42

*Corpus Decretalium* 105

Correctores Romani 47-48, 47n, 50, 59n, 62, 63, 64, 83n, 132n, 133, 136, 137; and Segni Fragment 59-60; and Vatican codex 59, 61

Cossart, G., 76, 107, 112
Councils, *see* Antioch (341); Bari (1099); Benevento (1102, 1108); Carthage (401); Clermont (1095); Guastalla (1106); Melfi (1100); Nîmes (1096); Pavia (850); Piacenza (1095); Poitiers (1100); Reims (1049; 1119); Rome (502; 864; 1078; 1079; 1080; 1095; 1099); Rome, Lateran (1102; 1105; 1110; 1112; 1116; 1123; 1139); Toulouse (1119); Troyes (1107)
Crescentius, archbp. of Spalato (1100-1110): at Lateran council (1102) 12, 18; and papal letter JL 6570 13
crusades 93
Cusanus, Nicholas, card. pr. of San Pietro in Vincoli, and bp. of Brixen (1401-1464) 116
Cyprian: *Liber de unitate ecclesiae* 69

Dacumarius, governor of Benevento 10
Daimbert, patriarch of Jerusalem (1102-1107) 26n, 27n; at Lateran council (1105) 28; restitution of 26-28
*decreta patrum* (and synonyms) 17, 52, 53, 55, 61, 64, 65, 68, 83, 90, 93, 96, 103, 119, 124, 125
*Decretals, see* Gregory IX, pope
*Decretales Pseudo-Isidoriani* 35n, 127; redaction of Lanfranc, archb. of Canterbury (1070-1089) 17n; Ps.-Lucius (JK†123) 68; Ps.-Sixtus II, ep. **2, 6** (JK†134) 69; Ps.-Stephanus I, ep. **2.12** (JK† 131) 64, 69, 83, 119, 136
Deusdedit, cardinal pr. of S. Pietro in Vincoli (ca. 1078-1098/99) 82; *Collectio canonum* 126; **2.40** 68; **3.47** 69, 83n, 119; **4.19** 70, 83n; **4.22** 70, 83n, 119; **4.54** 69, 83n, 119
Diani, Pietro (Petrus Placentinus), card. pr. of S. Cecilia (1188-1208) 44
Diernstein, Gottschalk von 66
*Digestum vetus*: at papal curia 10n
Disidenbodenberg, monastery at 22
*Diversorum patrum sententie* 111, 117, 136; c.**195** 69; c.**260** 69, 119, 126
Diviso, card. pr. of SS. Martino e Silvestro (ca. 1103-1121): at Guastalla 42n; at Troyes 79
Dol (Brittany), diocese of: and council of Troyes 81, 81n; and Ivo of Chartres 76; *and see* Even, archbp. of
Donatus, schismatic bp. of Carthage (d. ca. 355) 52, 53, 56, 57
Donizo, *Vita Mathildis* 36
Duchesne, L. 43, 44, 44n, 46n, 47, 48, 49, 49n, 50, 51
Dupuy, Pierre (1582-1651?), and Jacques (1591-1656): 88

Eadmer, monk of Christ Church, Canterbury: *Historia novorum in Anglia*, 16-17, 24, 30, 31, 97; *Vita Sancti Anselmi* 18
*Editio Romana, see* Aquino, Antonio d'; Correctores Romani
Egino, abbot of SS. Ulrich and Afra (1109-1120) 36n
Ekkehard of Aura: *Chronicon Universale* 3, 11, 33n, 41; *Chronicon* and council of Guastalla 36, 36n, 41, 42n, 54, 71; *Chronicon* and council of Troyes 76; *Chronicon* and Lateran council (1102) 13, 16, 20-21; *Chronicon* and Nordhausen assembly 34, 34n, 35n
Equitius 131; at Guastalla 42n
Erickson, J. 114
Erlung, bp. of Würzburg (1106-1121): at Châlons 82
Eugene III, pope (1145-1153) 112
Eulalius 83n
Even, archbp. of Dol 81n
Evramar of Chocques: and patriarchate of Jerusalem 27
Ewald, P. 107
excommunication 20, 22, 30, 30n, 31n, 34, 53, 60, 61, 64, 65, 71, 72, 82, 92, 93, 95, 97, 99, 119, 120

Fiesole, *see* John bp. of
Fliche, A. 2
Florence, *see* Santa Maria Novella, monastery
Fournier, P. 114
France 1, 55

Fransen, G. 19
Frederick I, Archbp. of Cologne (1100-1131): suspended with suffragans 77, 100
Frederick, bp. of Halberstadt (ca. 1090-1105) 77; at Guastalla (?) 39; deposed at Guastalla 39, 71; suspended in 1105 71
Friedberg, E. 133, 133n
Fruttaria, monastery of (Turin): papal letter JL 6258 108
Fuhrmann, H. 119

Galo, bp. of Paris (1104-1116): and Paschal II 80n; at Troyes 80
Galo, card. pr. of SS. Martino e Silvestro (1211-1227) 37n
Galterius, card. deacon (title unknown; ca. 1100) 131
Gasparri, L. 48
Gebehard, bp. of Trent (1106-1120) 39
Gebhard, bp. of Constance (1084-1110) 34, 100; at court of Mathilda of Tuscany 40; at Guastalla 40-41; papal letter JL 6143 82, 99, 100; and Rothard, archbp. of Mainz 100; suspension and pardon of 77, 100
Gebhard, bp. of Speyer (1105-1107) 73
Gelasius II, pope (1118-1119), see John of Gaeta
Gelmirez, Diego, bp. of Santiago de Compostela: papal letters JL 5822 8n; 5839, 5840 8
"generalis tractatus" 35n, 123
Gerard, bp. of Angoulême (1101-1136) 46n; papal letter 6154 80
Gerard, archbp. of York (1101-1108) 16n
Gerbert, abbot of St. Vannes, Verdun 41
Gerhoch of Reichersberg: *De edificio Dei* 122n
Germany (Empire) 52, 53, 55, 56, 73, 74, 81-82, 101, 106, 124-125; papal-imperial relations 33-36; Paschal's policy toward 33-35
Gervais, archbp.-elect. of Reims 98
*Gesta episcoporum Virdunensium* 98
*Gesta Treverorum* 25-26
Gisla, abbess of Remiremont 41n

Godfrey, bp. of Amiens (1104-1115); papal letter 6095 42; at Troyes 80
Godfrey, abbot of Vendôme 17
Göttweig abbey 41
Gonter, abbot of St. Lambert, Liesse 41
Gottlob, T. 21
Gottschalk, bp. of Minden 73, 100
Gratian: *Concordia discordantium canonum*/*Decretum* (ca. 1140) 61, 62, 63, 109, 127; C.**1** q.**1** c.**12** 109n; C.**2** q.**7** c.**60** 132, 133; C.**16** q.**7** c.**16** 59, 60, 62, 62n, 64, 65, 70, 132, 133, 137; C.**16** q.**7** c.**17** 59, 62, 64, 65, 71, 84n, 109n, 132; C.**16** q.**7** c.**18** 59, 60, 62, 64, 65, 69, 132, 132n, 138; C.**16** q.**7** c.**19** 60, 69, 132, 138; C.**16** q.**7** c.**24** 109n, 137; C.**16** q.**7** c.**25** 109n, 136, 137; C.**18** q.**2** c.**18** 70, 132, 133; 1106 canons in 62, 63, 64 137
Gregory I, pope (590-604) 116
Gregory VII, pope (1073-1085) 11, 81n, 116, 124, 127; and canon law 125; excommunication of Henry IV 21; and Paschal II 2; register of 5; see also Rome, council of (1075; 1078; 1079; 1080)
Gregory IX, pope (1227-1241): *Decretales* (*Liber Extra[vagantium]*) 12-13; see also papal letter 6570
Grossolan, archbp. of Milan (1102-1116, d. 1117) 29
Guarin, deacon of cathedral of St. Etienne, Châlons-sur-Marne: papal letter JL 6142 79
Guastalla, council of (1106) 25, 32-73, 77, 84, 99, 100, 119, 124, 137; agenda of 71-73; conciliar procedure at 52, 65, 125-126; and decrees of 1112 46, 57; investiture prohibited at 53, 60, 64-65, 69, 70, 71, 73, 106; and *Liber Pontificalis* 43-46; and truce with Henry V 50
Gui, bp. of Lescar (1115-1141) 108
Guy, archbp. of Vienne (later Pope Calixtus II): correspondence of 1111/1112 45, 122; papal letter JL 6325 125

Halberstadt, diocese of: canons from, at Guastalla 41, 71; see also Frederick, bp. of; Reinhard, bp. of

Haller, J. 2
Hardouin, J. 20, 24, 102n
Hartmann, abbot of Göttweig abbey 41
Hauck, A. 2, 33n
Hefele-Leclercq 27
Helmarshausen, monastery of (Paderborn) 36n, 41
Henking, C. 40
Henry, abbot of S. Salvatore 28
Henry, archbp. of Magdeburg 100
Henry, bp. of Paderborn (1090-1127): at Guastalla (?) 40
Henry IV, emp. (1054-1106) 25; break with Henry V 32; excommunication of 20; schism of German church under 72; and Walcher of Cambrai 73
Henry V, emp. (1105-1125) 25, 73, 75; assemblies at Nordhausen and Quedlinburg (1105) 33; break with Henry IV 32; capture of Paschal II 5, 45-46, 123; not condemned at Guastalla 73; control over German church 32n, 73, 100; embassies to Paschal II 25, 25n, 32, 39, 40, 75, 99, 106n; and investiture 32n, 73, 75, 99, 100, 106, 107n, 110; invitation for Paschal II 33n; negotiations at Châlons 97; negotiations with Paschal II 32-34; papal letter JL 6070 33; Paschal's 1111 privilege for 60n, 125
Henry I, king of England (1100-1135) 30; councillors of, excommunicated (1105) 30-31; embassies of 16n, 17, 30, 81, 123, 131; excommunicated 30n; homage, dispensation for 97, 123; investiture compromise 1, 18, 19, 97, 97n, 128
Herbert, bp. of Thetford-Norwich (1091-1119) 16n
heresy/heretic 21, 22, 53, 56, 64
Hermann, bp. of Augsburg (1096-1132): at Guastalla 39, 72; and Gebhard, bp. of Constance 40; and Udalschalk 40; see also papal letters JL 6119 and JL 6548
Hermann, bp. of Metz (1073-1090) 116
Hermann of Reinhausen, count 39
Hermet, abbot of monastery of Bergues-Saint-Winoc: papal letter 6138a 79
hierarchy, ecclesiastical 54, 57, 70, 96, 119, 127, 128

Hildebert of Lavardin, bp. of Le Mans, later bp. of Tours (1056-1134): papal letter 6154 80; and Paschal's 1110 decrees 121n
Hirsau, monastery of 100
homage (lay) 17-20, 31, 43; dispensation for 97
Horst, U. 133n
Hugh, abbot of St. Amand: papal letter JL 6137 79
Hugh, abbot of St. Gilles, Nimes 42
Hugh, archbp. of Lyons (1092-1106) 39, 42
Honorius II, pope (1124-1130) 43
Hungary 1; investiture 1; renunciation of investiture 38, 38n, 45, 49; see also Coloman, king of

Innocent I, pope (ca. 401-417) 124n
Innocent II, pope (1130-1143) 15, 61n, 112
Innocent III, pope (1198-1216) 46n, 81n
*Institutes*: at papal curia 10n
investiture (lay) 1, 18, 21, 43, 64, 73, 110, 115; and Empire 1, 45, 53, 55; and England 30; and Hungary 1, 38; prohibited 53, 60, 61, 64, 69, 70, 71, 73, 77, 83, 86, 92, 97, 100, 103, 105, 119, 123, 127, 129; with ring and staff 72, 75, 99, 100, 128-129; see also France; Henry I, king of England
Iusiurandum Wirziburgensium, see Würzburg
Ivo, bp. of Chartres (ca. 1040-1115/17) 127; *Decretum*, 55; **3.85** 70; **5.119** 70; **6.173** 92; *Panormia* 19, 62n; letters 20, 76, 86n; *Prologue* 52; and Reims conflict 98; not at Troyes 81; visit of Anselm, archbp. of Canterbury to 31; visit of Paschal II to 74

Jaffé, P. 23, 27, 83
Jerusalem, Latin Kingdom of: church of the Holy Sepulchre 26; papal letter JL 6175 26-27; see also Baldwin, king of; Daimbert, patriarch of
John, bp. of Fiesole (1101-ca. 1103): papal letter 5898 17

John, bp. of Thérouanne (1099-1130) 42, 122; at Troyes 80
John, card. bp. of Tusculum (d. 1119): at Melfi 9
John of Gaeta, deacon of S. Maria in Cosmedin, chancellor, later Pope Gelasius II (1118-1119) 131; at Guastalla 42n; at Lateran council (1102) 17; at Melfi 9; as pope Gelasius II 54, 108; represented Montecassino 9; at Troyes 79

Kehr, P. 3
Konrad, archbp. of Salzburg (1106-1141) 39, 73
Krantz, A.: *Ecclesiastica historia* 77-78
Kuttner, S. 47n, 48n, 61n

Labbe-Cossart 14, 24, 25, 30, 37, 38, 49, 49n, 77, 102n, 107n
Lambert, abbot of St. Bertin: at Troyes 81
Lambert, bp. of Arras 81n; at Troyes 80
Landulf, archbp. of Benevento (1108-1119) 43n, 102; *see also* Landulf, card. pr. of S. Lorenzo in Lucina
Landulf, card. pr. of S. Lorenzo in Lucina (ca. 1106/07): at Guastalla 42n; at Troyes 79, 80; *see also* Landulf, archbp. of Benevento
Landulf of S. Paulo: *Historia Mediolanensis* 24, 29
Landulf of Vareglate, later bp. of Asti 29
Lateran councils, *see* Rome: Lateran councils
Leo I, pope (440-461) 124n; epistle **12.6** (JK 410) 52, 53
Leo IV, pope (847-855) 133
Leo IX, pope (1048-1054) 5, 48, 125; and synod of Reims (1049) 94, 95
Leodegar, bp. of Bourges (1097-1120): papal letter JL 6154 80
Lescar, abbey of: cartulary of 14, 108
Lescar, diocese of 108; *see also* St.-Pé-de-Générez, monastery of
*Liber Censuum* 12, 36, 36n, 37n, 38, 42n, 44, 46n, 47, 48, 50
*Liber Extra(vagantium)*, *see* Gregory IX, pope
*Liber Pontificalis* 43-44, 51, 97
libertas ecclesiae 1, 18, 30, 64, 77, 126

Libri, Guglielmo Icilio Timoleone, conte Carucci della Somaia (1803-1869) 66
Liège, diocese and city of: and formula of anathema and obedience 23, 72; *see also* Otbert, bp. of
Liesse, *see* St. Lambert, monastery of
Lille, *see* St. Quentin, abbey of
Lohrmann, D. 41n
Lombardy 55
Louis VI, king of France (1098-1137) 97, 98; and meeting of St. Denis 75; pactum pacis of 86n
Lowenfeld, S. 104
Lucius II, pope (1144-1145) 112
Ludovicus de Interannis [Terni] 66
Luitprand, priest of Milan 24, 29; *see also* Landulf of S. Paulo
Lyons: Anselm, archbp. of Canterbury at 30; *see also* Agobard, archbp. of; Amoulo, archbp. of; Hugh, archbp. of

Mainard, bp. of Turin (1099-1116) 108
Mainz, archdiocese of: Disidenbodenberg monastery in 22; suffragans of 35; *see also* Rothard, archbp. of
Manasses, archbp. of Reims (1096-1106): and Cambrai 73
Manasses, bp. of Soissons (1103-1108); transferred from Cambrai 73
Mansi, G. D. (1692-1769), archbp. of Lucca 4, 5, 7, 14-17, 23, 24, 38, 50, 78, 82, 102n, 107, 133
Marca, Pierre de: *Histoire de Béarn* 14, 107n, 108
March, J. M. 43
marriage 94
Martène, E. (1654-1739) 49, 50, 78, 82, 89
Masson, Jean-Papire (1544-1611) 88, 89
Mathilda of Tuscany, countess (1074-1115) 35, 35n, 39, 40, 41, 73; allods of, at Mousay and Stenay 41n; *see also* Donizo, *Vita Mathildis*
Mathoud, Hugo 112
Mazzara, diocese of: papal letter JL 5841 8-9; *see also* Stephen, bp. of
Melfi, city of: and Normans 7n
Melfi, council of (1100) 7-11; ex-

communication of Benevento at 10; secular judges at 9-10
Messina, see Robert, bp. of
metropolitan oath 13
Metz, see St. Arnulph, cathedral of
Milan, archdiocese of, see Landulf of S. Paulo, *Historia Mediolanensis*; Luitprand, priest of
Milo, card. bp. of Palestrina: at Melfi (1100) 9; at Lateran council (1102) 17
Minden, diocese of see Gottschalk, bp. of; Widelo, bp. of
Modena, diocese of 52, 54
Montecassino, abbey of: against S. Maria, Capua 9; and controversy with Capua 12, 29; *see also* Bruno, bp. of Segni; John of Gaeta
Mordek, Hubert 110

Niccoli, Niccolò (1363-1437), Florentine humanist 66
Nicholaitism 91-92
Nicholas I, pope (858-867) 124n
Nicholas II, pope (1058-1061): *Synodica generalis*, c.3 92; c.5 93, 94; c.6 70, 93; c.8 92
Nîmes: council of (1096) 70; *see also* St. Gilles, monastery of
Nordhausen, synod of 34
Novatian (d. 258) 53, 56

oath of office 21
Oddo II, card. bp. of Ostia (d. after March 1101): at Melfi 9
Odo, abbot of St. Martin of Tours: elected bp. of Cambrai (1105) 73; supported by Paschal II 73
Odo, bp. of Cambrai (1105-1113): at Troyes 79
*Ordo de concilio celebrando* 125
Ormanetti, N., bp. of Padua (1570-1577) 62; *Liber Veronensis* 62n
Otbert, bp. of Liège (1092-1117) 73, 77; excommunicated at Guastalla 71, 72; papal letter JL 6099 22, 41, 72-73
Otto, bp. of Bamberg (1103-1139): at Châlons 82; and Gebhard, bp. of Constance 100; at Guastalla 39

Paciaudi, Paolo M. 67
Pagi, A. 24, 25, 30
Palermo, archbp. of (1102): and *Liber Extra(vagantium)* **1.6.4** 12
pallium 13, 22, 72, 81n, 100n
Pamfili, Joseph, bp. of Segni (1570-1581) 59n
Pandulf 43
papal curia 65, 123, 126
papal letters: JL 5201 118; JL 5348 124n; JL 5393 21n; JL 5812 124; JL 5818 124; JL 5820 124; JL 5822 8n; JL 5825 23n; JL 5835 124; JL 5839 8; JL 5840 8; JL 5841 8; JL 5855 124; JL 5864 8, 9, 10; JL 5875 130n; JL 5898 17; JL 5899 17; JL 5908 14, 15, 16, 17, 19, 20; JL 5909 18; JL 5921 131, 131n; JL 5922 131; JL 5923 131, 131n; JL 5924 131; JL 5925 131, 131n; JL 5926 131; JL 5927 131; JL 5928 16n, 20, 129, 131; JL 5929 16n, 124, 131; JL 5930 131; JL 5931 131; JL 5932 131; JL 5971 36, 45, 49, 61; JL 6028, 23n, 24, 30, 31; JL 6029 23n, 31, 31n; JL 6050 34, 72n; JL 6070 33; JL 6073 19n, 97n, 123; JL 6076 35n; JL 6093 41, 71n; JL 6095 42, 71n; JL 6096 71n; JL 6097 41n, 71n; JL 6098 42n; JL 6099 22, 41, 72; JL 6103 36, 37n; JL 6114 74n; JL 6115 74n; JL 6116 74n; JL 6117 74n; JL 6118 74n; JL 6119 36, 37n, 72n, 74n; JL 6120 74n; JL 6121 74n; JL 6125 79, 80; JL 6132 75n; JL 6134 75n; JL 6136 79; JL 6137 79; JL 6138 79; JL 6138a 79; JL 6139 79; JL 6141 79; JL 6142 72; JL 6143 82, 83n, 99, 100; JL 6144 78, 82, 83n, 99; JL 6145 35n, 69, 70, 78, 82, 84, 84n, 93, 99, 126; JL 6152 124n; JL 6154 80; JL 6158 78, 82, 97; JL 6173 78; JL 6175 26, 28; JL 6206 106; JL 6252 45; JL 6258 108; JL 6301 45; JL 6325 45, 125; JL 6453 83n; JL 6503 107; JL 6570 12-13, 45; JL 6608 133; JL 6609 133, 133n; JL 6610 133; JL 6611 110n; JL 6613 104; JL 6647 51n, 54
papal registers 2n
papal states 11

papal synods 6; importance of 5
Paris, *see* St. Denis, abbey of; St. Germains-des-Prés, abbey of
Parma, diocese and city of 52, 54, 71; *see also* Bernard degli Uberti, bp. of
Paschal I, pope (817-824) 62n, 133
Paschal II, pope (1099-1118) 133; and ancient precedents 124-126, and canonical collections 126; co-operation with Normans 7n; and decrees of Piacenza (1095) 32, 52, 53, 55, 57, 87, 113-114, 124, 126; difficulty of evaluating pontificate of 2-5; formerly Rainer, card. pr. of S. Clemente 124; French journey of 74; importance of synods of 5-6, 123; as negotiator 11n, 75, 97, 128; and peace and unity for the church 21-22, 52, 53, 69; register of 2, 44, 65, 84; vita of 43-47
Paulmy, Marquis de, Antoine-René de Voyer d'Argenson, vicomte de Mouzé (1722-1787) 88
Pavia, council of (850) 132
Pax and Treuga Dei (Peace and Truce of God) 14-15; at Clermont 87n; at Troyes 84, 85, 91
Pertz, G. H. 8n, 89
Peter the Apostle 83; gladius 106
Peter, bp. of Padua (1096-1106; d. 1119): deposed at Guastalla 71
Peter, papal notary 17
Petrus Pisanus 43
Petrus, Roman law judge: at Melfi 9
Petrus, son of Petrus Leonis (later Anacelete II): and *Liber Pontificalis* 43
Pflugk-Harttung, J. von 5, 23, 107, 113-114, 135
Philip I, king of France (1060-1108): death of 98; meeting at St. Denis 75; support for Paschal II 75
Piacenza, commune of 35, 44
Piacenza, council of (1095) 18n, 32, 34n, 36n, 52, 55, 113, 115, 135; c.**10** 53; c.**12** 52
Piacenza, diocese of 52, 54; *see* Aldo, bp. of
Platina, Bartholomew (1421-1481) 43
Poitiers, council of (1100): c.**3** 92; c.**15** 92

Poland, archbp. N. of: papal letter JL 6570 12, 45
*Polycarpus* 133n
Prato 112; cathedral of 112

Radulf, abbot of St. Fuscien-au-Bois (Amiens diocese): at Troyes 79
Radulf, abbot of St. Quentin 41
Radulf le Vert, prior of Reims cathedral 80, 98; elected archbp. of Reims at Troyes 98
Raimbald, Roman law judge: at Melfi 9
Rainaldi brothers 61n
Ravenna, archdiocese of: dismemberment of 36n, 44, 51, 52, 54; *see also* Wibert, archbp. of
Reggio (Emilia), diocese of 52, 54
Reims, archdiocese of 98; council of (1049); 95 council of (1119) 95; and Richard, bp. of Verdun 98
Reims, cathedral of, *see* Radulf, prior of
Reinhard, bp. of Halberstadt (1106-1123) 39, 82, 100; papal letter JL 6144 82, 99
Remiremont, abbey of 41n
Richard, archbp. of Narbonne (1106-1121): papal letter 6158 82
Richard, card. bp. of Albano (1096-1113): at Guastalla 39; at Lateran council (1102) 17; and pax decree of Troyes 77, 85, 87; at Troyes 80, 80n
Richard of Grand-Pré, bp. of Verdun, 98-99
Richardotus, Franciscus, bp. of Arras 59n
Richer, bp. of Verdun (1089-1107) 41
Riso, card. pr. of S. Lorenzo in Damaso (1105-1112) 42n; at Troyes 79
Robert, bp. of Messina: at Melfi 9
Robert Parisiensis, card. pr. of S. Eusebio (d. ca. 1119) 27, 28, 28n; at Melfi 9
Roger, bp. of Chester 16n
Roger, bp. of Syracuse: at Melfi 9
Roger, bp. of Volterra (1099-1131, tr. Pisa 1121) 28
Roger Borsa, duke of Apulia (1085-1111) 7n, 10
Rome: Anselm, archbp. of Canterbury at 30; Daimbert's embassy to 27; embassies to 16n, 25; Lateran (S. Giovanni in Laterano) 27, 118; St. Peter's basilica 21

Rome, council of (502), c.3 83; council of (864) 35n; council of (1075) 92; council of (1078) 93; c.3 93; c.13 120; council of (1079) 57; council of (1080) 93; council of (1099) 18, 18n
Rome, Lateran council (1102) 11-23, 128; anathema with a profession of obedience 13; Henry IV excommunicated at 22; investiture prohibited at 17; lay homage prohibited at 17-20
Rome, Lateran council (1105) 23-31; Capua-Montecassino conflict at 12, 29; investiture prohibited at 30, 31; Milan conflict at 29; *see also* Henry I
Rome, Lateran council (1110) 64, 69, 70, 71, 83n, 106-122, 126, 135, 136, 137; distinction of MSS classes of canons for 109; importance of 106, 109; shipwreck victims protected at 110-111, 120; transmission of canons of 109-111, 121
Rome, Lateran council (1112) 38, 45, 46, 125; breviarum of 46, 51, 57
Rome, Lateran council (1116) 62n, 107, 108
Rome, Lateran council (1123) 85, 96, 109n, 136
Rome, Lateran council (1139) 15, 61n
Roselli, Nicholas, titular card. of Aragon (d. 1362) 38, 47-48, 49, 50, 61, 64
Rothard, archbp. of Mainz (1088-1109) 72; papal letters JL 6050 34; JL 6076 35; JL 6145 82-83, 99, 100, 126; pardon of 100; and reinstatement of Udo, bp. of Hildesheim 34, 99; suspended at Troyes 35, 77, 99
Rowe, J. G. 26n, 27
Rudolf, abbot of St. Etienne in Fesmy: at Troyes 79
Rudolf, abbot of Montier-la-Celle: papal letter JL 6141 79
Runciman, S. 130
Rupert, bp. of Würtzburg (d. 1106) 39

St. Amand, abbey of (diocese Tournai) 79
Sant'Angelo in Formis, church of (near Capua) 12, 29
St. Arnulph, cathedral of (Metz) 117
St. Bertin, abbey of (St. Omer) 80
St. Denis, abbey of (Paris): meeting of Paschal II and French kings at 75, 97, 98; *see also* Suger, abbot of
St. Etienne, cathedral of (Châlons-sur-Marne) 79
St. Germain-des-Prés, abbey of (Paris) 89, 114
St. Gilles, monastery of (Nîmes) 42
St. Lambert, monastery of (Liesse) 41
S. Maria, convent of (Capua): abbess of at Melfi 9
S. Maria de Cingla, monastery of (between Capua and Montecassino) 9
Santa Maria Novella, monastery of (Florence) 112
S. Maria de Ripoll, abbey of, *see* Baluze, E. and *Codex Rivipullensis*
S. Maria Theodatae, convent of (near Padua) 42
Ste. Maria, cathedral church of (Arras) 80
St. Martin, abbey of (Tours archdiocese) 73
St. Mauritius, church of (Arras) 80
St. Omer, *see* St. Bertin, abbey of
St. Pé-de-Générez, monastery of (diocese Lescar) 108
St. Peter, abbey of (Chartres diocese) 80
St. Quentin, abbey of (Lille) 41
St. Sernin, abbey of (Toulouse) 85n, 87
S. Sophia, monastery of (Benevento), *see Annales Beneventani*
St. Trond, abbey of 79
SS. Ulrich and Afra, monastery of (Augsburg) 36n
St. Vaast, abbey of (Arras) 80
St. Vannes, abbey of (Verdun) 41
St. Vincent, monastery of (Besançon), 49
St. Vincent, monastery of (Volterra) 102n
Sance, bp. of Lescar (1095-1115) 108
Scheffer-Boichorst, P. 100, 115, 117
schism/schismatics 22, 23, 34, 50, 52-53, 55, 56, 64, 72, 73, 124, 126
Schmale, F.-J. 2n
Sdralek, M. 86, 89, 103, 104
Seckau, Chorherrenstift 66
Segni, *see* Bruno, bp. of; Pamfili, bp. of
Segni fragment, 64, 133; reconstruction of 59-60
Seher, abbot of Chaumouzey (d. 1128) 41

Sennes, archbp. of Capua (d. 1118) 12; at Lateran council (1105) 29
Sens, St. Pierre-le-Vif, monastery of 112
shipwreck victims 110-111, 120
Sicily 16
simony 53, 56, 95, 124
Siponto, see Albert, archbp. of
Sirmond, J. 112
Somerville, R. 6, 18n, 53, 113
Southern, R. W. 18
Spain 8
Spalato (Split), see Crescentius, archbp. of
Statius, Achilles 60n
Stephen, bp. of Mazzara: papal letter JL 5841 8
Suger, abbot of St. Denis 76, 77; *Vita Ludovici Grossi* 81, 82; *Vita Ludovici Grossi*—meeting at St. Denis 75
Susa 39
Symachus, pope (498-514): Roman council of (502) 83
Syracuse, see Roger, bp. of

Tarbes, diocese of: not represented at Lateran council (1110) 108
Tarré, J. 103n, 104n
Teutbald, bp. of Langres (849-859) 88
Theodoric, abbot of St. Trond: papal letter JL 6138 79
Thérouanne, diocese of: pax statute from 86-87; see also John, bp. of
Thietmar, abbot of Helmarshausen 41
Thomasius Taxaquet, Michael, bp. of Lérida (d. 1578) 48n, 135, 136n, 137
Thou, Jacques-Auguste de (d. 1617) 89
tithes 85n, 94
Torres, Francisco 113, 135
Toul 80; see also Chaumouzey, monastery of
Toulouse: council of (1119) 108; see also St. Sernin, abbey of
Tournai, diocese of, see St. Amand, abbey of
Tours, archdiocese of, see St. Martin, abbey of
*Tractatus de investitura episcoporum* (ca. 1109) 38n
Trent 25, 40

Trier, see Bruno, archbp. of
Trithemius, Johannes (1462-1516) 76
Troyes, council of (1107) 25, 35, 36n, 62, 64, 71, 74-101, 115, 124, 133; conciliar procedure at 84; crusading legislation 84, 85, 93; and French affairs 97; and German relations 99-101; investiture prohibited at 77, 83, 86, 92-93, 97, 100, 106, 120; and meeting at Châlons 76, 81-82, 97; no decrees against lay homage 97; pax legislation 85, 86, 91, 94
Tuscany 16, 55

Udalric, bp. of Regensburg (1106-1141) 73
Udalric, patriarch of Aquileia and abbot of St. Gall (1085-1121) 71, 77
Udalschalk, abbot, monastery of SS Ulrich and Afra (Augsburg) (ca. 1124-ca. 1150) 36n; *De Eginone et Herimanno* 36, 40
Udo, bp. of Hildesheim (1079-1114) 35, 99
Ugo, card. deacon of SS Cosma and Damiano (1105-1108) 29
Urban II, pope (1088-1099): addresses at Clermont 87; and convent of S. Maria (Capua) 9; excommunication of Henry IV 21; and Paschal II 1, 3, 19n, 23, 124-125; pedisequus of Gregory VII 124; see also Bari, council of (1099); Clermont, council of (1095); Nîmes, council of (1096); Piacenza, council of (1095); Rome council of (1099)

van Hove, A. 114
Verdun, see Richer, bp. of; Richard of Grand-Pré, bp. of; St. Vannes, abbey of
Victor III, pope (1086-1087) 126
Volterra, see Roger, bp. of; St. Vincent, monastery of
Vulgrinus (Bougrin) of Chartres, chancellor of cathedral chapter: at Troyes 81

Waitz, G. 89, 117
Walcher (Gaucher), bp. of Cambrai (1095-ca. 1106) 73n, 77; excommunicated 71, 73
Warelwast, William 81, 97
Wasserschleben, H. 86

Watterich, W. 43
Welf, duke of Bavaria: at Châlons 82
Weiland, L. 5, 46, 50-51, 78, 82, 84, 87, 90, 107, 109, 113, 115, 116, 135, 136
Wibert, archbp. of Ravenna (d. 1100) 52; and episcopal oath 22
Wido, bp. of Chur (1096-1122) 39, 40, 107; and Gebhard, bp. of Constance 100; papal letter 6503 107
Widelo, bp. of Minden (1097-1119) 77, 100; deposed at Guastalla 71; suspended in 1105 71

William, abbot of St. Peter's (Chartres) 80
William II, archbp. of Auch (1126-1166/70) 14-15
William, archdeacon of Paris: at Troyes 81
William, bp. of Sens (1168-1176) 37n
William of Tyre 28
Würzburg, city of: and formula of anathema and obedience 22

Zerbi, P. 2

Cel